Contemporary African American Fiction

Contemporary African American Fiction

NEW CRITICAL ESSAYS

Edited by

Dana A. Williams

 THE OHIO STATE UNIVERSITY PRESS / COLUMBUS

Copyright © 2009 by The Ohio State University.
All rights reserved.
Library of Congress Cataloging-in-Publication Data

Contemporary African American fiction : new critical essays / edited by Dana A. Williams.
    p. cm.
Includes bibliographical references and index.
ISBN-13: 978-0-8142-0576-1 (cloth)
ISBN-10: 0-8142-0576-3 (cloth)
    1. American fiction—African American authors—History and criticism. 2. American fiction—20th century—History and criticism. 3. African Americans—Intellectual life—20th century. 4. African Americans in literature. I. Williams, Dana A., 1972–
    PS153.N5.C643 2009
    813'.5409896073—dc22
                                    2008027394

This book is available in the following editions:
Cloth (ISBN 978–08142-0576-1)
CD (ISBN 978–08142-9183-2)
Paper (ISBN: 978-0-8142-5761-6)
Cover art: Raymond Saunders, Red Star, 1970
oil and metallic paint, with collage (paper, synthetic fabric, and gummed tape) on canvas 55 7/8 x 45 3/4 inches
Corcoran Gallery of Art, Washington, DC
The Evans-Tibbs Collection, Gift of Thurlow Evans Tibbs, Jr.
1996.8.18
© Raymond Saunders, Courtesy Stephen Wirtz Gallery, San Francisco

Cover design by Laurence Nozik
Typeset in Adobe Palatino

Contents

Acknowledgments   vii

Introduction
Dana A. Williams   1

1. Theoretical Influences and Experimental Resemblances: Ernest J. Gaines and Recent Critical Approaches to the Study of African American Fiction
Reggie Scott Young   11

2. Ideological Tension: Cultural Nationalism and Multiculturalism in the Novels of Ishmael Reed
Jennifer A. Jordan   37

3. The Politics of Addiction and Adaptation: Dis/ease Transmission in Octavia E. Butler's *Survivor* and *Fledgling*
Mildred R. Mickle   62

4. "When the Women Tell Stories": Healing in Edwidge Danticat's *Breath, Eyes, Memory*
Tara T. Green   82

5. The Coming-of-Age of the Contemporary African American Novel: Olympia Vernon's *Eden*, *Logic*, and *A Killing in This Town*
Dana A. Williams   99

6. Another Night, Another Story: The Frame Narrative in Toni Morrison's *Paradise* and *Alf Laylah Wa Laylah* [The Arabian Nights]
Majda R. Atieh   119

7. A Stranger on the Bus: Reginald McKnight's *I Get on the Bus* as Complex Journey
Sandra Y. Govan   136

8. Re-Imagining the Academy: Story and Pedagogy in Contemporary African American Fiction
Eleanor W. Traylor   160

List of Contributors   173

Index   175

Acknowledgments

I must first thank the contributors to this collection for their essays and for their commitment to the project. It is indeed their work that enhances the overall usefulness and variety of this collection. Additionally, I must thank a few people who ultimately helped make the collection better: Heather Lee Miller and Sandra Crooms, the acquiring editors at The Ohio State University Press, who understood the need for this collection; Eleanor W. Traylor, who selflessly shares her ideas about the literary tradition with her colleagues and who not only enables but encourages her students to write the books she could write effortlessly; John Valery White, a keen-eyed cultural critic who sees my projects through from beginning to end; Greg Carr, who complicates my ways of thinking about the literature, particularly as it relates to its liberating potential; and the students in my literature classes and graduate seminars here at Howard, who are ever asking *Why?* and *What do you mean?* and then turning my own words on me by challenging me to "prove it." I must also thank the Office of the Provost and its faculty Academic Excellence and Research Awards at Howard University for financially supporting my varied research efforts. Finally, I must thank my friends and family for their constant support and the ancestors for their unspoken but ever-felt encouragement of my perpetual quest to find the ways in which this great literature does indeed free us.

Introduction

DANA A. WILLIAMS

The discourses raised in and by contemporary African American fiction are as varied as the ideologies, themes, tropes, and discourses the fiction engages. While each of these discourses holds its own significance for readers and writers alike, the intertextual dialogues that hold especial significance for me are those that attempt to answer the question Sonia Sanchez raises in 1975 in the subtitle of a play: "How do it free us?" The play's full title—*Uh Huh, But How Do It Free Us?*—asserts a particular stance before the it ever opens, before the first line is uttered. The affirmation—*uh huh*—acknowledges (if somewhat sarcastically) an unstated position; something has indeed been achieved. The inquiry—*but how do it free us?*—however, highlights the need for clear connections to be made between general progress or achievement and communal and personal liberation.

The essays collected here investigate the ways in which contemporary African American fiction attempts *to free us*. Sensibly, they acknowledge that this attempt is not a new one. The African American literary tradition, as the emancipatory narratives remind us, has always been about survival and liberation. It has similarly always been about probing, challenging, changing, and redirecting accepted ways of thinking to ensure the wellness and the freedom of its community cohorts. In their acknowledgment of these truths' always, already-ness, the essays thus identify new ways contemporary African American fiction continues the tradition's liberatory inclinations; they interrogate the ways in which antecedent texts and traditions influence contemporary texts to create new traditions; and they reveal the ways in which contemporary African American fiction dialogues with broader literary and cultural traditions to better accommodate the complexity of the African American living in the contemporary moment.

While each of the essays deals with the broad concept of liberation, each does so quite differently. Liberation in the essay that purposefully opens the collection, for instance, has to do with finding ways to free the literature from its critics and their self-interested concerns. In "Theoretical Influences and Experimental Resemblances: Ernest J. Gaines and Recent Critical Approaches to the Study of African American Fiction," Reggie Scott Young enters into discussions of contemporary African American literary criticism, particularly as it relates to misreadings of contemporary writers' fiction. He begins his discussion by contextualizing the late-1980s debate between Joyce Ann Joyce, Houston Baker, and Henry Louis Gates Jr. about the future of black literary studies. His essay then moves into a discussion of canon formation, particularly as it relates to Henry Dumas's omission from *The Norton Anthology of African American Literature*, an omission that, according to Young, "marks him as a causality of the lingering critical wars of the previous decades." Like Dumas, who still rests on the periphery of the African American canon, Ernest J. Gaines did not become a canonical writer until the publication of *A Lesson Before Dying*. Forced to find ways to deal with him critically, scholars began to highlight similarities between Gaines and major black authors like Ellison, Wright, and Baldwin, despite Gaines's frequent comments that he did not read any of these writers while he was developing his skill as an author. A crucial recognition that Young makes in this regard is how such readings reduce Gaines's texts (and other contemporary texts read primarily in terms of their intertextuality with antecedent texts) to little more than acts of textual revision. Thus, a central task of Young's essay is to highlight how critics overuse and oftentimes exploit the politics of textual revision, insisting that all black writers have been influenced (almost exclusively) by earlier major black authors. Ultimately, Young argues effectively that "when the act of reading a literary text is done for reasons other than to seek an understanding of the work in relationship to the author and to the culture from which it was produced, we must question if the critical exercise offers any real illumination of the subjected work." It is only when we read the work in the context of its broad culture (and this often exceeds narrowly conceived ideas of African American culture) that we can ensure "the advancement of the literature in its relationship to the plight of African American people."

I would argue that Jennifer A. Jordan's essay, "Ideological Tension: Cultural Nationalism and Multiculturalism in the Novels of Ishmael Reed," especially meets Young's call for scholarship that reads literary texts to seek an understanding of the works as they relate to both the author and to the culture out of which they emerge, thereby offering real illumination of the texts. Jordan conducts close readings of Reed's novels to investigate whether Reed's representation of himself as a multiculturalist rather than as a cultural nationalist is one that his fiction supports. Arguing that "a careful examination of Reed's novels from *Free-Lance Pallbearers* to *Japanese by Spring* reveals an ongoing cultural nationalism which is consistent with many of the precepts of the Black Arts Movement and which deconstructs the multiculturalism that coexists with it," Jordan points out that even *Japanese by Spring*, Reed's last novel, "despite a continual attempt to reinforce cultural diversity, returns to a black cultural nationalism which represents African culture as a solution to the trauma inflicted by an increasingly aggressive and global conservatism." To develop her argument, Jordan conducts, first, a thorough review of the varied representations of the black nationalism of the 1960s, citing both primary and secondary texts, and, second, an equally effective examination of the advent and subsequent growth of multiculturalism. She then traces Reed's struggle to balance his nationalist impulses with what she calls his eclectic "intellectual and social inclinations" before highlighting Reed's use of satire and parody in his novels to critique the Black Arts and Black Nationalist movements. After the decline of these movements, Reed shifts his most aggressive critique to global capitalism, which, as Jordan points out, he presents as "the major source of racism," even as his "responses to the problem of the domination of global capitalism vary greatly." Finally, she investigates how effectively or ineffectively Reed's fiction promotes the multiculturalism he claims to espouse.

Multiculturalism assumes a broader meaning in Mildred R. Mickle's essay "The Politics of Addiction and Adaptation: Dis/ease Transmission in Octavia E. Butler's *Survivor* and *Fledgling*." Here, Mickle highlights how Butler uses alien species and their struggle with humans for dominance to critique humans' relentless quest for power and their obsession with discrimination as a way of asserting superiority. In her examination of these novels, Mickle uses "addiction as a lens for exploring human dis/ease" and argues that "Butler's point in focusing on the addictiveness of racism in *Survivor* and *Fledgling* is to stress that if humans continue to engage in racial addiction, they will not progress." In this sense, Butler's novels have liberating possibilities, as they encourage the reader to recognize the concept of race and racial deviancy as an addiction that causes and feeds dis/ease. If there are to be survivors in the fictional worlds of *Survivor* and *Fledgling* or in the real world that is Earth, unfruitful addictions must be replaced with adaptation and with respectful tolerance of *Other*s.

The essay that follows Mickle's focuses less on the communal liberation and survival that informs Butler's two novels and more on the personal liberation the protagonist in Edwidge Danticat's *Breath, Eyes, Memory* seeks as she tries to achieve psychological healing. Examining the mother-daughter relationship and its corresponding connection to healing in the novel, Tara T. Green's "'When the Women Tell Stories': Healing in Edwidge Danticat's *Breath, Eyes, Memory*" invokes other texts by black women writers with similar interests (Paule Marshall's *Praisesong for the Widow*, Alice Walker's *The Color Purple,* and Gloria Naylor's *The Women of Brewster Place,* for example) to show how Danticat's text, unlike its counterparts, insists on the existence of a working mother-daughter relationship in order for the daughter's healing to take place. "Unlike the authors of [earlier] novels where the mother-healers are not the biological mothers of the women they nurture," Green argues, "Danticat reenvisions the role of the biological mother as being essential in her daughter Sophie's movement toward renewal and healing." Thus, it is only from her mother that Sophie can learn that "healing cannot occur without removing herself from the site of sexual violation nor without acknowledging the abuse and thereby confronting the abuser." To develop this point, Green conducts, first, a close reading of Martine's failed journey toward healing and, then, one of Sophie's more successful journey toward healing, highlighting how Martine's failure to transcend her sexual violation and to move toward healing actually helps her facilitate Sophie's healing. Accordingly, Green's essay makes a considerable contribution to both scholarship on mother-daughter relationships and the varied ways they are portrayed by black women writers and to scholarship on healing as it is illustrated in their texts.

My essay, "The Coming-of-Age of the Contemporary African American Novel: Olympia Vernon's *Eden, Logic,* and *A Killing in This Town,*" looks to an emerging novelist to investigate ways contemporary fiction continues the tradition's propensity to alter discourses and thereby to be liberating. Vernon, like our most valued writers, insists upon finding ways to make old stories new. To do so, she carves out her own niche within the broader literary tradition, even as her writing inevitably remembers and redirects its antecedent American texts. It is the carving of space, in fact, that I argue has become a central undertaking of contemporary fictionists like Vernon. Borrowing Eleanor W. Traylor's interpretation of African American literature as "discourse altering," I suggest ways Vernon's novels engage three American literary traditions—the female pastoral, the Southern gothic, and lynching as trope—to highlight these novels' willingness to challenge traditions that support the falsity of American myths of innocence and purity and their corresponding oppressiveness. I chose Vernon's novels not only because of my confidence in the inevitability of her eventual emergence among critics as a major writer, but because of her willingness to investigate the beauty and the horror of the human condition and to offer alternative ways of *seeing* and *being* that critically and authentically reflect contemporary African American experiences. The central achievements of the essay, as I see them, are its critical engagement of three of the most innovative novels published in this millennium and its willingness to read Vernon's novels within varied traditions without limiting the achievements of the novels by imposing neat categorizations upon them.

The final three essays, written by Madja R. Atieh, Sandra Y. Govan, and Eleanor W. Traylor, highlight the ways in which contemporary African American fictionists express their knowledge of world traditions, the ways in which these writers situate their texts among these traditions, and the ways in which broader traditions can be useful in projects of liberation. Atieh's "Another Night, Another Story: The Frame Narrative in Toni Morrison's *Paradise* and *Alf Laylah Wa Laylah* [The Arabian Nights]" illustrates how *Paradise* emerges as "a new frame narrative, how it adopts and adapts the taxonomic characteristics of the frame by employing innovative techniques, all the while linking *Paradise* to the heritage of the life-giving fame narratives and showing how *Paradise* is a new version of the celebrated Arabic story cycle of *Alf Laylah Wa Laylah*." Atieh grounds her analysis in an especially useful review of the characteristics of framing as a narrative device. She then highlights the ways in which *Paradise* fashions new techniques to engage the taxonomies of the frame narrative, before moving into a comparative reading of *Paradise* and *Alf Laylah Wa Laylah* as exemplary frame narratives. This comparative reading is significant on two corresponding levels. First, it highlights the "affinity between the Arabic and African American modes of narration and organization," suggesting how "the kinship between these two modes is based on the Arabic and African American traditions and experiences, which are linked through the African culture, and on their oral and communal art of storytelling." Second, it highlights the similar ways women of different cultures use storytelling both as a device of resistance and a tool for survival. Significantly, Atieh's comparative reading of the texts ultimately suggests that two seemingly disparate cultures are as much alike as they are dissimilar.

In "A Stranger on the Bus: Reginald McKnight's *I Get on the Bus* as Complex Journey," Govan offers one of too few insightful readings of McKnight's first novel. Govan centers her reading of the novel on its engagement of DuBoisian notions of double-consciousness. The novel's protagonist, Evan Norris, is an American-born Peace Corps volunteer who finds himself in Senegal, West Africa. As Govan notes, Evan's narrative voice and syntax, as revealed in the novel's opening pages, offer readers the first indication that the novel will likely explore its protagonist's psychological state in its subtext, especially since Evan is literally making the figurative journey "back to Africa." What the early pages do not suggest, however, and what Govan points us to in her essay is McKnight's manipulation of the familiar trope to present it differently. The novel transcends more traditional interpretations of double-consciousness. "In several instances," Govan notes, "[Evan] unaccountably finds that his consciousness has *shifted* and he has fused with another person, actually *becoming* the other. This transit of souls, so to speak, affectively illustrates DuBois's [double-consciousness] in a manner quite distinctive" (emphasis in original). Having examined the ways in which the novel consciously and unconsciously engages double-consciousness as trope, the essay then moves into an investigation of the ways in which the novel explores questions of identity, particularly as they relate to antecedent texts' similar questioning. Invoking Countee Cullen's "Heritage," James Weldon Johnson's *Autobiography of an Ex-Colored Man*, and Ralph Ellison's *Invisible Man*, for instance, Govan notes how McKnight situates Evan firmly in the African American tradition. Yet McKnight does not limit himself to this tradition. He willingly admits to Govan that "*I Get on the Bus* is almost a virtual rewriting, under the guise of blackness, of Albert Camus's *The Stranger*," and it is on the basis of this admission that Govan conducts a fascinating comparative reading of the two texts at the end of her essay. Ultimately, the essay proves quite effective its argument that *I Get on the Bus*—perhaps both because of and despite its characterization of its protagonist as a lost, existential African American in the tradition of Camus's Meursault rather than Richard Wright's Cross Damon (from *The Outsider*)—is a novel that will change and enrich the canon of African American literature.

Finally, Eleanor W. Traylor's "Re-Imagining the Academy: Story and Pedagogy in Contemporary African American Fiction" takes a forward look at what literary historians of the next century will find when they begin to investigate the "generative power of language" as it manifests itself in our contemporary moment. What they will find, she argues, is a focus on *story* rather than on *myth*. They will similarly find a narrating posture of interrogation rather than one of declaration. Probing Toni Cade Bambara's avowal to tell stories that "save lives," Traylor also posits that historians will find pedagogies of survival embedded in "fictions." In their determination to save lives, these fictions are not only what Traylor calls "discourse altering"; they are "discourse making." To support these claims, Traylor peripherally engages Bambara's *The Salt Eaters* and Henry Dumas's "Ark of Bones," both of which are aggressively concerned with (meta)fiction as a way of conveying knowledge and of negotiating survival through cultural memory. The essay then moves into an astute reading of Morrison's *Paradise* as an exemplary text of fiction as pedagogy. Inherent to this reading of the novel, however, is Traylor's recognition of antecedent texts that teach characters and readers alike "how to learn to see yourself for yourself" in hopes of ushering in transformation, rebirth, and survival. Among this essay's many strengths, then, is Traylor's awareness of world literary traditions—she effortlessly engages Plato's cave; the Zoroastrian vision of redemption; Homeric and Virgilian travelers; Cartesian, Aristotelian, and Acquinian oppositional binaries; "infernal and paradisical visions of Dante, Milton, and Goethe"; and the "modern angst" of Chinua Achebe's *Things Fall Apart*. Of even greater value, perhaps, is her ability to situate contemporary African American fiction within this tradition, all the while rememorying W. E. B. DuBois's veil, Charles Chestnutt's conjurer, Langston Hughes's river, Ralph Ellison's invisibility, Richard Wright's native son, Amiri Baraka's slave, and Toni Morrison's bluest eye. Smartly, she closes the essay with the subtle contention that what literary historians will likely find upon their investigation of our contemporary moment are the many ways in which contemporary African American fiction acts as this moment's guiding light toward universal manifestations of and investigations into the human condition.

As the preceding summaries reveal, the essays collected here are varied. A select few are overtly theoretical, while others are more probing and analytical. Still others—Young's and Traylor's, for example—are more assertive than they are exploratory. The diversity of the critical approaches utilized here is among the collection's strengths, as more can be learned from different approaches to the literature than from uniform approaches to it. In this sense, the book inherited the obvious benefits an edited collection has over a single-authored book, particularly the willingness to offer varied insightful perspectives and its corresponding ability to cover a wide range of ideas in broad yet focused analyses. The contributors' range of interests and their differing professional ranks undoubtedly enhanced the collection's overall effectiveness as an offering of commentary on contemporary African American fiction and its relationship to earlier African American, American, and broader literary traditions. In the sense that the essays included here investigate many of the key inquires that inform discussions about this fiction and examine the trends and ideas that loosely characterize it, the strength of the collection rests more with its articulation of suggested ways of reading, seeing, thinking, writing, and being than with its comprehensiveness.

By engaging the authors examined here and other authors whose fiction is significant but not examined here—authors like William Melvin Kelley, John Edgar Wideman, Clarence Major, Gloria Naylor, Gayl Jones, Leon Forrest, Charles Johnson, Alice Walker, Percival Everett, Edward P. Jones, Nathaniel Mackey, Samuel Delany, and Tananarive Due, among others—scholars of contemporary African American fiction, using the discourses these essays raise and the critical approaches they initiate, must continue to ask the hard questions if we are to garner from this literature all it has to offer. The range of queries is, and ever must be, wide and varied. How does African American fiction represent the changing times in America and in the world? How are these changes reflected in narrative strategies or in narrative content? How do contemporary fictionists engage diasporic Africanisms, or how do they renegotiate Americanisms? In what ways do these fictionists invoke vernacular forms such as oratory, myth, and music in ways that are different from antecedent authors? On what traditions are they building? In what ways are they reconstructing traditions or constructing new ones? What is the impact of cultural production, gender, sexuality, nationality, and ethnicity on this fiction? What is the impact of popular culture fiction and what Bernard Bell refers to as *paraliterature* (science/speculative fiction; gay and lesbian fiction; and detective, mystery, and romance fiction) on more traditional literature and their literary forms? All of these questions and more must be probed further.

While the essays included here do, indeed, attempt to initiate (in some cases) and to participate in (in others) much needed conversations about contemporary African American fiction, even a cursory review of the literature on scholarship specific to contemporary African American fiction reveals just how much work there is to be done to explore fully its complexity, even as such a review also reveals how the hard work of this scholarship has already begun. It was a literature review, in fact, that birthed the idea for this collection initially. After reviewing a number of texts for the specific purpose of identifying the wide-ranging though innately connected tendencies of contemporary African American fiction, I was somewhat surprised to find that no such collection as this one (which focuses specifically on fiction written and published from 1970 to the present) existed. Earlier collections and books that attempt to investigate the latest movement(s) in African American literature examine texts that date back as early as 1940 (with the publication of Wright's *Native Son*) and end in the mid-1990s (typically with a Morrison novel). Thus, this collection has filled a void in scholarship on contemporary African American fiction, particularly as it relates to established literary traditions and to a new one that is emerging. Heretofore, this void could be justified largely by contemporaneity, following the traditions of scholarship that typically allow primary texts to lie dormant for years before returning to them critically. The critical examination of these texts is now imminent.

In the tradition of critical texts emerging from the Harlem Renaissance, the Protest Movement, and the Black Arts Movement that identify these movements' aesthetics, much of the work here begins to chart the course of scholarship on contemporary African American fiction and to reveal responses to the questions raised above. Building on these essential questions, future scholarship is likely to reveal the many ways this fiction offers fruitful responses to the overarching Sonia Sanchez title-as-query that loosely frames this text: *Uh Huh, But How Do It Free Us?* As scholars of liberation, we must take Toni Cade Bambara's words literally when she intuits that she and many of her contemporaries write stories that save lives. Our job, then, is to query and to preserve their stories.

Theoretical Influences and Experimental Resemblances

Ernest J. Gaines and Recent Critical Approaches to the Study of African American Fiction

REGGIE SCOTT YOUNG

> The premise of Black Studies is that self knowledge is the key to all knowledge ... these courses provide the student with a perspective and understanding of culture, history, psychology and economic characteristics of black people that cannot be attained in other departments within the University. ... Students enrolled in the Black Studies program are encouraged to view the black community as a classroom where lessons can be learned and taught.
> —*San Francisco State University Black Studies Department Web site*

1.

Scholars, teachers, and advanced students who are involved in the study of African American studies today should be familiar with the late-1980s debate between Joyce Ann Joyce, on one side, and Henry Louis Gates and Houston A. Baker, on the other, that appeared in the pages of *New Literary History*. The discussion centered on the views expressed by Joyce in her essay "The Black Canon: Reconstructing Black American Literary Criticism," especially regarding the direction of contemporary African American literary criticism and the use of critical theory by "black scholars." In addition to Joyce's essay, the journal included responses from Gates and Baker and a final rebuttal from Joyce. The exchange is important for a number of reasons, especially since it illustrates the shift that occurred in African American critical thought when it moved from domination by scholars with black aesthetic approaches to the leadership of those who rose to prominence in the aftermath of the "Reconstructionist" movement of African American literary studies in the late 1970s.[1] Although the issues debated concerning what Karla Holloway, in *Moorings and Metaphors*, has described as the "language of contemporary criticism and the membership of interpretive community" (190n6) were important at the time, as they are still today, the underlying currents of hostility and distrust stand out more than any of the particular ideas that were expressed by the participants.

The exchange between Joyce and her two male respondents, Gates and Baker, came at a time in the late twentieth century when Black Studies program initiatives were being assimilated into mainstream academic departments. No matter how one responds to the ideas expressed in her essay in terms of either quality or method of expression, Joyce's perspective is nationalistic, whereas Gates and Baker's responses are more in line with the integrationalist thought of earlier decades. Neither of the critics who opposed Joyce in the debate can be described as less black than she, despite their efforts to open up the study of African American literature to all interested scholars, since nationalism alone cannot be used as a barometer of blackness. However, the participants in this debate should be considered in light of the contentious factions that have historically represented the pull by some in the direction of cultural autonomy and the push by others toward social inclusion that has existed since the first New World Africans arrived on North American shores. My purpose is not to evaluate this debate, which many saw as an embarrassing public spectacle, but to suggest it as one of the pivotal moments in the recent history of the field and one that helped pave the way for many of the subsequent trends that have developed in the study of the literature, especially the works of African American fiction writers.

Joyce's essay begins with an illustration about reading, one drawn from a meeting she had with one of her African American students over that student's difficulty in understanding an essay by James Baldwin from a popular magazine. One of the major points of contention between Joyce and the two respondents, particularly Gates, involves their different conceptions of reading and varying notions of literacy itself. Each of the scholars, including Joyce, fails to consider the complexities faced by individuals attempting to cope with, much less master, multiple literacies and the difficult adjustment individuals must make in their efforts to move from one to another as their primary way of learning and knowing. All acts of reading entail acts of interpretation, whether they involve the reading of linguistic signs in printed scripts or, as Ron Welburn has noted, finding "great poetry in a flock of birds rising to the air and changing shape" (25). Welburn, in fact, states that "outside of Eurocentrism, the world is perceived and understood in holistic and intuitive terms" (32), and that "people of color in America have lived in a cultural literacy and diversity and know more than one vocabulary" (34). It is important to consider some of the various dimensions of literacy (as a means of learning and knowing) that influence works produced by certain African American writers that are not exclusively related to acts of reading and acquiring knowledge through books. When scholars in the field are unable to recognize and explicate them because of their limited understanding of the experiential matters from which many African American writers draw source materials, it places severe limitations on the work they are able to do. Instead of being able to draw from the realities of black life to help in the process of understanding the fictional narratives they treat in their scholarly endeavors, these particular critics too often approach the works as if they are little more than intertextual exercises in language.

2.

> The universe is in motion. If this is the case, what is the function of criticism? It is merely a way into things. And is it important only insofar as it relates to the nature of the changing world? There are, consequently, no steadfast critical values.
> —Larry Neal, "Cultural Nationalism and Black Theatre/Two on Cruse: The View of the Black Intellectual"

One of the jobs of professional literary scholars is to shape canons. According to Gates, "None of us are naïve enough to believe that 'the canonical' is self-evident, absolute, or natural. Scholars make canons" ("Canon-Formation" 38). In participating in this process, scholars determine the works that are available for study by students, and they are influential in the process of establishing the value of selected writers and works. They are, in fact, instrumental in influencing how literary works from various cultural communities and social perspectives are to be read or not read at all. An example of the latter is the de facto prohibition against extraliterary considerations in the study of African American literature that came into practice with the Reconstructionist shift to "formal" readings several decades ago. No one has been as concerned with the exertion of power in shaping the African American literary canon as Gates and some of the others who assumed positions of prominence and influence in the academy after the overthrow of the black aesthetics agenda that was central to the study of the literature in Black Studies programs. Gates and Nellie McKay make this clear in their preface to the *Norton Anthology of African American Literature* when they state, "We have endeavored to choose for the Norton Anthology works of such a quality that they merit preservation and sustain classroom interest" (xxxvii). They explained their task was "to bring together into one comprehensive anthology texts ... 'that introduce students to the unparalleled excellence and variety' of African American literature" and to create an anthology that contains "texts that, in the judgment of the editors, define the canon of African American literature at the present time" (xxxvii). Although anthologies most often celebrate writers who have already achieved major status, however that is defined, they also make available the works of overlooked or underappreciated writers who were important contributors to a literature's development during the eras when they wrote or in the movements with which they are associated. They also focus attention on writers whose experimentations have proved influential in expanding the possibilities of expression for writers of ensuing generations. In a response to earlier statements by Gates concerning the forthcoming publication of the *Norton Anthology* and the canonization of the literature, Donald Gibson argues, "canons are formed as the result of needs having nothing to do with literature" (45). Gibson is correct in pointing out that inclusion in a canon is not a determinant of a work's actual value and its possible significance to potential readers, but only of its importance to the shapers of that particular canon.

One writer who might be considered a victim of the exertion of canonical power by the Norton editors is Henry Dumas, whose works are excluded from both editions of the anthology despite the fact that he was significant enough to merit discussion by Baker in his introduction to the section titled "The Black Arts Movement, 1960–1970" in the first edition, and retitled "The Black Arts Era, 1960–1975" in the second. Dumas's exclusion is important because no other anthology is as influential as the Norton, and exclusion of a writer means her or his works are less likely to be taught and that unfamiliar readers will not receive exposure to that writer for future reference. It is not unusual, after all, for a reader to obtain an author's books after first encountering that writer in anthologized collections. In terms of the Black Arts era, especially in the 1970s when his works were made readily available, Dumas emerged as one of the literature's most important writers, especially when his impressive body of fiction, all published posthumously, is considered together with his extensive collection of poetry. It is worth wondering if

Dumas's advancement of ideas in some of his works that were consistent with those articulated by Black Arts–era theorists diminished his value in the eyes of Baker and the anthology's other editors and led to Dumas's being judged as having less value than writers from other periods who have arguably not contributed as much to the development of the literature.[2] Dana A. Williams and Trudier Harris have written about Dumas's "Ark of Bones" as a thematic forerunner to August Wilson's *Joe Turner's Come and Gone,* and Harris has detailed Dumas's almost certain influence on the works of Toni Morrison. There are not many writers in the Norton who share such strong connections with writers of this magnitude in the tradition.

Baker's introductions seem more concerned with extraliterary controversies involving the Black Arts–era writers and their political and aesthetic ideas than with the actual advancements in African American writing made during the period—advancements that are seen in the expressions of today's hip-hop generation of writers and spoken word artists. In terms of understanding some of the developments in black writing that took place in the years accorded to the Black Arts era and the writers who made their earliest contributions to the literature at that time (including Ernest J. Gaines, Alice Walker, Toni Cade Bambara, Lucille Clifton, Ishmael Reed, Toni Morrison, John Edgar Wideman, and others), it is important to note the following comment by Wideman, who is often thought of as a Black Arts Movement antagonist:

> [I]f you look back now and ask what was produced, what came out of the sixties and that remains of some significance to Afro-American literature, then I would hope that people would say that we [Gaines, Walker, Bambara, etc.] were part of it, the Black Arts Movement.... In other words, there were many, many things happening. It was a multifaceted cultural event, this growth, this consciousness that was arising in the sixties, and the artwork that was being produced in the sixties. (Rowell 90)

He goes on to say, "I hope we've carried forward the ideas that are most significant, profound, important. I see continuities, rather than simply a break with or repudiation of the Black Arts Movement of the sixties" (Rowell 91).

The anthology's treatment of the Black Arts Movement, however, does appear to be a repudiation of the era, especially in the first edition, which limits the Black Arts' span of years to the decade of the sixties and offers only a scant representation of notable writers and works, as if the Black Arts era represents more of a momentary break than part of the ebb and flow in the literature's progression. Gibson had previously expressed concern that the drive for canonization that the publication of the *Norton Anthology* would entail might "do to a number of black writers what the New Criticism did to Longfellow, Whittier, Lowell, and Holmes" and reduce them to "canon fodder" (46). At the time, he pointed to the need to "carry forward the tradition of black writing that has seen it as functional, as having more to do with our social and political well-being than with our need for enjoyment and entertainment" (45). Few writers in the closing decades of the twentieth century expressed in their writing a passion for the plight of African American people equal to Dumas, but in the pages of the *Norton Anthology of African American Literature*, he is both reduced to canon fodder and used as a scapegoat for what the anthology sees as the era's aesthetic deficiencies. Despite Morrison's earlier pronouncement that "a cult has grown up around Henry Dumas—a very deserved cult" and that "he had completed work the quality and quantity of which are almost never achieved in several lifetimes" ("On Behalf" 310), Baker remarks:

> In the 1960s, only the short stories of the tragically short-lived Henry Dumas took up the themes of Africa. His work resonated with the overt attention to Africa found in the poetical rhythms and nationalistic politics of the Black Arts movement. Yet Dumas's stories were often only roughly polished polemics. (*Norton* 1st ed. 1798)

Baker's statement attempts to justify Dumas's exclusion from the Norton and the editors' criteria of selection for their newly constructed African American canon. Anyone who has studied Dumas's "Ark of Bones," the story included in *The Literature of the South*—the Norton anthology dedicated to Southern literature—and other Dumas works such as "Echo Tree," "A Boll of Roses," "For Six Days You Shall Labor," and "The Voice," must think it ironic that a black writer whose works are allegedly polemical and not worthy of any significant literary merit has been canonized in the bible of Southern literary anthologies after being deemed unworthy of inclusion in the sacred text of African American writing.[3] (It should be noted that Dumas is also prominently included in *Call & Response: The Riverside Anthology of the African American Literary Tradition*, which, for many, offers a more holistic and less elitist representation of the African American tradition in writing.) Baker fails to point out how Dumas's most meaningful stories are set in the South and that they bear witness to something Jean Toomer pointed out decades earlier in *Cane*:

that "the Dixie Pike has grown from a goat path in Africa." (12) In fact, one of Toomer's most important contributions to African American letters is the example he left of a writer drawing from the rich bedrock of folk material that black life in the South provides. Even if Dumas did not live long enough to shift the northern/urban emphasis of the 1960s Black Aesthetic agenda back to the South, it would not be far-fetched to draw a relationship between him and the South's preeminent African American writer, Ernest J. Gaines. But whereas critics, with a few exceptions, have yet to claim marks of influence on Dumas's work from what they might theorize to be his reading of earlier black writers, Gaines now finds himself stigmatized for not being forthright in addressing the issue of his alleged "black" literary influences. Like Dumas, he resided on the periphery of the African American literary canon for years (some might take exception with this, but other than a special issue of *Callaloo* on his work in the late 1970s, he received little critical attention until the late 1980s), but because of the success of *A Lesson Before Dying*, critics have since rushed to find ways of explicating Gaines's works,[4] even through means that lead to faulty conclusions.

3.

> Literacy customarily is defined as the assigned meaning of a body of information that a group shares.
> —Kimberly Rae Connor, Imagining Grace

> I'm still writing those letters for the old people on that plantation. I've published eight books and all of the stories take place in that general area, but I have still not told all of their stories.
> —Ernest J. Gaines, "Louisiana Bound"

As a writer, Gaines exemplifies what might be best seen as a "Leadbelly" tradition that draws on extraliterary influences from the lives of those whom Ralph Ellison once described as blues people who "accepted and lived close to their folk experience" (qtd. in Jones 176). This aspect of the larger tradition in African American fiction dates back to Charles Chesnutt, Jean Toomer, and Zora Neale Hurston, and includes individuals whose works are informed by a Southern folk perspective based on experiential knowledge and beliefs. These writers do more than observe, theorize, and comment on black vernacular expressions as Frederick Douglass does in his autobiographical narratives, or write about these vernacular expressions in a classical style as DuBois does in *The Souls of Black Folk*. Instead, they write from a perspective of cultural immersion and in the voices of the folks who created nonwritten narratives of their human experience in spiritual, gospel, and blues songs; tall tales and toasts; and other kinds of oral narratives. At the same time, Gaines acknowledges a formal "Mozart" or "learned" influence in his work.[5] He has expressed his ideas about these dual and seemingly antithetical influences in published talks and interviews throughout his career, many of which are collected in his eighth and most recent book, *Mozart and Leadbelly: Stories and Essays*.

Like Dumas, Gaines's explorations of black Southern folk culture and the fact that his work lends itself to comparisons with the aforementioned Toomer indicate that both draw from similar sources in their efforts to portray a particular dimension of African American life.[6] Their portrayals of black Southern experience in fiction suggest fertile ground for comparative study of the two, but the way young scholars are now trained to play critically in the works produced by creative writers, it would not be surprising to find such a study proclaim a read literary relationship between the two built around speculation and circumstantial bits of information for the purpose of supporting the critic's own agenda. In doing so, the critic could argue that one or more of Gaines's works is a retelling or extension of something Dumas wrote before his untimely death (or that Dumas rewrote something of Gaines's, depending on the objectives of the critic). It would not matter if Gaines has never read anything by Dumas, or if Dumas had never read Gaines, because it is the critic who determines influence from her reading of selected texts. Writers in these studies are permitted little input on the pronouncements made about their work; those, like Gaines, who have spoken extensively about most aspects of their histories as writers and the influences that helped to shape their writing are often ignored and at times disparaged.

Gaines has stated, in a personal interview, that he has never read the works of Henry Dumas, just as he has stated in print that he did not read any African American writers during his early literary development and that his novels and stories have not been influenced by other African American writers, something a few critics have found puzzling.[7] No doubt, the two writers do have much in common: They were born a year apart in neighboring Southern states, and both left for "the North" during their youth—California and New York, respectively—before returning to the South as adults. But before either embarked upon physical journeys back "home," they first did so through their writing—Gaines resettled in

Louisiana much later than Dumas's move back southward, but Dumas's return took him to southern Illinois, as opposed to his native Arkansas, in an area of the state that borders Missouri and is much closer in miles and culture to Arkansas, Tennessee, and Mississippi than it is to Chicago, and its history of race relations rivals that of any other southern region. Another similarity is that both spent time in the military before attending college and eventually attended prestigious schools on their respective coasts: Gaines attended Stanford and Dumas attended Rutgers. In fact, the two began their careers as writers around the same time. To borrow from Ralph Ellison's concept of literary relatives and ancestors in *Shadow and Act,* one writer does not have to exert an influence on the other for the two to share a kinship, especially a cultural one, such as the kinship that existed between Ellison and Richard Wright. Ellison, in an essay directed at Irving Howe, claimed

> [H]e [Wright] did not influence me if I point out that while one can do nothing about choosing one's relatives, one can, as artist, choose one's "ancestors." Wright was, in this sense, a "relative"; Hemingway an "ancestor." Langston Hughes, whose work I knew in grade school and whom I knew before I knew Wright, was a "relative"; Eliot, whom I was to meet only many years later, and Malraux and Dostoievsky [sic] and Faulkner, were "ancestors"—if you please or don't please! (140)

Although it is difficult to believe Ellison received no influence from Wright or that his fiction is in no way indebted to someone who once served as his mentor, that does not diminish the validity of his remarks about relatives and ancestors. Writers have cultural relationships with their relatives that are often no more than a matter of circumstance and not choice, whereas the relationships they have with other writers through reading entails not circumstance but deliberate choice. A writer can obviously receive influence from cultural relatives, but that influence is not always literary and can be transmitted through other forms of expression.

No matter how one reads Ellison's statement, it is interesting to note the connection made between Gaines and Ellison in Herman Beavers's *Wrestling Angels into Song: The Fictions of Ernest J. Gaines and James Alan McPherson.* Beavers's strategy is to read Gaines through Ellison's work, as if Gaines is a writer in the Ellisonian tradition. When asked in an interview about Ellison, Gaines is clear: "No I hadn't read anything at all by Ralph Ellison until I had formed my own style of writing" (Fitzgerald and Marchant 13). Furthermore, Arnold Rampersad in *Ralph Ellison: A Biography* reveals something that Gaines has expressed only to his closest confidants, something he has sought to keep out of print to avoid offending Ellison devotees: that he has little regard for Ellison's work in fiction and believes that *Shadow and Act* is a much better book than *Invisible Man*. In terms of the *literary* influence he received during his development, Gaines asserts he "had to get it from Faulkner and from Joyce, but not from Richard Wright or Ellison or Baldwin or anybody like that. They [Faulkner and Joyce] showed me how to get it much better than the black writers had done because so many of them really dealt with style, whereas I think the black writers are much more interested in content" (Fitzgerald and Merchant 13–14). But he also explains that he had to get what he needed from white writers because works by black writers were not available to him when he was a boy in the South and a teen in the seaport town of Vallejo, California (*Mozart and Leadbelly* 7), and few if any works of black literature were included in the English curriculum when Gaines attended San Francisco State and Stanford.

Beavers's conception of a relationship between Ellison and Gaines employs the critic's license to compare the thematic threads found in different writers' works in an effort to discover various literary connections in the writing, but he does not overstate his case. He was attracted to Gaines because of the author's devotion "to an interrogation of American experience in ways that *resemble* Ellison's refusal to accept narrow definitions of diversity" (6; emphasis added). Furthermore, Beavers states that similar to Ellison, Gaines's fiction is "peopled by characters who valued acts of storytelling and whose stories were attempts to understand their lives in terms larger than those afforded by race" (6). Unlike several recent studies that now circulate in the field of African American literary studies, Beavers does not go so far as to claim that Gaines's work is all or in part the consequence of influence exerted by Ellison that could have stemmed only from Gaines's reading and then consciously or unconsciously rewriting his relative. However, there are critics in the academy who allege what is best described as an anxious literary influence on Gaines's work by other relatives in the tradition, including Wright. In trying to impose selected relationships of influence on Gaines, these critics assume, like Irving Howe did of Ellison and Wright, that they share a direct relationship of literary ancestor and progeny because of their common racial designations (recalling the old stereotype that claimed "all 'Negroes' are alike"). This allows critics to reduce the descendant's (Gaines) work to little more than a response to her or his relative forerunners (Wright et al.) when no more than thematic similarities—or what Beavers sees as resemblances—are evident. Although comparative critiques of writers based on matters of craft, style, and theme have long been an important methodological tool, the recent trend in the study of African American fiction is for critics to go beyond the act of pointing out resemblances to demonstrating how a writer's efforts in fiction can be boiled down to little more than an act of textual revision.

If two writers share a relationship by virtue of both being African American and not because of an immediate or discernable literary influence by one on the other's writing, the relationship between the two, based on Ellison's premise, makes them no more than literary cousins ("literary" by virtue of their common involvement with creative writing), not fathers and sons: They are related, but relatives do not always relate to or with each other, and people often go through life without ever having much contact with their more distant relations. In terms of Gaines and Dumas, it would be appropriate to view them as relatives who are linked not only because of "race" but also because of their shared Southern heritage and works steeped in a Leadbelly tradition of writing; however, it would be a mistake, if not a dishonest act by critics, to claim a direct literary relationship *through reading* between the two based on little other than circumstantial matters of resemblance. No matter what compels writers from various perspectives to express themselves through the use of fictional narratives, African Americans dating back to the production of the earliest imaginative expressions of New World African slaves have most often written because of the need to interpret through art their unique experiences as a people in bondage and the lingering effects of that bondage in their ensuing generations. Because of the circumstances from which black writing was forced to develop in the United States, writers have often explored similar thematic concerns while constructing plots that share common threads. Since literary criticism is primarily a process of textual analysis—although the conception of what we think of as a text has been expanded in recent years to include various kinds of nonwritten expressions—the nature of the work that most critics involve themselves with is most often limited to words written on the printed page. This is especially true in the study of African American narratives and has been that way since the domination of the field by "professional" critics beginning in the Reconstruction era, meaning it is growing more common to find commentators on the literature whose only excursions into the "black experience" are through the novels and stories they read and use for their specialized critiques. Unlike students who used to receive an education in Black Studies, critics today are no longer encouraged to view the black community as a classroom where they might learn valuable lessons about the very texts they seek to explicate.

It is important to keep in mind that African American fiction writers can also belong to other traditions and that assessments of their works can and should be based on factors other than race, although I would argue that readings should never ignore the cultural influences in the writing. (The word *race* is often confused with culture, but race in its Americanized conceptualization is most often used to signify little other than color, whereas culture entails a group's patterns of knowledge, belief, and behavior that are transmitted from one generation to the next.) African American writers might share common cultural influences that are not literary in nature, but they also have relationships with non–African Americans for a variety of reasons. For example, Dumas and Mark Twain are not only writers who have contributed to the tradition of Southern literature, but both have offered unique yet related depictions of the racial realities in the Southern environs of the Mississippi River, even if it turns out that Dumas never read a single work by Twain. Dumas and Gaines are both recognized as part of the tradition of Southern writing, whereas Toni Morrison is generally excluded (although some have tried to place her there because of her use of Southern settings in several of her works). Dumas could correctly be considered one of the recent pioneers of black speculative writing and a forerunner to Morrison in this area.[8] He is also one who helped to usher in an age of exploration into the spiritual realism of African American life by writers of fiction in the post–Black Arts Movement era, while Gaines seldom strays beyond traditional realistic representations—although there is a profoundly deep spiritual dimension in his writing that anxiety of influence studies tend to find antithetical to their specific agendas—something James W. Coleman has identified as an African American faithful vision.[9]

As Carolyn A. Mitchell has so perceptively pointed out, Dumas is a black Southern writer in the tradition of Jean Toomer in his "comparable forays into higher, spiritual consciousness" (309). But it is also important to note Mitchell's admission of the possibility "that Dumas may not have had Toomer consciously in mind, but that both authors 'resonated' at a vibratory level that made the younger man an automatic heir to what the older had begun" (309).

Just as an effort to form a connection of read literary influence between Dumas and Gaines would be problematic, so also is the insinuation of a relationship that certain scholars of black women writers once claimed existed between Zora Neale Hurston and Toni Morrison. When the critical euphoria over Hurston and Morrison was at its zenith, some assumed a direct influence on Morrison from her reading of Hurston's works, despite Morrison's insistence that she had not read Hurston's novels before she began her writing career. In a discussion with Gloria Naylor, Morrison states:

> The fact that I had never read Zora Neale Hurston and wrote *The Bluest Eye* and *Sula* anyway means that the tradition really exists. You know, if I had read her, then you could say that I consciously was following in the footsteps of her, but the fact that I never read her and still there may be whatever they're finding, similarities and dissimilarities, whatever such critics do, makes the cheese more binding, not less, because it means the world as perceived by black women at certain times does exist. (Morrison and Naylor 214)

The critics who, in Morrison's statement, do "whatever" are potentially damaging to the integrity of African American literature as a field of study, especially since it is a discipline that Morrison once said lacks the necessary systematic standards to help govern its related critical production (McKay 152).[10] Whether one agreed with their positions or not, the early Reconstructionists seemed involved in the task of establishing standards, as did Gates and Baker with their vernacular theories and some of the significant works of black feminist criticism of the 1980s and early 1990s, but today the field seems to lack recognized scholars who are entrusted to define the central goals and concerns of African American literary studies in the early twenty-first century. There are a number of influential scholars in the field, but the literature today is also infested with those who participate in what Trudier Harris has described as "the commodification of and exploitation of African American literature" ("Mis-trained or Untrained?" 462). Her statement is applicable to a significant amount of the scholarship being produced on works of African American fiction and published in journals and books by university presses. This is not to disparage the majority of academic studies that have been produced in the field in recent years, but it is important to wonder if the kind of scholarship being produced by Morrison's "whatever" critics would be tolerated in more traditional areas of study. In African American literary studies today, some scholars are no more than strollers through the field, and the nature of their critical inquiries can at times be compared to the pseudoscientific speculations into "black" subject matter performed by Adam Nehemiah in Sherley Anne Williams's *Dessa Rose* and Reema's boy in Naylor's *Mama Day*. Since they often write to a largely uninformed audience, at least in terms of the culture, they are frequently rewarded for their efforts.

An example of this can be seen in the efforts recent scholars have made to connect Gaines's composition of *A Lesson Before Dying* to that of other writers in the African American tradition, especially to Richard Wright's *Native Son*. Gaines claims in several interviews and in his own "Writing *A Lesson Before Dying*" that the story was influenced by the situation of a young man who was on death row in South Louisiana.[11] Based on Gaines's discussion of the research he did before writing the novel, none of it involved reading Wright's *Native Son*. Much of it entailed discussions he had with faculty colleagues and individuals from the local community, including several lawyers who were students in his creative writing courses at the University of Louisiana at Lafayette. Those individuals put him in touch with former law enforcement officials from the area who offered him details on how capital punishment cases were handled in small South Louisiana towns in the 1940s (*Mozart and Leadbelly* 53). Even the decision to set the novel in the 1940s—Gaines's original intention was for the fictional events to take place in the 1980s—was influenced by suggestions made by one of his former colleagues who informed him of several cases that had taken place in South Louisiana during that time. However, in *Black Metafiction: Self-Consciousness in African American Literature,* Madelyn Jablon declares that the novel was set in an earlier decade because of the influence of Wright's novel. Regardless of Gaines's prior statements about his not being influenced by other African American writers, Jablon writes of Gaines's work as a product of Wright's influence based on the critic's own circumstantial consideration of the text. Her attempt to create an influential link between *A Lesson Before Dying* and *Native Son* ignores prior statements by Gaines concerning the actual influences of the work.

Although one can argue that any act of writing fiction is a metafictional endeavor that involves such elements as revision, dialogism, and intertextuality, it is still surprising to see Ernest J. Gaines, of all writers, located in a study that seeks to promote awareness of black postmodern and experimental writing. It is even more surprising when a writer as postmodern and experimental as Henry Dumas has been completely overlooked in favor of Gaines. However, a critic must have a fairly thorough knowledge of the literature to have awareness of the experimentation found in the works of someone like Dumas.[12] Since he is so often associated with the Black Arts Movement and its inherent Black Arts aesthetics, which Jablon tactfully disparages in her study, it would not be surprising to discover that the critic never bothered to consider his work, much less examine it, to observe his investigations into new ways of fictionalizing the realities of African American life. But in this chapter of a study of "self-consciousness" in "black" literature, Jablon reduces the scope of conscious (and what she sees as unconscious) acts of black writing to specific responses to the reading of other black writers' texts.

In the chapter that discusses Gaines's novel, Jablon states, "Any study of metafiction must include a discussion of influence, for in the acknowledgment of literary predecessors, fiction demonstrates an awareness of its own status" (81). This might sound good, but literary fictions are the imaginative constructions of writers—human beings who respond not only to the texts they read but also to the world of human experience. The above statement speaks of fiction as if it is some kind of sentient entity that can act upon its own awareness, but in order to read someone like Gaines metafictionally using that kind of rationale, the critic must commit to finding influence even in places where real influence may not exist in order to justify the inclusion of the writer's work. The discussion goes on to say that "'if writing is a conversation with reading,' as Giovanni suggests, Ernest Gaines's *A Lesson Before Dying* is conversant with the genre of African American crime fiction, particularly Richard Wright's *Native Son*" (81–82). Crime fiction is a convenient categorization of the novels and one that actually places them in the same tradition occupied by the likes of Chester Himes's Harlem-set detective novels and Walter Mosley's Easy Rawlins chronicles. Conceiving of the two as crime novels is not difficult since both involve crimes in their plots; but despite the fact that *Native Son* is a thriller (an important trait in crime fiction) that was marketed as such to promote sales and make it a more appeasing read to mainstream audiences, it is important to ask if either author intended his work to be read in that manner. Of greater importance is how the novels fit or fail to fit within the generally accepted framework of the genre. Neither work is mentioned in the entry that discusses African American contributions to "Crime and Mystery Writing" in the *Oxford Companion to African American Literature*. Based on Stephen F. Soitos's discussion, it is obvious that neither work tries consciously to transform and signify on the "Euro-Americentric detective formulas" as African American works of crime fiction most often tend to do (182–84). In terms of *A Lesson Before Dying* and *Native*

Son, there is little about the novels' crimes as plot devices that are really similar enough to see one as a revision of the other or in dialogue with it. But how better to link Gaines's spiritually redemptive, understated Southern narrative to Wright's naturalistic urban exposé than to categorize both as works of crime fiction? There are obvious similarities in the two plots, but nothing that supports a reading of one as a rewriting of the other. In trying to make a connection between Gaines and Wright, it would be more understandable to see a critic compare Wright's stories set in the South in *Uncle Tom's Children* to some of Gaines's earlier works, such as *Of Love and Dust* and "Three Men."

Although Jablon claims the need "for a theory regulated by the historical contexts and cultural specifics definitive of black literature" (Napier 216), and proclaims her work to be devoid of the politics of the Black Arts Movement and the dialectics of Donald Gibson, a highly respected veteran scholar of African American literature whom she calls out for the use of "faulty logic" (15), Charles Scruggs finds those same elements "at the heart of her own book whose subject is ultimately not so much aesthetics as having the right ideas" (201). Those ideas, according to Scruggs, privilege concepts such as "improvisation, hybridity, and intertextuality" (202), but in doing so we are left to wonder how much the critic actually has to tell us about Gaines's novel or the other works she discusses in her study. Instead of offering illumination into a work of African American fiction, the critic seems more concerned with the advancement of the theoretical ideas she was trained to use, according to the introduction, during her graduate school training. The literature, therefore, becomes reduced to little more than a theoretical playground.

Keith Clark, in an otherwise enlightening study on literary black manhood, also argues for an influential literary relationship between Gaines and Wright in a study published several years after Jablon's. Clark draws his connection between the two through the trope of black manhood, but in doing so he also argues that *A Lesson Before Dying* figuratively converses with *Native Son*, making Gaines Wright's "literary native son whose father's words are indelibly etched into his literary memory despite his [Gaines's] attempts to minimize the kinship" (73). Although the literary native son metaphor is a clever one, Clark's attempt to place Gaines into a kind of forced paternal relationship with Wright raises ethical concerns. A literary father/son relationship implies that the son learned something from the father about the craft of writing—about style—as opposed to there being only relative thematic ties between them that could have resulted from various sources, both literary and extraliterary. Ellison's words must be considered here: Writers, including black writers, should be able to choose their literary ancestors, and a literary father is a writer's most immediate ancestral figure. It is curious to see academic critics try to fix Gaines with a black literary father such as Wright when Gaines came along in a place and time when black literary figures were not readily available for aspiring writers. How can the words of a previous writer in a tradition be etched into another writer's memory when those words went unread?[13] Should we label Gaines a liar in order to make the declarations of these critics ring true? Gaines admits little connection to Wright other than that they are both black men with Southern origins who have written novels about black men on death row. However, Sister Helen Prejean, who is, like Gaines, from South Louisiana, also wrote a book, although nonfiction, about a (white) man from the state on death row. Does that make her a theoretical literary cross-racial daughter to Wright and a mixed-genre half-sister to Gaines? To quote the title of one of the Last Poets' LP's from the Black Arts Movement era: "This is madness."

4.

> I ain't singing for you,
> I'm singing for a people who
> feel the same way that I do.
> —John Lee Hooker, "Heartaches and Misery"

Why is it so troubling for some to hear important African American writers proclaim they had not read or been significantly influenced by certain other black writers in their process of writing works that have since been picked up for study by those who are involved in the reconstructed field of African American literary studies? How do we respond when contemporary black writers claim that their stories and novels owe no real ties of influence to earlier canonized African American masterworks? Do we challenge the integrity of those writers because their testimonies do not jive with our theories of signifyin(g) "black" textual influence, especially when we see the evidence of possible textual influence from our own subjective reading of their works? It is one thing to point out resemblances in plots and themes, but it is entirely another to contradict a writer's personal testimony of her or his stated influences because of our own critical agendas. This is not to discount the valuable work critics perform in pioneering new and different readings through various methods of theorizing and experimentation, because this kind of scholarly activity is crucial to advancing our understanding of the works of individual writers and the literature as a whole. However, when the act of critiquing a work is done for reasons other than understanding it in relation to the author and the culture from which it was produced, we must question whether the critical exercise offers any real illumination of the subjected work.

Should Gaines have lied over the course of his illustrious career about his indelible influences and his relationship to a black literary establishment with whom he has not always had good relations? In terms of the validity of his claims about his background and influences, any newcomer to the study of his work can discover without much effort that Gaines has always shown disdain for aesthetic ideas that privilege a commitment to political dogma over artistic craft. After the publication of his early works in the sixties and early seventies, his background as a southerner who chose to write about the black Southern experience and his acknowledgment of non-black literary influences seemed so antithetical to the quest for blackness that dominated Black Arts at the time that many in black intellectual circles failed to look closely enough at his work to see that his portrayals of the black experience were as culturally "black" as any writer could hope produce. Because of Gaines's focus on the South and his construction of humanistic depictions of black life as opposed to the use of a more politically based aesthetic approach, his works were deemed by many black cultural nationalists as irrelevant to the cause and led to his exclusion from the circle of "acceptable" black writers.[14] Outside of the South, his works received little more critical attention, even after the advent of the Reconstruction Movement, than those of Henry Dumas until the success of *A Lesson Before Dying* (obviously helped by its selection for Oprah Winfrey's book club) pushed Gaines into a prominent place in the black canon. His emergence in the 1990s as one of the most important living African American writers—not a bold claim considering *A Lesson Before Dying* has been adopted by dozens of diverse public citywide reading programs from Seattle to Miami, and *The Autobiography of Miss Jane Pittman* has been adopted in a one-book reading program by the entire nation of France and many of its former francophone colonies—raises a crucial question for those of us involved in critical considerations of African American works: How do we construct a black literary tradition that includes prominent figures whose literary influences are not necessarily from black forerunners? One answer is that we challenge scholars who venture into the field to seek a more comprehensive and in-depth understanding of the literature, its traditions, and its influences, including those that are experiential.¹⁵

Jablon is correct in her study when she speaks of the need to counter the notion that African American writers, like Gaines, are influenced only through their relationships with white writers, but she, like the other critics who claim their own discoveries of particular "black" literary influences on his work, fails to realize that his black influences are not necessarily literary ones. This is interesting since there are writers, such as Morrison, who have tried to distance themselves from the often inaccurate and otherwise misleading imposition of white literary influences on their works by professional critics; in fact, when Morrison spoke of having "no systematic mode of criticism that has yet evolved from us," she also made the following declaration:

> I am not *like* James Joyce; I am not *like* Thomas Hardy; I am not *like* Faulkner. I am not *like* [sic] in that sense. I do not have objections to be compared to such extraordinarily gifted and facile writers, but it does leave me sort of hanging there when I know that my effort is to be like something that has probably only been fully expressed in music, or some other culture-gen[re] that survives almost in isolation because the communities managed to hold on to it. (McKay 152; emphasis in original)

It is the culture thing, what Gaines calls the Leadbelly tradition, that is increasingly neglected in critical considerations of African American fiction today, because too many critics lack those kinds of insights, and they find it more comfortable, if not expedient, to read works of African American fiction only in relation to other works, with the emphasis now shifting to black authorial influences. African American fiction writers such as Gaines, Morrison, and Wideman often write about those from the culture who, to borrow from John Lee Hooker, "feel the same way that I do." This feeling, one conveyed through their composition of black letters on white printed pages, often stems from a shared cultural experience that also manifests its influence in related expressions of the blues, gospel, jazz, r&b, and hip-hop, as well as other written genres (i.e., poetry, drama, and film) by African American expressive artists.

Wideman, like Morrison, has addressed the issue concerning the relationship between critics and writers. Critics, according to Wideman,

> are important if you want your stuff to be read, because they are the vehicle by which you are presented to the public. But I think very often

critics frustrate this ideal function. I think that a lot of times, because of ego, because of their own limitations, they stand in the way of the work. That's frustrating, and I get furious. It's a very unfair competition because there is no real forum in which authors can answer critics' charges. . . . But as I said before, the whole vexed relationship of black literature to the mainstream, the inability of critics to use black literature as technique, as art, the tendency of critics to use black literature as a way of trying to put forward certain ideological concerns and points of view—that has been a disaster for all black writers. (Samuels 30)

It is important to go back to the issue Joyce raised years ago when she argued that *black scholars* should base their work on a love of the literature and Gates's response on behalf of the *critics of African American literature* in which he said, "What's love got to do with it?" Love as a requirement to work in the field is as tricky of a proposition as it is in affairs of the human heart, but the need for fidelity is not. In opening up the field, the Reconstruction of Instruction movement made it possible for the next generation of scholars to embark on careers centered on the formal study of African American fiction and other genres of writing, but it also opened up the field to "dabblers," as Harris has described them—individuals who "locate a few points of entry" into the literature, identify selected writers and works for focus, and ignore the bulk of the literature and culture" ("Mis-trained or Untrained?" 462). Harris uses strong words in her discussion of these critics, because their incursions into the literature for the sake of academic capital not only create what Wideman describes as a "disaster" for the writers, but they also leave in their wake assorted pitfalls that future students and scholars will need to avoid. Although some may take issue with this claim, I do not believe scholars have the right to proclaim themselves as authorities or experts in African American literature until they have seriously read the contributions made by the many and various Henry Dumas-figures to the literature's history and traditions, even if their works cannot be found, conveniently, in the pages of major anthologies.

Notes

1. Reconstructionist critics in African American literature proclaimed their mission was to reconstruct the pedagogy and study of Afro-American literature so that it would reflect the most advanced thinking of a contemporary universe of literary-theoretical discourse. The early Reconstructionists were associated with the Modern Language Association's publication of *Afro-American Literature: The Reconstruction of Instruction*, edited by Dexter Fisher and Robert B. Stepto, in 1978. According to Hazel Arnett Ervin in *African American Literary Criticism, 1773 to 2000*, these critics tend to "separate the language of criticism from the vocabulary of critical ideology and establish sound theory and aesthetic values," and they still dominate the present age of African American literary criticism (17). As Keith Byerman notes, the Reconstructionists shifted considerations of the literature to the "formal and literary-historical" and away from it being used as a conduit for understanding the social and political plight of African American people (190). Several of the major Reconstructionist critics, including Stepto and Gates, opposed any dimension of African American literary criticism that were extraliterary in nature and instead focused on explications of language and their intertextual possibilities.

2. The entire Black Arts Movement section stands out in the anthology's first edition, and although it was revised for the second edition, the changes made were minor and merely consisted of shifting several writers to the Black Arts section from the much larger "Literature since 1970" section, which concludes the anthology.

3. Baker's comments may have been influenced by a consideration of only one story, "Will the Circle Be Unbroken," Dumas's most distinctive cultural nationalist piece in fiction, and one that was derided in reviews and comments by several scholars after the Random House publication of *Ark of Bones* in 1974. Reaction to this story was split along the Black Arts/Reconstructionist divide—it was considered one of the era's most poignant works by those who identified with Black Arts aesthetic ideas while being denounced as propaganda by those who ascribed to more traditional Western conceptions of art.

4. After the 1978 special issue of *Callaloo* on Gaines's work, notable discussions of Gaines's work include Marcia Gaudet and Carl Wooden's book-length interview, *Porch Talk with Ernest Gaines* (1990), and Valerie Babb's study, *Ernest Gaines* (1991). Other than those, there were as few as five other scholarly publications on Gaines in the 1980s, including one annotated bibliography and two published interviews, meaning there were only two critical treatments of his work during that time. On the other hand, *Black American Literature Forum* dedicated an entire issue to Henry Dumas in 1988 featuring contributions from notable scholars and writers, although few, if any, from Reconstructionist scholars. The issue appeared after the republication of selected works of Dumas's fiction and poetry in *Goodbye, Sweetwater* and *Knees of a Natural Man*.

5. For Gaines, the term *Mozart* represents a way of expressing the formal and classical influences on his work as a writer, whereas *Leadbelly* represents a folk or nonlearned influence that he sees as equal in value. According to Marcia Gaudet and Reggie Young in the introduction to Gaines's *Mozart and Leadbelly: Stories and Essays*, his early "exposure to classical and canonical influences in literature, art and music were important to his development as a writer . . . but he does not privilege these over those of his own cultural heritage" (xvi).

6. Of all of the writers of the African American tradition, Gaines most closely identifies himself with Toomer. In *Porch Talk with Ernest Gaines* he states, "one book

by a black writer that would have had as much influence on me as any other book would be *Cane* by Jean Toomer. What he does in those short little chapters are things that I wish I could do today, those short chapters, those little songs, the poetry between chapters. That is still my favorite novel of any black writer" (222).

7. Gaines has been queried several times in published interviews about the influence of African American writers such as Richard Wright, Ralph Ellison, and James Baldwin on his work. He has always offered the same basic response. Several examples can be found in *Porch Talk with Ernest Gaines* and John Lowe's *Conversations with Ernest Gaines*.

8. Sandra Govan examines African American speculative fiction in the *Oxford Companion to African American Literature*. Speculative fiction is a term that has been used by selected scholars and critics since the 1960s to categorize works that speculate on or explore various possibilities of existence beyond the more conventional literary representations of naturalism and reality. Speculative fiction is often used as a blanket category that covers many of the modes of genre writing that involve elements of the fantastic, such as science fiction, magical realism, fantasy, and utopian fiction. (I also include African American spiritual realism under this category.) Although the concept was most popular in scholarly and critical circles in the 1980s and 1990s, according to Govan, African American speculative fiction dates back to the publication of Martin R. Delany's novelistic slave narrative, *Blake, or the Huts of America*. Delany and other early African American writers who reflected "a speculative sensibility" included "those whose speculative vision projected a transformed world, a social revolution, or a radical change in the depiction of an altered reality" (Govan 683). The most noted African American writers of speculative fiction today are arguably Samuel R. Delany, Octavia Butler, and Nalo Hopkinson, but others such as Toni Morrison, Gloria Naylor, John Edgar Wideman, and Jeffery Renard Allen must also be considered. Although Ernest J. Gaines is not often thought of as a writer of speculative fiction, his works such as *A Cold Day in November* and *The Autobiography of Miss Jane Pittman* contain speculative elements of Southern folk culture, including acts of conjure.

9. Coleman's notion of faithful vision is similar in many way to what I call *spiritual realism*, although my focus largely entails a consideration of the rituals and beliefs that inform literary explorations of African American folk culture, whereas Coleman concentrates on the religiocosmic aspects of African American postmodern works. Coleman's study *Faithful Vision: Treatments of the Sacred, Spiritual, and Supernatural in Twentieth-Century African American Fiction* is important, however, because it is one the few extended critical studies that treats the "suprarational" aspects of the literature.

10. In a 1983 interview with Nellie McKay, Morrison confessed her disappointment in many of the critical treatments of her works because very few of them evolved out of the culture from which she writes. According to Morrison, "other kinds of structures are imposed on my work, and therefore they [her novels] are either praised or dismissed on the basis of something I have no interest in what[so]ever," and she called for critics who understand her works in terms of "how they function in the black cosmology" (151). It is in this discussion that Morrison called for "some pioneering work to be done in literary criticism," especially by black women, because of the lack of a systematic mode of criticism at the time. Many will argue that the major theoretical works produced in the 1980s by Gates (*Signifying Monkey*) and Baker (*Blues, Ideology, and Afro-American Literature*) represent the kind of criticism Morrison called for, but it is important to wonder if either begins to address her concerns about black cosmology. A number of black women critics such as Karla F.

C. Holloway (*Moorings and Metaphors: Figures of Culture and Gender in Black Women's Literature*) have come closer to addressing Morrison's concern, but these studies have not had the lasting influence of Gates's and Baker's works on the larger field of African American literary studies.

11. The discussion has been published as part of Gaines's collected essays in *Mozart and Leadbelly*. It is based on a highly popular talk he has presented about his process of writing the novel, including his influences.

12. According to John S. Wright in the introduction to *Echo Tree*, Dumas's most recent collection of fiction, "we find Dumas interlacing traditional Southern black folklore, legend, and myth with occult histories of the world and 'instauration' themes linked in sixties 'sidestream' fiction to utopian subversions promulgated by 'Pariah Elites' or 'Secret Masters,'" along with "elements of Gothic romance, the ghost story, biblical parable, the psychological thriller, and inner-space fiction . . . " (xii). In terms of what had been traditionally accepted as black or African American fiction when Dumas's works were first published, many of his stories had no readily available predecessors, meaning he had few apparent literary "ancestors," either black or white, to whom scholars could compare his works.

13. Despite the number of times I have used the term *tradition* in this discussion, as a concept, it is a problematic one. Wahneema Lubiano, for one, over a decade ago, asked "What is a tradition in African American literature?" but seldom have other scholars attempted to address her inquiry. From our perspective as specialists of African American literature, it is important to see the forerunners—such as Wright and Ellison—in the assumed tradition as having cleared out space for literary descendants such as Ernest Gaines to follow because of the work they had already done. However, this kind of thinking about African American writing, especially in fiction, relates to the way scholars try to rationalize writers in relation to their predecessors, but it has little to do with the way most actually engage the process of constructing works of literary art. Similarities in the works of black writers of different generations mean, to paraphrase Morrison, that "the world" as lived in and perceived by black people at different times does exist and that black writers, even those of different generations, are often exposed to similar social and cultural realities. That means resemblances in the writing are sometimes not from literary sources but because of black people's common experiences (and their common views of those experiences) in the world.

14. John Lang's entry on Gaines in the *Oxford Companion to African American Literature* calls attention to the criticism Gaines once received "for not embracing the tradition of social protest literature represented by Richard Wright's fiction" (308), and Valerie Babb notes how he was criticized "for his seemingly political neutrality" (136). Gaines has often elaborated on his relationship to the Black Arts Movement in interviews, private discussions, and small group talks. For example, he is still amazed that the only "damning" review he received of *The Autobiography of Miss Jane Pittman* was from "a black woman poet from Chicago, one of those Black Arts Movement people," who said the novel "was the most boring book she had read, and the only reason she read it was that she was supposed to review it" (personal interview; Lowe 318). Some more militant-minded critics thought "the book sent the wrong message in having a little old black lady drink from a water fountain" as opposed to the character taking a more pronounced stand against the white oppressor (personal interview). Gaines said, "And even after the book was published, I was still attacked by many of the black militants for having spent my time working on this [*The Autobiography of Miss Jane Pittman*] when I should have been out there fighting cops" (Lowe 317). Gaines himself has stated of his early career:

> . . . you had to write a *Soul on Ice* [Cleaver] or LeRoi Jones–type stories to get attention from the black kids on campus. I don't know whether it was fortunate or unfortunate that my books were beginning to be published at the time when a lot of the militant demonstrations were going on, and I wasn't considered part of that crowd. I wasn't writing in *The Black Scholar,* or *Black World,* or some of the more militant papers, so I was not accepted as that kind of writer. (Tarshis 78)

15. There is not a particular approach to the study of African American fiction that I would recommend, but I would suggest that if fiction is a cultural expression, and if human experience is the lifeblood of fiction (as many writers are taught), then critical studies of black fiction, no matter what approach scholars use, should show sensitivity to the culture and experiences that inform the literature. This is not to say that we must take a cultural studies approach but that we should at least avoid assertions that come off as arrogant and paternalistic toward the writers. Beavers's study, for example, offers a close analysis of Gaines's and McPherson's novels and stories, and he also argues for a kindred relationship between the two and Ellison. His primary focus is literary, but in discussing what he sees as the relationship between Gaines and McPherson and their predecessor (not "father") in the African American tradition, he also offers respectful consideration of the writers' biographies and their comments about their literary influences and histories as readers. He does not make unsubstantiated claims, and the kinship he sees between the latter two and their literary forerunner is based on their being writers whose footprints in the tradition seem to most closely resemble the ones that Ellison left behind—not on their having consciously or unconsciously mimicked Ellison in their writing.

Two useful examples of critical studies that view works of African American fiction in relationship to cultural influences are A. Yemisi Jimoh's *Spiritual, Blues, and Jazz People in African American Fiction: Living in Paradox* and James W. Coleman's *Faithful Vision: Treatments of the Sacred, Spiritual, and Supernatural in Twentieth-Century African American Fiction.* As their titles indicate, Jimoh reads works of African American fictional narratives in relationship to the musical expressions that are often a crucial dimension of black texts, and Coleman approaches African American works of fiction through a consideration of what many critics tend to dismiss as religion, although the study is far from limited by simple religious concerns. Jimoh's study offers a historical overview of the influence of musical idioms beginning with the era of blackface minstrelsy in the mid-nineteenth century through the 1960s. Even though she focuses on contemporary works of black fiction, Jimoh offers a useful approach to reading recent works of African American fiction and for relating contemporary works to those produced by earlier writers, since the development of black musical forms most often parallels those found in literature. *Faithful Vision* treats novels produced in the second half of the twentieth century and illustrates how works of African American fiction often blur the lines between secular and nonsecular realities through what Coleman conceives of as the work's faithful vision. Although he does not examine any works by Gaines or Henry Dumas, both would comfortably fit into this study, whereas Richard Wright would not.

Works Cited

Babb, Valerie Melissa. *Ernest Gaines.* Boston: Twayne, 1991.

Baker, Houston A., Jr. "The Black Arts Era: 1960–1970." In Gates and McKay 1831–50.
———. "In Dubious Battle." *New Literary History* 18 (1987): 363–69.
Baker, Houston A, and Patricia Redmond. *Afro-American Literary Study in the 1990s*. Chicago: University of Chicago Press, 1989.
Beavers, Herman. *Wrestling Angels into Song: The Fictions of Ernest J. Gaines and James Alan McPherson*. Philadelphia: University of Pennsylvania Press, 1995.
Byerman, Keith. "Criticism since 1965." In *Oxford Companion* 190–92.
Clark, Keith. *Black Manhood in James Baldwin, Ernest J. Gaines, and August Wilson*. Urbana: University of Illinois Press, 2002.
Coleman, James W. *Faithful Vision: Treatments of the Sacred, Spiritual, and Supernatural in Twentieth-Century African American Fiction*. Baton Rouge: Louisiana State University Press, 2006.
Dumas, Henry. *Goodbye, Sweetwater*. New York: Thunder's Mouth Press, 1988.
Ellison, Ralph. *Shadow and Act*. New York: Vintage, 1972.
Ervin, Hazel Arnett., ed. *African American Literary Criticism, 1773 to 2000*. New York: Twayne, 1999.
Fitzgerald, Gregory, and Peter Marchant. "An Interview: Ernest J. Gaines." In Lowe 3–15.
Gaines, Ernest J. *A Lesson Before Dying*. New York: Vintage, 1994.
———. *Mozart and Leadbelly: Stories and Essays*. Comp. and ed. Marcia Gaudet and Reggie Young. New York: Knopf, 2005.
———. Personal interview. August 17, 2004.
Gates, Henry Louis. "Canon-Formation and the Afro-American Tradition." In Baker and Redmond 14–39.
———. "'What's Love Got to Do with It?' Critical Theory, Integrity, and the Black Idiom." *New Literary History* 18 (Winter 1987): 345–62.
Gates, Henry Louis, and Nellie Y. McKay, eds. *The Norton Anthology of African American Literature*. New York: Norton, 1997; 2nd ed. 2004.
Gaudet, Marcia, and Carl Wooton. *Porch Talk with Ernest Gaines*. Baton Rouge: Louisiana State University Press, 1990.
———. "Talking With Ernest Gaines." In Lowe 221–40.
Gibson, Donald. "Response to Gates." In Baker and Redmond 44–50.
Govan, Sandra Y. "Speculative Fiction." In *Oxford Companion* 683–87.
Harris, Trudier. "August Wilson's Folk Traditions." In *August Wilson: A Casebook*. Ed. Marilyn Elkins, 49–67. New York: Garland, 1994.
———. "Mis-Trained or Untrained? Jackleg Critics and African American Literature (Or, Some of My Adventures in Academia)." In Ervin 461–70.
———. *South of Tradition: Essays on African American Literature*. Athens: University of Georgia Press, 2002.
Harrison, Paul Carter. "Mother/word: Black Theater in the African Continuum: Word/song as Method." In *Totem Voices: Plays from the Black World Repertory*. Ed. Harrison, xi–lxiii. New York: Grove, 1989.
Hill, Patricia Liggins, et al., eds. *Call & Response: The Riverside Anthology of the African American Literary Tradition*. Boston: Houghton, 1998.
Holloway, Karla F. C. *Moorings and Metaphors: Figures of Culture and Gender in Black Women's Literature*. New Brunswick, NJ: Rutgers University Press, 1992.
Jablon, Madelyn. *Black Metafiction: Self-Consciousness in African American Literature*. Iowa City: University of Iowa Press, 1997.
Jones, LeRoi. *Blues People: The Negro Experience in White America and the Music That Developed from It*. New York: Morrow, 1963.

Joyce, Joyce A. "The Black Canon: Reconstructing Black American Literary Criticism." *New Literary History* 18 (1987): 335–44.

———. "Who the Cap Fit: Unconscionableness in the Criticism of Houston Baker and Henry Louis Gates, Jr." *New Literary History* 18 (1986): 371–84.

Lang, John. "Ernest Gaines." In *Oxford Companion* 307–8.

Lowe, John. "An Interview with Ernest Gaines" (1994). In *Conversations with Ernest Gaines*. Ed. Lowe, 297–328. Oxford: University of Mississippi Press, 1995.

McKay, Nellie. "An Interview with Toni Morrison." In Taylor-Guthrie 138–55.

Mitchell, Carolyn A. "Henry Dumas and Jean Toomer: One Voice." *Black American Literature Forum* 22 (Summer 1988): 297–309.

Morrison, Toni. "On Behalf of Henry Dumas." *Black American Literature Forum* 22 (1988): 310–12.

Morrison, Toni, and Gloria Naylor. "A Conversation: Gloria Naylor and Toni Morrison." In Taylor-Guthrie 188–217.

Napier, Winston. Review of *Black Metafiction* by Madelyn Jablon. *MELUS* 23 (1998): 216–19.

The Oxford Companion to African American Literature. Ed. William L. Andrews, Frances S. Foster, and Trudier Harris. New York: Oxford University Press, 1997.

Prejean, Helen. *Dead Man Walking: An Eyewitness Report of the Death Penalty in the United States*. New York: Random House, 1993.

Rampersad, Arnold. *Ralph Ellison: A Biography*. New York: Knopf, 2007.

Rowell, Charles H. "An Interview with John Edgar Wideman." In TuSmith 86–104.

Samuels, Wilfred D. "Going Home: A Conversation with John Edgar Wideman." In TuSmith 14–31.

Scruggs, Charles. Rev. of *Black Metafiction* by Madelyn Jablon. *American Literature* 70 (March 1998): 202–3.

Soitos, Stephen F. "Crime and Mystery Writing." In *Oxford Companion* 182–84.

Tarshis, Jerome. "The Other 300 Years: A Conversation with Ernest J. Gaines, Author of *The Autobiography of Miss Jane Pittman*." In Lowe 72–79.

Taylor-Guthrie, Danille, ed. *Conversations with Toni Morrison*. Oxford: University Press of Mississippi, 1994.

TuSmith, Bonnie, ed. *Conversations with John Edgar Wideman*. Oxford: University Press of Mississippi, 1998.

Welburn, Ron. "Seeing and Listening: A Poet's Literacies." In *Multicultural Literature and Literacies: Making Space for Difference*. Ed. Suzanne M. Miller and Barbara McCaskill, 21–36. Albany: SUNY Press, 1993.

Williams, Dana A. "Making the Bones Live Again: A Look at the 'Bones People' in August Wilson's *Joe Turner Come and Gone* and Henry Dumas's 'Ark of Bones.'" *CLA Journal* 42 (1999): 309–19.

Wright, John S. "Introduction." In *Echo Tree: The Collected Short Fiction of Henry Dumas*. Ed. Eugene B. Redmond. Minneapolis: Coffee House Press, 2003.

2

Ideological Tension

Cultural Nationalism and Multiculturalism in the Novels of Ishmael Reed

JENNIFER A. JORDAN

> A foolish consistency is the hobgoblin of little minds, adored by little statesmen and philosophers and divines. With consistency a great soul has simply nothing to do.
> —Ralph Waldo Emerson, Emerson, Spiritual Laws

> What goes round comes round—African American folk origin.
> —OED

Ishmael Reed has represented himself, since the early 1970s, as an opponent of the Black Arts Movement and an advocate of multiculturalism. His conflict with critics that he associated with the Black Arts Movement, such as Addison Gayle and Houston Baker, is well documented (Martin 41–62). But a careful examination of Reed's novels from *Free-Lance Pallbearers* (1967) to *Japanese by Spring* (1993) reveals an ongoing cultural nationalism that is consistent with many of the precepts of the Black Arts Movement and that deconstructs the multiculturalism that coexists with it. Of course, *Mumbo Jumbo* (1972) is the most overtly nationalistic text, so much so that Houston Baker in a *Black World* review designated it as "a guide for the contemporary black consciousness intent on the discovery of its origins and meanings" ("Books Noted: *Mumbo Jumbo*" 63). But even Reed's last novel, *Japanese by Spring*, despite a continual attempt to reinforce cultural diversity, returns to a black cultural nationalism that represents African culture as a solution to the trauma inflicted by an increasingly aggressive and global conservatism.

There are many ways of defining the black nationalism of the sixties.[1] However, most nationalists espoused the notion of black people as a separate nation—a nation that voluntarily segregated itself from white America, that possessed its own culture and that strove to define and control its own institutions. Nationalists represented white America as oppositional and oppressive, but they varied in terms of their involvement in political activism—an activism that ranged from community organizing to calls for revolution. Some focused on economic development and institution building or were primarily interested in cultural issues, including religion. Black cultural nationalists during the sixties tended to privilege culture over politics and economics, but even among cultural nationalists there were ideological disagreements. Nationalist critics and artists occupied spaces on the political continuum from the extreme left to the right. Despite the political differences, most cultural nationalists argued that African American culture possessed special characteristics and a definable history. This culture required a specific aesthetic by which it could be understood and evaluated. Depending on their orientation, various artists and critics perceived the true black culture to be either the folk culture of African Americans or a kind of essentialist African culture. A few artists like Ishmael Reed and Amiri Baraka (then LeRoi Jones) were fascinated by a variety of manifestations of Africanist culture, whether they be African American folk culture, their notion of authentic African culture/s, or the manifestations or carryovers of Africa in African American culture.

The nationalist impulse of the sixties resulted in a notion of the primacy of the African/African American culture and in a binary approach that juxtaposed that culture to an essentialized European culture. Carole Boyce Davies argues that both Eurocentrism and Afrocentrism function out of the same logic that implies dominance and control in relationship to other cultures, although she makes clear that Afrocentrists cannot wield the power necessary to actualize that domination in the real world (96). Although Ishmael Reed insists on his belief in a multicultural world, there exists in his novels a continual inclination to resort to a chauvinistic representation of African/African American culture and to revert to the Africanist versus European binary that dominated Afrocentricity in the sixties and that dominates Afrocentric discourse now.

Ishmael Reed's nationalism has, since *Mumbo Jumbo*, coexisted uneasily with a type of multiculturalism, but multiculturalism, like nationalism, has proven to be protean in its manifestations. In an excellent article that examines the history of the critical response to multiculturalism, Timothy Powell identifies the most superficial type of diversity as a *boutique multiculturalism*, a term coined by Stanley Fish in a 1997 *Critical Inquiry* article. The boutique multiculturalism focuses on superficial manifestations of culture, such as foods and festivals, to be sampled primarily by the consumer (cited by Powell 154). Such a multiculturalism is the most easily exploited and commodified.[2] It also results, according to Fish, in a type of "universal identity." This sort of patchwork universality is actually embraced by Ralph Ellison in the essay "The Little Man at Chehaw Station." He describes a six-foot-six-inch "light-skinned, blue-eyed, Afro-American-featured individual," dressed in an African dashiki, English Jodhpurs, and a Homburg and driving a Volkswagen Beetle with a Rolls-Royce front. To him this theatrically costumed "homeboy" and his purposeful eclecticism serve as a challenge to white America's rejection of cultural integration and an example of the "new possibilities of perfection" in a multicultural nation (22–24).

Powell argues that multiculturalism as it has been defined and practiced in the last thirty years has been either superficial or mildly disruptive in the aesthetic manner described by Ellison. According to Powell, proponents of a more political multiculturalism have been activist, subversive, and multifocal (159–64).[3] Powell seems to promote a polycentric multiculturalism[4] in which "fiercely independent cultures continually come together and come apart" (157) but in the long run create an effective whole that will transform the academy and America. Boyce Davies argues that a polycentric multiculturalism based on each group's culture, ethnicity, and history is doomed to ineffectiveness and argues for a polycentricism based on the class, social, and political commonalities around which everyone can unite to challenge neocolonialism and capitalism (102–3).

It is Powell's notion of multiculturalism that is most consistently reflected in Ishmael Reed's activism and art. As early as 1968 Reed called for "a cooperation of autonomous groups" ("When State Magicians" 13). For him, multiculturalism allows for a centering through one's own culture and a cooperative struggle with other ethnic groups against the enemies of equality and diversity. Part of that struggle for Reed was a pragmatic involvement in cultural institutions that challenged the notion of a monoculture. In 1976 Reed founded the Before Columbus Foundation with a group of artists from a variety of ethnic groups, including Simon Ortiz, an American Indian poet; the Asian artist/designer Bob Onodera; the Asian writer Shawn Wong; and Bob Callahan, the Irish American editor of Turtle Press. The purpose of the foundation was to challenge the idea that American culture was essentially European and to reinforce the notion that all ethnic and racial groups not only had contributed to the overall cultural production of the United States but also had influenced each other (Reed, "The Great Tenure Battle" 262). The foundation began the kind of multicultural conversation that thirty years later seems the norm. It sponsored readings for writers and poets as far away as Alaska, served as a national and international book distributor for 125 multiethnic small presses and magazines, and in 1976 instituted the American Book Awards ("Interview" with Helm 156; Reed, "And That History" 268–69). Selections from the writings of the winners, who frequently included world-famous writers like Toni Morrison and Louise Erdrich, have been collected in two anthologies, *The Before Columbus Foundation Fiction Anthology* and *The Before Columbus Foundation Poetry Anthology*, both published in 1992. Reed also cofounded a publishing company—Reed, Cannon and Johnson—which over the years published a wide range of works, including the second book of the Native American poet Joy Harjo, *What Moon Drove Me to This* (1979), a rare and highly collectible volume, which can be had for a minimum of $175 on Amazon.com. One of the most recent texts of the company is a collection of poems by Amiri Baraka, *Un Poco Low Coup* (2004).

A great believer in the necessity and power of the small magazine to promote his vision of a multicultural America, Reed has over the years edited a number of journals. In 1971 he founded the journal *Yardbird Reader* with a group of volunteers to publish minority writers and European American writers who he felt had been ignored by mainstream publishers and periodicals ("Interview" with Abbott and Simmons 78–79, 92). *Yardbird Reader, Volume 3*, for instance, was a highly praised anthology of Asian American writers. *Yardbird Reader* was followed by *Y'Bird*, *Quilt*, and *Konch*, which started as a print journal in 1990 and moved online in 1998 (Reed, "Konch at 16").

Despite Reed's philosophical interest in multiculturalism and his continual struggle to sustain multicultural institutions, his writings frequently gravitate toward a nationalism that belies his insistence that various ethnic and racial groups can come together in progressive struggle as cultural equals. Although he consistently insists that African and African American cultures are expansive and syncretic enough to incorporate the cultural influences of other groups in America (Martin 70–74, 76–77; "Ishmael Reed: A Conversation with John Domini" 137), the result of that syncretism seems to be simply a stronger Africanist presence in his literature. Most of his novels, from the earliest to the latest, insist on the primacy of African culture and/or fail to incorporate a viable representation of the multicultural possibilities.

Early in his career, Ishmael Reed began the struggle to balance his nationalist impulses with the eclecticism that defined both his intellectual and social inclinations. He was a member of Umbra, a group that many critics and the participants in the Black Arts Movement credit as an early battlefield in the struggle to define the black aesthetic. Reed's position in the battle is impossible to define, and he has, perhaps wisely, refused to explain. According to a number of the participants, Umbra was essentially nationalist in that its participants, even the white ones, were interested in work that expressed "a certain consciousness using materials, using subject matter and trying to explore certain techniques in poetry that are consciously and definitely from African American experience" (Oren 242). But participants recollect that the movement was troubled by a number of divisions—nationalism versus integration, political activism versus aestheticism, and even class resentments. Michael Oren argues that Ishmael Reed was, at the point of the greatest conflict over ideology, " the spokesman and principal strategist" (241) for the cultural nationalist dissidents, most of whom eventually migrated from the East Village to Harlem and Baraka's Black Arts Repertory Theater/School. Reed was housemates with the nationalists who were evidently taking advantage of his hospitality by not paying their share of the rent. Calvin Hernton describes the breakup with the nationalist faction. According to Hernton, the group began to criticize Reed for the Eurocentric references in his poetry and for his romantic involvement with a Jewish woman. These differences resulted in the end of the living situation and the move of several of the more nationalistic members of Umbra to Harlem with Baraka (Oren 246).

Umbra members have offered a variety of conjectures about Reed's inconsistent political positions during the period. There were those who felt he simply liked a good fight. Less charitably, Hernton argued that he was essentially an opportunist who lined up with whichever side was winning. On the other hand, Art Berger, one of the few white members of Umbra, felt Reed liked the challenge of being in opposition to power. Jane Poindexter, an ex-girlfriend, contends that Reed had no real "thought-out coherent political analysis." She tells Oren, "I don't think he's incapable of taking [an ideological or political position] or having one, but I think he's very capable of renouncing it the next month" (247).

According to Oren, by the time Ishmael Reed edited *19 Necromancers from Now* in 1970, he was openly hostile to the Black Nationalist Movement. But Reed's real anger was directed toward nationalist academics, Addison Gayle and Houston Baker. Even as he sparred with those two and "disown[ed]" the Black Aesthetic ("Interview" with Young 44), he continued to publish his poetry and essays in *Black World*, the primary journal of the black consciousness movement for artists and critics.[5] Reed tends to lump Baker and Gayle together as elitist intellectuals who were distant from the culture of the average black American, but Baker and Gayle are very different critics.

Although Addison Gayle praises Ishmael Reed as "the best black satirist since George Schuyler" (*The Way* 332) and includes Reed's introduction to *19 Necromancers from Now* in his anthology *The Black Aesthetic* (1971), Reed rejects Gayle's love of orthodoxy and the notion that the scholar rather than the artist should be a definer of an aesthetic. Reed finds especially egregious the idea that all Black writers had to follow the dictates and restrictions of one particular aesthetic and accuses Gayle of threatening to "machine-gun" those writers who fail to meet certain standards ("Ishmael Reed: A Conversation with John Domini" 135–36). Actually Reed misunderstands a metaphor Gayle uses in his introduction to *The Way of the New World*. Gayle cites a reference to the machine gunner from both Wright and Baraka and represents the novelist as "the machine gunner in the cause of mankind" (xxiii). Gayle uses this metaphor to reinforce a notion of the Black Aesthetic Movement that creative literature could be used as a weapon to transform America both culturally and politically. Gayle, basically a conservative thinker, saw this transformation as primarily cultural, an assumption with which Reed agrees. Reed is accurate in his belief that Gayle saw himself as defining guidelines for black writers. Reed perceives this dogmatism as a hindrance to the creativity of the artist and contends that the academic practitioners of the Black Aesthetic were giving "Marxism a black veneer" ("Ishmael Reed: A Conversation with John Domini" 141). If Reed had read Gayle more closely, he would have discovered that Addison Gayle was extremely hostile to Marxism (*The Way* 192–93).

What Reed is trying to identify is a fascistic tendency in Black Arts Movement, a tendency which, in its milder version, was essentially a kind of peer pressure typical of your average high school and in a weirder, more aggressive manifestation resulted in Larry Neal's being shot and Baraka run out of Harlem (Baraka, *Autobiography* 226–29). Reed later calls the attempt to define a black aesthetic "an urban professor's movement," which was "closer to Nazism or super-race philosophies" than to the black aesthetic of the Western hemisphere ("Interview" with Zamir 299).

Ishmael Reed's attacks on Houston Baker stem primarily from Baker's negative review of *The Last Days of Louisiana Red* (1974).[6] Baker was never a doctrinaire promoter of the Black Arts Movement and was interested primarily in putting the ideas of that movement into a form and vocabulary more acceptable to a wider—and not necessarily black—scholarly audience. Reed and Baker had more in common than Reed recognized, since both were at one point great admirers of Booker T. Washington (Reed, "Booker versus the Negro Saxons" 76–91; Baker, *Modernism* 37–41). But Reed reads his reviews and is sensitive to negative criticism. He speaks admiringly of what he perceives as a more accurate representation of *Mumbo Jumbo* in Henry Louis Gates's *Signifying Monkey* ("Interview" with Zamir 290), although Baker had given an equally positive review of *Mumbo Jumbo* (see above).

Certain aspects of the Black Nationalist Movement in the sixties receive harsh treatment in Reed's fiction. The academics of the Black Arts Movement are conflated with the old white left in Reed's representation of Bo Schmo and his neosocial realist gang in *Yellow Back Radio Broke-Down* (1969). Both are criticized for their disregard for the individual freedom of the artist. In *Free-Lance Pallbearers*, *Black World* becomes *Poison Dart*, a journal whose symposium on the role of the black writer includes discussions about whether the writer should "kinda stick out his lower lip and look mean" and "whether the brothers should part their hair on the side or part it down the middle" (80).

The early novels satirize the asceticism of the Black Nationalist Movement, which is represented by socially conservative elements like the Nation of Islam and Haki Madhubuti (Don L. Lee),[7] and illustrate the contradictions manifested by those who preached an anti-white separatism but availed themselves of the largesse of white academia and the government. In *Free-Lance Pallbearers* Elijah Raven, who wears the conservative dress of the Black Muslims and greets everybody with "Flim Flam Alakazam" (9) instead of "As-Salaam-Alaikum," is an agent of Harry SAM, the white tyrant who controls all. Raven claims a desire "to expose SAM, remove some of these blond wigs from off our women's heads and bring back ruckus juice and chitlins," but wears cufflinks from Sargent Shriver—at the time the head of the Lyndon Johnson's War on Poverty.[8] At the end of the novel Raven is exposed as the kidnapper of black children who are eaten by SAM. In *Mumbo Jumbo* the puritanical Abdul Hamid is represented in a kindlier fashion, but he is criticized for his hatred of pleasure and culture and for his love of "factories, schools, guns" and "dollars" (37). (The irony of this critique, given the focus of the *The Last Days of Louisiana Red*, will be explored later.) Abdul's greatest fear is sexual, and he destroys the Egyptian Book of Thoth, which is supposed to provide control and continuity to the

Africanist cultural energy, Jes Grew. Jes Grew is centered in the African American world and counteracts the rigidity, power, and racism of those who believe in Atonism, a monoculture of one God. But Abdul burns the text because it is "a lewd, nasty and decadent thing" and a "fabrication by the infernal fiend" (231).

Reed presents several parodies of the poetry of the Black Arts Movement in his novels. Reed's versions are simplistic, anti-white harangues that trivialize the notion of revolution. The first example in *Yellow Back Radio Broke-Down* is provided by the pseudomilitant Indian Chief Showcase, who ultimately is an agent of the white man and uses his anti-white poetry as entertainment at the wedding of Drag Gibson, the powerful white who controls the economics and politics of the West. The chief's poem, "The Wolf-tickets of Chief Showcase," excoriates the white man but is applauded by the white audience, who find it amusing and titillating. In *Free-Lance Pallbearers* Elijah Raven claims that he is creating revolution by "going round saying muthafucka in public" (73). Another parody of the style appears when Dupeyduk, the naive protagonist of *Free-Lance*, takes a job with a gay performance artist, Cipher. Cipher plays a tape of anti-white poetry during one of the performances, and the white audience is thrilled with the harangue, part of which reads, "WHITEY ... YOU WILL MEET YOUR DEMISE [...] CAUSE YOU CAN'T HOLD A CANDLE TO US VIRILE BLACK PEOPLE .... IF YOU DON'T WATCH OUT WE WILL BREAK INTO THOM MCCANN'S TOMORROW AND STEAL ALL THE SHOES" (77). Probably the most specific parody occurs in *Mumbo Jumbo* in a burlesque that almost replicates Haki Madhubuti's "Poem to Complement Other Poems" (Lee, *Directionscore* 104–5). Abdul Sufi Hamad's letter to Papa LaBas ends: "We must change these niggers! Change niggers! Niggers Change! Change! Change! Niggers! Make them baaaaaaad niggers!" (*Mumbo Jumbo* 230).

Ironically, the critics who promoted the Black Aesthetic Movement considered Reed one of their own with the publication of *Mumbo Jumbo*, a novel dominated by black-white binaries of power and culture. The novel, which juxtaposes Jes Grew and Vodoun against the Atonism of Europe, the Catholic Church, and the power structure, was highly praised. However, *The Last Days of Louisiana Red* earned Reed the wrath of some nationalists. That publication and his antifeminist positions cause many to continue to perceive him as a right-wing neoconservative. The review by Houston Baker in *Black World* that so angered Reed pronounced *The Last Days* as the unimaginative product of a "sophomoric consciousness" (52) and urged Reed to turn his rapier wit against the white power structure rather than the hustlers of the black left. Baker began and ended the review with a somewhat condescending tribute to Reed's abilities as a writer. Evidently the part of the review that angered Reed the most was Baker's assumption that he lived in the primarily white hills of Berkeley (Reed, "You Can't Be a Literary Magazine" 284). Baraka also responded to Reed's ostensible turn to the right. In a poem entitled "Red Eye," published in *Target Study*,[9] the nationalist Baraka offered to kill both Reed and Calvin Hernton for unnamed reasons (*Selected Poetry* 84). And as a Marxist, Baraka condemns Reed as a "traitor" who fails to support the subversive elements of the Black Arts Movement and who is guilty of an extreme individualistic and bourgeois orientation ("Afro-American Literature" 10–12).

The primary target of *The Last Days of Louisiana Red* is not the Black Nationalist Movement. Indeed, by 1974 a purposeful attack on the Black Arts Movement would have been the beating of a slowly dying horse. The movement had been greatly reduced by Baraka's switch to Marxism and the critical ascendancy of highly productive women writers like Toni Morrison and Alice Walker. The novel instead satirizes the New Left, the Panthers, feminists, and unproductive Negroes. The leader of the Moochers is Max Kasavuba, a white radical professor, who proves to be a racist. The Moochers recruit Street Yellings, the criminal son of the heroic businessman Ed Yellings, to serve as a nominal head of the organization. He is in exile in Africa and is described in a manner that evokes the famous poster of Huey Newton sitting in a large wicker chair holding a spear and a rifle. Street sits on "a huge hollow wooden throne" and holds "an archaic weapon in each fist" (83). Andy and Kingfish from the old radio and television show *Amos and Andy* are used to criticize another level of moochers—freeloading blacks who resent their more prosperous brothers, represented in the novel by Amos. In *Mumbo Jumbo* Reed had satirized both Haki Madhubuti for his poetic denunciations of the flawed masses and the Last Poets (he calls them the First Poets) because they went around Egypt telling the Egyptians "that they weren't ready . . ." (187).[10] In *Last Days*, however, Reed adopts a similar critique of what the nationalists would have considered the self-defeating habits of the Negro.

The heroes of *The Last Days of Louisiana Red* are the black middle class—businessmen like Ed Yellings, who serves as a model for his workers, each of whom is to continue his work, "taking care of Business, teaching, improving the quality of the product, giving the customer a fair deal, making only enough profit to sustain him or herself" (187). The "spit and polish" operation of Booker T. Washington (43) is Reed's standard for the black business world. Washington, an anal and self-righteous believer in the Puritan ethic, seems a strange hero for a man who promotes liberality, sensuality, and cosmopolitanism in the earlier *Mumbo Jumbo*. However, in an introduction to Booker T. Washington's *Up from Slavery*, later expanded in *Another Day on the Front*, Reed celebrates Washington's promotion of entrepreneurship, his lack of interest in integration, and his creation of a lasting educational institution. Reed even tries to ignore Washington's patronizing nigger jokes and his fawning over the English aristocracy in *Up from Slavery* to argue that Washington possessed a pride in his blackness ("Booker" 81). In *The Last Days* Reed also reveals his admiration for small businesses by including in his novel free advertisements for actual businesses that existed in the Oakland area during the period—the Roxie Theater; the Potluck; Narsai's; Casa de Eva; Ruthie's Inn, which promoted rhythm-and-blues acts; and the Tenth Street Inn, a venue for blues acts (49). Reed's later novels continue the promotion of entrepreneurship. Nance Saturday, the black detective in *The Terrible Twos* (1982) and *The Terrible Threes* (1989), quits law school to become a small businessman. In *Japanese by Spring* Reed includes a half-page listing of real small businesses in the Oakland area (223).

Reed's admiration of the business world and of the black middle class seems on one level to put him in direct conflict with the values promoted by the Black Arts Movement. Baraka, even before he proclaimed himself a Marxist in 1972, was especially hard on the black middle class.[11] But Reed's promotion of business and the middle class is not alien to the more conservative wing of black nationalism. Marcus Garvey, like Ishmael Reed, was a great admirer of business and of Booker T. Washington. Garvey had written to Washington from Jamaica and had planned to visit Tuskegee, a visit prevented by Washington's death in 1915. T. Thomas Fortune, a significant part of the Tuskegee Machine, later edited Garvey's *Negro World* from 1923 until 1928 (Verney 36).

The nationalist interest in ideas promoted by Washington and Garvey was reflected in a number of ways during the sixties. Lorenzo Thomas argues that one ideological inclination within Umbra was "the Booker T. Washington, Garveyite tradition of black self-reliance and self-sufficiency" (Oren 171). The ideals and practices of the Nation of Islam, with its desire for separate land within the United States, its small businesses, and its repudiation of involvement in American politics, have much in common with the programs promoted by Garvey and Washington. Don Lee (Haki Madhubuti) was and is a great believer in the building of black institutions and businesses, and his poetry and essays from the late sixties reflect his great respect for the discipline and work ethic of the

Nation of Islam (Jordan 50–51). Maulana "Ron" Karenga, the inventor of the commercially overexploited Kwanzaa and the cultural nationalist whose US organization influenced Baraka's establishment of his Spirit House after his move from Harlem back to Newark, encourages blacks in his *Quotable Karenga* to form businesses within the structure of American capitalism (36). In 1995 Ishmael Reed provided a black nationalist rationalization for his interest in business. In an interview with a group of writers, he argued that his study of Yoruba had revealed an African "hierarchical" civilization, based on "property and market economy" (Reed, "Gathering" 367).

Despite his fascination with business enterprises and the possibilities of success in a free market place, Ishmael Reed has throughout his writing career opposed the excesses of global capitalism. On various occasions he has expressed interest in socialist ideas (Oren 246; "Interview" with Helm 160). However, he sees communism as simply the flip side of capitalism—another monoculture violating individual rights ("Interview" with Helm 150). Reed provides a critique of global capitalism in the pro-business novel *The Last Days*. Ed Yellings is motivated to create a business that provides a sanctuary for workers who are "bedazzled by modern subliminal tendencies [and] manipulated by politicians and corporate tycoons, who posed as their friends, while sapping their energy" (9). Most of his novels, including *Yellow Back Radio Broke-Down* and *Free-Lance Pallbearers*, mock the unholy alliance between business tycoons and the American government. In *Flight to Canada*, Swille (a thinly disguised Nelson Rockefeller) controls both the Union and Confederate armies. He brags, "[E]verybody salutes our flag. Gold, energy and power: that's our flag" (48). As the country moved to the right with the Reagan years, the stranglehold of corporate capitalism and the conservative religious right on the government becomes the major target of *The Terrible Twos* and *The Terrible Threes*. In *Japanese by Spring*, Jack Only, a wealthy oilman, chairman of a right-wing think tank, and a member of a group similar to the Trilateral Commission, heads a kind of shadow government with tremendous power in the government, economy, and academia. Only and his group are described by the militaristic Dr. Yamato as "the people who are really in charge" and "who run things while the president is out jogging and commuting up to Kennebunkport" (184).

Reed presents global capitalism as the major source of racism. In *The Last Days* corporate capitalists manipulate racial tensions in order to exploit white workers (9). In *The Terrible Twos* the conservatives are motivated by racism to celebrate Hitler and Nazism and to form a coalition with the supposedly white Soviet Union to prevent the world from "turn[ing] brown and muddy and resound[ing] with . . . mad savage drumming and the strumming of guitars"(54). The conservatives concoct a scheme called Operation Two Birds, which involves bombing New York to get rid of the surplus people of color and the poor, blaming the bombing on Nigeria, and then dropping an atomic bomb on Nigeria to destroy the "black niggers who had the H-bomb" (141). Jack Only in *Japanese by Spring* wants to segregate black people in a South Carolina colony and finances the fascist student newsletter *Koons and Kikes* at Jack London College.

In his novels Reed's responses to the problem of the domination of global capitalism vary greatly. In *Free-Lance Pallbearers* the destruction of HARRY SAM simply leaves another group of tyrants in place, and the mocking of Bukka Doopeyduk's crucifixion implies the impossibility of salvation. The most hopeful ending takes place in *Flight to Canada,* which ends with the death of Swille and the triumph of Uncle Robin through subterfuge and the mask of submission. Most of the other novels—*Yellow Back, Mumbo Jumbo, The Terrible Twos, The Terrible Threes,* and so on—end with no resolution but with the survival of a resistance in various forms. In *Japanese by Spring* a weakening of global capitalism is implied by the physical appearance of Jack Only, who looks like "a giant craggy-faced cucumber with flippers" (192) and has to be carried by his black chauffeur. A fictional Ishmael Reed, who is a character in the novel, at one point insists that his organization will have no dealings with capitalists, but at the end of the novel he convinces Jack Only to replace the conservative board members of his foundation with a list suggested by Reed. Only asks Reed to be the chairman of the board, and the fictional Reed implies that such cooperation with the powerful may be a sacrifice necessary to prevent conservative forces from destroying the world. This suggestion, however, implies a compromise with the present economic system that is far from progressive.

Reed's resistance to global capitalism and attraction to a more primitive form of capitalism does not place him outside the pale of black cultural nationalism. However, his insistence on a multicultural world in his essays and interviews seems in complete contradiction with the separatist rhetoric of the Black Arts Movement. Yet there is no consistency about the role of other ethnic groups in the black nationalist tradition. According to Matthew Guterl, Marcus Garvey very actively supported Irish nationalists in their fight against British colonialism (323–37) despite the traditional racial tensions between black people and the Irish in America. During the Black Arts Movement, Larry Neal frequently exhibited an interest in the struggles of other people of color. In his seminal essay "The Black Arts Movement," Neal wrote, "When we speak of a 'Black Aesthetic,' several things are meant.... Essentially it consists of an African American cultural tradition. But this aesthetic is finally, by implication, broader than that tradition. It encompasses most of the usable elements of Third World Culture" (64). In defining the "question of national liberation for black America," Neal insisted that "our struggle is one with the struggles of oppressed people everywhere, and we alone must decide what our stance will be toward other nations struggling to liberate themselves from colonial and neocolonial domination" ("Black Power" 137). In 1966 Baraka—then called LeRoi Jones—implied a solidarity with at least other people of color when he attacked America as "a policeman working feverishly to keep nonwhite peoples down, in colonial or semi-slave positions, whether they are American Negroes, Africans, Asians, or Latin Americans. It is all the same ... " ("last days" 198). And Maulana Karenga, in Ishmael Reed's *MultiAmerica*, claims that his Afrocentric organization, US, trained and cooperated with Latino community organizations during the late sixties (201–2). Unfortunately, his inability to get along with his fellow black radicals—the Panthers—made it easy for the FBI's Counterintelligence Program (COINTELPRO) to manipulate the two groups into an armed confrontation that had deadly consequences.[12]

Ishmael Reed's continued interest in multiculturalism is reflected in his fiction. In his early novels *Yellow Back Radio Broke-Down* and *Free-Lance Pallbearers*, white youth are represented as a strong opposition to the tyranny of his wealthy white villains. In *Free-Lance Pallbearers*, the young black student, M/Neighbor's son, and his white sidekick, Joel O, are arrested, tried, and sentenced to thirty years on fabricated charges in a courtroom procedure oddly prescient of the Chicago 7 trial that took place two years after the novel was published. The treatment of the two defiant young defendants is similar to that suffered later by Bobby Seale, a Black Panther accused of conspiring with white radicals, who, after verbal outbursts, was bound and gagged in the courtroom during the trial. Reed's *Mumbo Jumbo* features a multicultural band of art thieves, Mu'tafikah, whose mission is to restore the art treasures stolen by the Western world from colonized and oppressed cultures of color. In *The Terrible Twos* President Dean is a positive white character who, once he discovers the perfidy of his conservative advisers, calls for disarmament, the nationalization of utilities, and the appropriation of the Rockefeller and Dupont estates for the landless. He proclaims in a speech that all people have "a right to exist which means the pursuit of happiness as well as the right to eat" (155). Oswald Zumwalt, a leftist who deserts liberal and radical causes and sells himself to big business, reunites with his progressive wife, Jane. *The Terrible Threes*, modeled after the Christmas story, finds the conversion of various white conservatives to liberal, pro-black agendas. Judge Nola Payne, after a visit from St. Nicholas and a penitent Judge Taney of Dred Scott fame, reverses the government's confinement of the newly enlightened President Dean. James Way, a conservative columnist modeled after George Will, suddenly gets religion after a similar dream, invites the homeless to Christmas dinner, and calls himself a "petty little son of a bitch whose whole career is built on baiting black people" (117).

However, Reed's promotion of multiculturalism is not effectively supported by its representation in his fiction. In the first two novels, interracial cooperation is a very minor theme. In *Mumbo Jumbo* the multicultural Mu'tafikah is hampered by conflict and is eventually destroyed when its only white member, Thor, proves to be more loyal to his race and class than to the organization.[13] The black leader of the group, Berbelang, who has encouraged Papa LaBas to integrate other cultural elements into his organization and who defends the traitorous Thor when the Asian Yellow Jack expresses his distrust, is killed by the police. In *Japanese by Spring* the Japanese who take over Jack London College are simply a different version of racism and fascism. At the end of the novel, they join with the capitalist Jack Only to stifle democracy in Japan. Reed's version of multiculturalism does not evidently include African people, despite his glorification of African culture. In *Japanese by Spring* the African who heads the African Studies department, Mutata Musomi, is a traitor imported by the capitalist Jack Only to lead African Americans astray. Musomi is a fictional representation of one of Reed's ideas repeated in various interviews during the seventies. Reed attacks West Indian and African intellectuals as opportunists "imported by mischievous whites to preside over [the African American's] political and cultural life, to stifle his rage and show him up" ("The Writer as Seer" 73; see also "Interview" with Abbott and Simmons 91). Reed ends *Japanese by Spring* with a weak version of boutique multiculturalism, a festival of ethnic foods and music. His parting symbol of multiculturalism, the black butterfly with yellow spots, is an illogical signifier of effective multiculturalism given the betrayal of the Japanese characters in the novel.

Reed makes a valiant effort to incorporate whites into his multicultural scheme. Bob Callahan has served as the token Irishman in the Before Columbus Foundation, and Reed has made much of the Irish genes in his own biological inheritance. But Reed has difficulty maintaining a consistent vision in his novels of whites who function as equal partners in a multicultural endeavor. Prior to *The Terrible Twos* and *The Terrible Threes*, white characters, whatever their class and political leanings, are usually flawed, if not completely traitorous, participants in any progressive endeavor. In most of the novels the archvillain is a ruthless white capitalist of unlimited funds and power. But the white left is also presented in a negative light. In *Free-Lance Pallbearers* the Marxist Nosetrouble, an ineffectual pedant married to a black woman, is later discovered having sex with HARRY SAM, the tyrant who controls everything. The aforementioned Thor Wintergreen in *Mumbo Jumbo* betrays Beerbelang, the black leader of Mu'tafikah who defended Thor when Yellow Jack, the Asian member, challenged the presence of a white person in their group.

White academics, even those who claim to be liberals or leftists, are portrayed as racists and turncoats. Max Kasavuba, the white English professor who is the head of the Moochers in *The Last Days of Louisiana Red*, is obsessed with the idea of black men having sex with white women and is ultimately using the organization for power and money. When the Japanese take over Jack London College in *Japanese by Spring*, William Hurt, the liberal dean who had previously insisted on the value of multiculturalism, eventually aligns himself with the neo-Nazi students to protect his self-interest, maligns black welfare mothers, and denies the existence of the Holocaust. Ishmael Reed, as a character in the novel, names white women as the biggest benefactors and exploiters of academic multiculturalism. According to him, these women dominate multicultural studies while "people of color" are denied jobs (109).

The white youth who represented resistance to white supremacy and global capitalism in *Yellowback Radio* and *Free-Lance Pallbearers* return to the safety of white privilege in *The Terrible Threes*. When Black Peter turns out to be a fake, "most of the white dreds who'd followed him had returned to their suburbs.[. . .] Many had moved on to prep school or joined" the religious right (57). In *Japanese by Spring* the young college students are more racist than their elders. They even attack the conservative Chappie Puttbutt, who is a firm believer in the American Dream. The text cites Herman Melville as the source of the idea that the "true savages" live in the "suburbs of upstate New York." These same suburbs are the sites of "drugs, alcoholism, incest, spousal abuse, child abuse, violence [and] fractured families" (100). White male students are portrayed as rapists and perpetrators of crime. Indeed, according to the text, they are responsible for "15 percent" more crime than "the communities surrounding their colleges and universities" (135).

Amiri Baraka, in an essay in Reed's *MultiAmerica: Essays on Cultural Wars and Cultural Peace*, contends that while fighting capitalism and Eurocentric cultural hegemony, all ethnic groups should appreciate the "accomplishment of European humanism" (393). But Ishmael Reed usually redeems his white characters by having them commit a kind of race suicide. When Judge Taney of the *Dred Scott* decision visits the conservative judge Nola Payne in *The Terrible Threes*, he regrets that he has not had Black Studies where he could have studied with Ivan Van Sertima, author of *They Came before Columbus*, a history of Africans in the pre-Columbian Western hemisphere much admired by black nationalists, or been exposed to James Spady, a contemporary black journalist and jazz critic. The detective Nance in *The Terrible Twos* and *Threes* has a Russian girlfriend who alienates her family by insisting that she is not of European descent but is instead of Tartar or Asian heritage. Reed feels the need to state that his wife, Carla Blank, is not "white" but rather is a "Semite" who "belongs to the same race as the Arabs" ("The Great Tenure Battle" 255). In *Japanese by Spring* Professor Crabtree, a Milton scholar, is forced to learn and teach Yoruba. He is transformed by the experience. He not only is able to speak Yoruba flawlessly, he attacks his former Eurocentric colleagues as intellectual "rednecks" (155). At the Yoruba ceremony near the end of the novel he appears in full Yoruba dress and sings a Yoruba song during the religious ritual.

Ishmael Reed's novels reflect numerous principles and ideas identified with the cultural nationalism of the sixties. Although Reed insists on the value of multiculturalism, several of his novels are based on a binary typical of black nationalism. A Eurocentric value system is juxtaposed with an African-based one. In *Yellow Back Radio* the pope battles the powers of Vodoun (also called voodoo or HooDoo). In *Mumbo Jumbo* European Knights of the Wallflower Order fight against black practitioners of an African-based Hoo Doo whose origins are Egyptian. In his last novel, *Japanese by Spring*, Reed returns to this binary by combating a European capitalism (even the Japanese are subject to it) with the world view of the Yoruba.

Reed's use of an iconology or mythology adapted from African and African American culture is similar to the approach taken by the artists/definers of the Black Aesthetic Movement. Larry Neal speaks of the need to replace traditional European symbols and archetypes in "The Black Arts Movement." According to Neal, "the Black Arts Movement proposes a radical reordering of Western cultural aesthetic. It proposes a separate symbolism, mythology, critique and iconology" (62). Neal, citing Karenga, lists mythology as one of the seven major components of culture (68).[14] According to Neal, Baraka's play/pageant *Black Mass* is his "most important," "mainly because it is informed by a mythology that is wholly the creation of the Afro-American sensibility" (73). The source of this mythology is the Nation of Islam's myth of the creation of whites by the evil scientist Yacub.

Ishmael Reed also makes use of both African and African American sources in the symbiology that informs his work. Decrying his Eurocentric education at the University of Buffalo, he speaks of his need to "create a mythology closer to me.[. . .] That's why I got into Egyptology and voodoo" ("The Great Tenure Battle" 268). Reed, on occasion, has admitted the influence of the Black Arts Movement in his use of African-influenced mythology. In 1973 he compared his use of Egyptology to the practice of the Black Arts poet Askia Muhammad Toure, who during the sixties made extensive use of Islamic and North African references. Both Toure and Amiri Baraka are praised as "revolutionaries" who rejected the "Judeo-Christian culture" of the West and "sought other sources for their material" ("Interview" with Gaga 54, 56). In 2003 Reed again acknowledged the influence of the Black Arts Movement writers who, like him, were seeking an alternative source of iconography and mythology. His earlier study of Egyptian culture was followed by a more detailed investigation of the culture and languages of West Africa, specifically Yoruba ("Battle of San Diego" 26–28).

According to Carole Boyce Davies, this focus on specific culture is central to Afrocentrism. She writes, "The varying and necessary positions and types of Afrocentricity [. . .] share a commonality [. . .]. in their culturalism and in their attempt [. . .] to find that center, that single source or originary point from which all emanate" (103). So Reed, as he moves through Egyptology and voodoo to the emphasis on Yoruba in *Japanese by Spring*, continues the search for a mythic base that began with the writers of the Black Arts Movement during the sixties. But the move to Yoruba as a cultural base is a move away from a polycentric multiculturalism. One of the virtues of neo-hoodooism, according to Reed, was its catholicity and ability to incorporate elements from all other cultures with which it comes in contact. Yoruba, in contrast, seems exclusory. The interest in Yoruba also replicates an early focus of black cultural nationalists. Baraka was briefly a student of Yoruba in the sixties (Baraka, *Autobiography* 215–17, 240), and during that period Larry Neal was married by a Yoruba priest ("Interview" with Rowell 12).

Another aspect of the Black Arts Movement shared by Reed is the insistence on the primacy of culture over politics and economics. In the late sixties some cultural nationalists argued that the transformation of black people's consciousness to a truly African one would be tantamount to a political revolution. Others contended that the political revolution could not take place until the cultural transformation was complete (Jordan 35–36). In a 1978 public conversation with other members of the Before Columbus Foundation, Reed contended that the weaponry of the powerful made violence an unlikely tool. He argued, however, that "[c]ulture can work more effectively than shooting it out with them. Yet, unless we see ourselves in warfare, guerilla warfare against illiteracy, against the numbing powers of mono-culture, then we're in danger of just becoming some kind of old lady's reading society" ("Before Columbus" 172). The notion of artist as fighter is reminiscent of the language of the sixties. Larry Neal in the essay "And Shine Swam On" states, "[T]he black artist must link his work to the struggle for his liberation and the liberation of his brothers and sisters.[. . .] The artist and the political activist are one. They are shapers of the future reality. Both understand and manipulate the collective myths of the race. Both are warriors, priests, lovers and destroyers" (22–23).

Reed, like the cultural nationalists of the Black Arts Movement, believes that creative art is a powerful tool for social and political change. In *Mumbo Jumbo* the narrator cites some anonymous author who "suggest[s] that the Nursery Rhyme and the book of Science Fiction [sic] might be more revolutionary than any number of tracts, pamphlets, manifestoes of the political realm" (20). Reed describes *Yellow Back Radio Broke-Down* as

> artistic guerilla warfare against the Historical Establishment. I think the people we want to aim our questioning toward are those who supply the nation with its mind, tutor its mind, develop and articulate its mind, and these are the people involved in culture . . . . What it comes down to is that you let the social realists go after the flatfoots out there on the beat and we'll go after the Pope and see which action creates a revolution. ("Ishmael Reed" with O' Brien 37)

In *Flight to Canada* Raven Quickskill, the writer, tells 40s, who is stockpiling guns, "Words built the world and words can destroy the world" (92). This statement seems to be a play on the biblical "In the beginning was the Word." But it also reflects the African concept of Nommo, which was much utilized by black nationalist theorists. In the traditional African worldview, the universe is energized by Nommo, a force that can be activated only through the power of language. It is through language that man and the gods control Nature and all inanimate objects.

Both the life force that makes all things happen and the verbal power that activates this force is called Nommo (Jahn 124–26).

Ishmael Reed's claims of multiculturalism are much hampered by his insistence on the centrality of Africa in world culture and history. Boyce Davies argues that Afrocentricity tends to "widen its center and locate everything in itself. Thus at its furthest reach it is not unusual to hear Afrocentrists claim that the entire world is Afrocentric, including All Europeans and their cultures, using the available archeological evidence to support this claim" (103). On some levels Ishmael Reed is guilty of the J. A. Rogers syndrome. Rogers, a newspaperman and amateur historian who began writing in the twenties, had a tendency to ferret out any hint of African genes in a famous individual and to claim the personage for the race in publications like *World's Greatest Men of Negro Descent* (1931) and *Five Negro Presidents, According to What White People Said They Were* (1965). Reed follows Rogers's example in a number of novels. In *The Terrible Threes* John James Audubon, whose African ancestry is not supported by most biographies, is called the "black illustrator" (96), and in *Yellow Back Radio* Cervantes is a Moor. *Mumbo Jumbo*, of course, makes the broadest claims. According to the novel, Dionysus, the Greek counterpart of Osiris, learns his art in Egypt; indeed, Homer's *Odyssey* is merely an appropriation of the Osiris myth. Moses marries the daughter of Jethro, an Egyptian, to learn the secrets of Osiris but becomes simply "a 2-bit sorcerer practicing the Left Hand" (205) or the distorted version of the rituals. Judaism is not the only religion influenced by the Egyptian mysteries. Mary is the Christian version of Isis, Jesus a white perversion of Osiris, and the Catholic mass an Egyptian invention. Even the negatives of Western civilization are products of the Egyptian Set, who is monotheistic, antinature, antiart, war-mongering, and hostile to nature and art. He is an anal disciplinarian, the "deity of the modern clerk," and perhaps the inventor of taxes (185). Both *The Terrible Twos* and *The Terrible Threes* predict an African Renaissance in which African nations combine the powers of their traditional cultures with technology to become world powers again. Despite revealing the dangers of European and Japanese nationalism, *Japanese by Spring* offers Yoruba culture with its social values, its conservational appreciation of nature and dedication to entrepreneurship as a model for the world.

Ishmael Reed has consistently maintained a type of cultural nationalism in his writings, but the rise of conservatism in the United States has provoked a stronger nationalist response from him. In the introduction to *Another Day at the Front* (2003), Reed replies to the notion that he is becoming "too black":

> Well, a racist society will often force you to engage in "essentialism" from time to time. I would prefer living as a world person on a planet that accepts differences instead of on one that is dull and monochromatic. But a funny thing happened to me while en route to this perfect world. I was fined for living while black. Being "universal" is difficult in a country where African-Americans are defined by the police, by the red-liners, by the racial and retail profilers, by the rude treatment in everyday life by people who are prejudiced. (xliii)

In a 1988 interview he complains that supporting a journal of African American literature controlled by whites is indicative of a "slave mentality" ("Interview" with Zamir 290). In *The Terrible Threes*, Nance, the black detective, explains his residence in a black ghetto. "Some [blacks] are marooned by choice from American society. . . . They don't want to integrate [. . .], and these ghettos as you call them are enclaves for the marooned. They have their own law, and their own leadership, like the Indians . . . , so on this block I'm the 'King'" (121–22).

In a 1995 report on the MLA conference held in San Diego and published in the *San Diego Reader*, Reed seems to have arrived at some sort of rapprochement with the Black Arts Movement. Although he had earlier been a harsh critic of the nationalist journal *Black World*, he celebrates it as a publication that challenged the New York publishing world's "control over the trends in African-American culture and thought" ("Battle of San Diego" 22). He expresses admiration for the Chicago-based Organization of Black American Culture (OBAC), whose members—Haki Madhubuti, Mari Evans, Carolyn Rodgers, and Gwendolyn Brooks—created an environment that produced black-owned publications and presses, such as *Black World* and Third World Press. Reed is an admirer of Joyce Ann Joyce, whom he sees as an independent critic willing to confront feminists ("Battle of San Diego" 22–23). In his 1997 introduction to the anthology *MultiAmerica*, Reed places himself on the side of the Black Arts Movement and Afrocentricity when he condemns the black conservative intellectuals who are rewarded by the establishment for "denouncing the black populist writers of the 1960s, or for opposing Afrocentricity" (xvi). He includes in the anthology former nationalists Amiri Baraka, Maulana Karenga, and Haki Madhubuti.[15]

Of course, any attempt to explain Ishmael Reed's novels and prose by pointing out the threads of cultural nationalism and multiculturalism that course through his work over the decades is reductive by nature. On one level his varying and sometimes contradictory positions validate DuBois's notion of the double-consciousness of the African American.

Even during his early days as a doctrinaire Marxist, Richard Wright was forced to acknowledge the power of nationalism. Despite his insistence in "The Blueprint for Negro Writers" that Marxism provides the proper perspective for black writers, Wright argues that "Negro Writers must accept the nationalist implications of their lives, not in order to encourage them, but in order to change and transcend them. They must accept the concept of nationalism because, in order to transcend it, they must *possess* and *understand* it" (1406; emphasis in original). According to Wright, black writers must comprehend the power of nationalism as long as America remains a nation divided by race. Amiri Baraka also struggles to balance black nationalism and Marxism. In his seminal essay, "Afro-American Literature and Class Struggle," he reaffirms his belief in the revolutionary nature of the majority of the participants of the Black Arts Movement and arrives at an archaic position very similar to the impractical ones of the Communist Party of the thirties and the Nation of Islam under the leadership of Elijah Muhammad. Wright contends that blacks must have "self-determination," one of the reasonable demands of both the Communist Party and the Black Power Movement, but, like the American Communist Party and the Nation of Islam, contends that this self-determination must exist "for the Afro-American nation in the Black Belt" (a now-imaginary place in the southeastern United States that was a more realistic demographic and political entity when the Communist Party promoted a similar program in the thirties). Baraka then calls for "equal rights—democratic rights for the black oppressed nationality everywhere else they be!" (11). Ishmael Reed obviously is not the first writer to have the need to rationalize the emotional pull of nationalism with the intellectual demands of other ideological positions. Reed need not resist his ethnocentric impulses or apologize for his inconsistent response to black nationalism. This very inconsistence reflects the history of the African American literary tradition and places him in some excellent literary company.

Notes

1. See Jordan 29–33.
2. There is an academic version of this boutique multiculturalism—the dissertation that carefully examines one white American, one African American, and one Hispanic text to explore superficially their thematic differences and similarities and to ensure a wide sea in which to cast the job search net.
3. See Powell for an examination of the leftist and feminist critics who argue that multiculturalism is a hindrance to the universality necessary to confront capitalism or patriarchy.
4. Another name for polycentric multiculturalism is "particularistic" (David Ravitch, cited by Reed in *MultiAmerica* xxi).
5. Reed published in *Black World* as late as 1974. His "Self Interview," republished in *Shrovetide*, first appeared in *Black World* in June of that year.
6. Baker published a review of *Louisiana Red* in *Black World* (51, 53) in 1975. Reed's angry response appeared in his literary magazine *Yardbird V* in an article called "You Can't Be a Literary Magazine and Hate Writers."
7. The Nation of Islam influenced many cultural nationalists who were impressed by its strict discipline, asceticism, and belief in entrepreneurship. Haki Madhubuti, especially abstemious about matters of diet and censorious of black social and sexual behavior in his lectures and poetry during the sixties, promoted similar emphases in a Pan-African framework during the sixties. See Jordan 35–36, 48–51.
8. Baraka's Black Arts Repertory Theater was funded largely by Har-You, a unit of the War on Poverty in New York. Funding for the group was ultimately cut off because of the anti-white rhetoric of the organization (Baraka, *Autobiography* 214).
9. The publication date of the poem is not clear, but *Target Study*, which was included in Baraka's *Selected Poems*, included poems written between 1961–67.
10. See poems like "Die Nigga!" on the album by the Original Last Poets, *Right On*.
11. For an example of Jones/Baraka's negative representation of the middle class, see Baraka's "Black Art," *LeRoi Jones/Amiri Baraka Reader* 219.
12. The COINTELPRO program of the FBI targeted , infiltrated, and manipulated black and white radical groups and even civil rights leaders like Dr. King. Their extraconstitutional activities were documented in the *Report of the Select Committee to Study Governmental Operations with Respect to Intelligence Activities of the United States Senate, 94th Congress, 2nd Session 1976*. The committee is also known as the Church Committee after its chairman, Senator Frank Church. See excerpts on a Web site posted by Paul Wolf, a human rights lawyer, at www.cointelpro.org.
13. David Mikics argues that Reed destroys Mu'tafikah because Reed rejects their belief in racially pure types. He cites Yellow Jack's remarks to Berbelang that African Americans lack militancy as evidence of dissension within the group (15, 26). Oddly Mikics ignores Thor's treason, and his evidence of dissension between Jack and Berbelang is discounted by Yellow Jack's later repudiation of his remarks about black Americans and Jack's contention that his only concern is his lack of trust in Thor.
14. Neal provides no citation for either the Knight or Karenga quotes. But the Karenga list of cultural components appears in the self-published monograph *The Quotable Karenga*. Patterned after the Little Red Book of Chairman Mao, it contains short, simplistic quotations from Karenga. The green softback cover has a picture of Karenga in the Buba designed and worn by the group US.
15. All these former stars of the Black Nationalist Movement of the sixties make some slight concessions to multiculturalism in their essays. Baraka mainly attacks

Eurocentrism. Karenga argues for multiculturalism but presents African Americans as playing "their historical vanguard role" in leading the way to change. Madhubuti simply reaffirms the need to fight white supremacy by establishing independent Afrocentric schools; calls for greater communication between English-speaking Africans in America and Portuguese-speaking Africans in Brazil; and speaks to the need to "tackle, absorb, decipher, reject and appreciate European-American culture" while remaining "first and foremost concerned" about one's own African culture ("Cultural Work" 448). He makes no mention of other ethnic groups in America.

Works Cited

Baker, Houston A, Jr. "Books Noted: *The Last Days of Louisiana Red.*" Review. *Black World* 24, no. 8 (1975): 51–52, 89.

———. "Books Noted: Mumbo Jumbo." Review. *Black World* 22, no. 2 (1972): 63–64.

———. *Modernism and the Harlem Renaissance*. Chicago: University of Chicago Press, 1987.

Baraka, Amiri. "Afro-American Literature and Class Struggle." *Black American Literature Forum* 14, no. 1 (1980): 5–14.

———. *The Autobiography of LeRoi Jones/Amiri Baraka*. New York: Freundlich Books, 1984.

———. *The LeRoi Jones/Amiri Baraka Reader*. Ed. William J. Harris, New York: Thunder's Mouth, 1991.

———."Multinational, Multicultural America versus White Supremacy." In Reed, *MultiAmerica* 391–94.

———. *Selected Poetry of Amiri Baraka/LeRoi Jones*. New York: William Morrow, 1979.

Boyce Davies, Carole. "Beyond Unicentricity: Transcultural Black Presences." *Research in African Literatures* 30, no. 2 (1999): 96–109.

Ellison, Ralph. "The Little Man at Chehaw Station." *American Scholar,* December 13, 1977. Rpt. in *Going to the Territory*, 3–38. New York: Random House, 1986.

Gates, Henry Louis, Jr. *The Signifying Monkey: A Theory of Afro-American Literary Criticism*. Oxford: Oxford University Press, 1988.

Gayle, Addison. *The Way of the New World: The Black Novel in America*. Garden City, NY: Anchor Press, 1976.

Guterl, Matthew Prat. "The New Race Consciousness: Race, Nation and Empire in American Culture." *Journal of World History* 10, no. 2 (1997): 307–52.

Jahn, Janheinz. *Muntu: The New African Culture*. New York: Grove Press, 1961.

Jones, LeRoi [Amiri Baraka]. "the last days of the american empire (including some instructions for black people." In *Home: Social Essays*, 189–209. New York: William Morrow, 1966.

Jordan, Jennifer. "Cultural Nationalism in the 1960s: Politics and Poetry." In *Race, Politics, and Culture: Critical Essays on the Radicalism of the 1960s*. Ed. Adolph Reed Jr., 29–60. Westport, CT: Greenwood Press, 1986.

Karenga, Maulana. "Black and Latino Relations: Context, Challenge and Possibilities." In Reed, *MultiAmerica* 189–204.

———. *The Quotable Karenga*. Ed. Clyde Halisi and James Mtume. Los Angeles: US Organization, 1967.

Lee, Don L. [Haki Madhubuti]. *Directionscore: Selected and New Poems*. Detroit: Broadside Press, 1971.

Madhubuti, Haki R. "Cultural Work: Planting New Trees with New Seeds." In Reed,

MultiAmerica 443–50.
Martin, Reginald. *Ishmael Reed and the New Black Aesthetic Critics*. New York: St. Martin's Press, 1988.
Mikics, David. "Postmodernism, Ethnicity and Underground Revisionism in Ishmael Reed." *Postmodern Culture* 1, no. 3 (1991). Project Muse, http://muse.jhu.edu/journals/postmodern_cultue/v001/1.3mickics.html. Retrieved January 26, 2005.
Neal, Larry. "The Black Arts Movement." Black Theatre Issue. *The DramaReview (TDR)*, 12, no. 4 (1968): 29–39. Rpt. in *Visions* 62–78.
———. "Black Power in the International Context." In *Visions* 133–43.
———. "An Interview." With Charles Rowell. *Callaloo*. Larry Neal: A Special Issue (Winter 1985): 11–35.
———. "And Shine Swam on." In *Visions* 7–23.
———. *Visions of a Liberated Future: Black Arts Movement Writings*. Ed. Michael Schwartz. New York: Thunder's Mouth Press, 1989.
Oren, Michael. "A 60s Saga: The Life and Death of Umbra." *Freedomways* 24, no. 3 (1984): 167–81; 24, no. 4 (1964): 237–54.
The Original Last Poets. *Right On*. Juggernaut Records, Jug-st/LP 8802. N.d.
Powell, Timothy. "All Colors Flow into Rainbows and Nooses." *Cultural Critique* 55 (2003): 152–81. Project Muse, http://cassell.founders.howard.edu:2070/journals/cultural__critique/v055/55.1powell.html. Retrieved February 25, 2005.
Reed, Ishmael. "And That History Is Subject to the Will." In *Talking Poetry*. Ed. Lee Bartlett, 167–78. Albuquerque: University of Mexico Press, 1987. Rpt. in *Conversations* 258–70.
———. *Another Day at the Front: Dispatches from the Race War*. 2003. New York: Basic Books, 2004.
———. "The Battle of San Diego." In *Another Day* 5–38.
———. "Before Columbus Foundation: Interview." With Bob Callahan et. al. *Before Columbus Foundation Catalog One, 1978–1979*: 1–12. Rpt. in *Conversation* 161–80.
———. "Booker versus the Negro Saxons." In *Another Day* 76–91.
———. *Conversations with Ishmael Reed*. Ed. Bruce Dick and Amritjit Singh. Literary Conversations Series. Jackson: University Press of Mississippi, 1995.
———. *Flight to Canada*. 1976. New York: Avon, 1977.
———. *Free-Lance Pallbearers*. 1967. New York: Avon, 1977.
———. "Gathering of the Tribes: Conversation with Ishmael Reed." With Steve Cannon et. al. *Gathering of the Tribe Magazine* 6 (Spring 1995). Rpt. in *Conversations* 361–81.
———. "The Great Tenure Battle of 1977." Interview with Jon Ewing. *The Daily Californian*'s Friday Magazine January 18, 1977. Rpt. in *Shrovetide* 253–72.
———. "Interview: Ishmael Reed." With Al Young. *Changes*, November 1972. Rpt. in *Conversations* 41–50.
———. "An Interview with Ishmael Reed." With Ruth Abbott and Ira Simmons. *San Francisco Review of Books* 1975: 13–20. Rpt. in *Conversations* 74–95.
———. An Interview with Ishmael Reed." With Shamoon Zamir. *Callaloo* 17, no. 4 (1994): 1131–57. Rpt. in *Conversations* 271–302.
———. "Interview with Ishmael Reed." With Gaga [Mark S. Johnson]. *Mwendo* (Fall 1973): 32–35. Rpt. in *Conversations* 51–58.
———, ed. Introduction. *MultiAmerica:Essays on Cultural Wars and Cultural Peace*, xv–xxviii. New York: Penguin, 1997.
———. "Ishmael Reed." Interview with John O'Brien. *Fiction International* 1 (1973): 61–70. Rpt. in *Conversations* 25–40.

———. "Ishmael Reed: A Conversation with John Domini." *American Poetry Review* 7, no. 1 (1978): 32–36. Rpt. in *Conversations* 128–43.
———. "Ishmael Reed: An Interview." With Michael Helm. *City Miner Magazine* 3, no. 4 (1978): 7+. Rpt. in *Conversations* 144–60.
———. *Japanese by Spring*. 1993. New York: Penguin, 1996.
———. "Konch at 16: A Publication for the Rest of Us." *Ishmael Reed's Konch* (Spring 2007). http//www.ishmaelreedpub.com. Retrieved May 23, 2007.
———. *The Last Days of Louisiana Red*. 1974. New York: Avon, 1976.
———. *Mumbo Jumbo*. 1972. New York: Avon, 1978.
———. *Shrovetide in Old New Orleans*. 1978. New York: Avon, 1979.
———. *The Terrible Twos*. 1982. New York: Avon, 1983.
———. *The Terrible Threes*. 1989. London: Allison & Busby, 1993.
———. "When State Magicians Fail: An Interview with Ishmael Reed." With Walt Shepperd. *Nickel Review*, 28 August–10 September 1968: 4–6. Rpt. in *Conversations* 3–13.
———. "The Writer as Seer: Ishmael Reed on Ishmael Reed." *Black World* 23, no. 8 (1974): 20–34. Rpt. in *Conversations* 59–73.
———. *Yellow Back Radio Broke-Down*. Garden City, NY: Doubleday, 1969.
———. "You Can't Be a Literary Magazine and Hate Writers." *Yardbird* 5 (1976): 18–20. Rpt. in *Shrovetide* 283–85.
Report of Select Committee to Study Governmental Operations with Respect to Intelligence Activities of the United States Senate, 94th Congress, 2nd Session, 1976. Excerpts on Web site posted by human rights attorney Paul Wolf. www.cointelpro.org. Retrieved May 27, 2007.
Verney, Kevern. *The Art of the Possible: Booker T. Washington and Black Leadership in the United States, 1881–1975*. New York: Routledge, 2001.
Wright, Richard. "Blueprint for Negro Writing." *New Challenge* 2 (1937): 53–65. Rpt. in *The Norton Anthology of African American Literature*. Ed. Henry Louis Gates Jr. et al. 2nd ed., 1403–10. New York: Norton, 2004.

3 The Politics of Addiction and Adaptation

Dis/ease Transmission in Octavia E. Butler's Survivor *and* Fledgling

MILDRED R. MICKLE

A major force in contemporary African American literature, science fiction, and speculative fiction, Octavia E. Butler uses her fiction as a forum to move beyond what we accept as the norm. Her agenda is to encourage readers to think about *what addicts us*—the fear of change that leads people to cling to outmoded concepts or beliefs or the positive and negative forces of change that can push us to new realms of awareness and progress. And she encourages readers to think about *how we can adapt* our ways of thinking and acting, particularly when our ways are destructive. One of the ways in which she innovates is to change the discussion of the addictiveness of racism so that it is seen under the larger rubric of the addictiveness of speciesism. This is a powerful narrative strategy because it increases readers' awareness of how ignorant we are about the species that we influence and that we are influenced by. The struggle for dominance between humans and alien species is perhaps far more catastrophic than the struggle between races, but ironically it can be a way to make humans look past the arbitrary pettiness of skin color and hair texture. In two of her works, *Survivor* (1978) and *Fledgling* (2005), Butler examines ranges of addiction and adaptation, showing that neither addiction nor adaptation need be completely negative if humans can learn from the dis/ease they cause and make progress toward more constructive behavior.

Addiction refers to a compulsion toward self-destructive agents that affect an individual on a mental and/or a physical level. The addictive source may be a concept or belief that one holds to rigidly and that compels one to act in a certain way, or it may refer to an ingested substance that propels one toward continuous, excessive consumption. bell hooks urges readers to look beyond the typical association of "addiction" to tangible things like drugs. She wants us to acknowledge how addiction to self-destructive and illogical concepts like racism, white supremacy, black inferiority, and so on have invaded black communities and the larger American society. In "Growing Away from Addiction," she writes:

> I have found it meaningful to connect the struggle of people to "recover" from the suffering and woundedness caused by political oppression/exploitation and the effort to break with addictive behavior. In contemporary black life, disenabling addictions have become a dangerous threat to our survival as a people. Still many black people refuse to take addiction seriously, or if we accept the harm to individual and community that addictions cause, we may refuse to take seriously what it means to create an environment where people can recover.[...] As early as 1975, Stanton Peele explained:

> Addiction is not a chemical reaction. Addiction is an experience—one which grows out of an individual's routinized subjective response to something that has special meaning for him—something, anything, that he finds so safe and reassuring that he cannot be without it.... We still find that we learn habits of dependency by growing up in a culture which teaches a sense of personal inadequacy, a reliance on external bulwarks, and a preoccupation with the negative or painful rather than the positive or joyous. Addiction is not an abnormality in our society. It is not an aberration from the norm; it is itself the norm. (67–68)

This essay will discuss how Octavia Butler's third science fiction novel, *Survivor*, and her last novel, *Fledgling*, use the ranges of addiction and adaptation as lenses for exploring human dis/ease. Butler's point in focusing on the addictiveness of racism in *Survivor* and *Fledgling* is to stress that if humans continue to engage in racial addiction, they will not progress. Instead, they will regress further into an even larger addiction to the illogical concept of speciesism, discriminating against other species with the assumption that humans are the superior species and underestimating how other species can affect humans' ability to survive in countless ways. In *Survivor* dis/ease is represented in the addictive alien fruit, "meklah," a metaphor for cultural, mental, and physical inflexibility. In *Fledgling* Butler uses the Ina people's addiction to their human symbionts and vice versa as a force for destruction and creation. Without their bond to their human symbionts, the Ina will die, and without the meklah, the Garkohn will die.

With the human and Garkohn addiction to meklah and the Ina-human symbiotic bond, Butler investigates the dynamics of human control versus anarchy. She questions to what extent humans can adapt beyond what addicts them. Addiction becomes a social and political tool for structuring and dividing a society. Also, addiction to the alien meklah in *Survivor* and the Ina-human symbiosis in *Fledgling* provide an intriguing parallel to the alien clayark disease that the Missionaries leave behind on Earth in *Survivor*. Butler suggests that alien compulsion and/or addiction is not as easy to discard as humans may think. Butler's uncompromising view of the ease and dis/ease of the meklah addiction and the Ina-human symbiotic relationship becomes the next stage in an ironic natural selection of humans, thereby preempting human control over the ability to survive and adapt and raising questions about the very nature of survival.

America is a society addicted to the concept of race and racial deviancy, and it is this addiction that is a dis/ease. Dis/ease refers to both the sense of people being mentally uncomfortable—cognitive dissonance, if you will—and of people being physically ill due to an infection or withdrawal from an addictive substance. But not all blacks or Americans or even humans in the larger global community of Earth have yielded to the dis/ease of addictively negative thinking about race or species. Many have learned to adapt their thinking. Adaptation refers to self-constructive agents that affect an individual on a mental and/or a physical level. The adaptive source may be a concept/belief that one holds to for as long as it serves a person and that one chooses to modify or discard at will, or it may refer to a physical change that one accepts and uses to one's advantage. Catastrophes in both *Survivor* and *Fledgling* are the motivating factors that help Alanna in *Survivor* and Shori in *Fledgling* adapt.

An underlying question in Butler's *Survivor* is: What causes dis/ease and addiction? The answer in *Survivor* is adaptation. Addiction and dis/ease are tied to change because in the novel they are metaphors for cultural, physical, and mental health differences among the alien Kohn peoples, the human Missionaries, wild humans, and the clayark-infected humans. Both addiction and dis/ease play a role in the human struggle between adapting to and resisting change. Even when we think we are prepared for upheaval, when a catastrophic event occurs, it can be difficult to handle. We cannot predict how we may respond. We would like to think that we will rise to the challenge, but there can be variables that we cannot control that complicate our success. A change in *Survivor* that causes dis/ease in one's effort to survive is addiction. When one becomes addicted—whether the decision is conscious or not—one simultaneously embraces and resists change. One can become addicted to a new substance or idea, and the act of embracing that substance/idea brings about a change in that person. If the addiction colors one's viewpoint until one cannot think or function without that substance/idea, it curtails freedom and can lead to self-destructive behavior. Once the person is addicted to the substance/idea and changed by it, the person resists further change. It hurts physically and mentally to withdraw from the addiction. In some cases, withdrawal may kill the person. In *Survivor* Butler explores layers of addiction that range from racism to speciesism, showing the tempting ease of clinging to preconceived notions of superiority and the difficulty of adapting to changing conceptions of being.

In Butler's *Survivor*, upheaval comes in the form of alien invasions. On Earth the clayark symbiont infects humans, controlling their will to live as they had been. The loss of control over Earth brings dis/ease to humans, ironically enough, because the dis/ease, or cognitive dissonance, arises from the clayark disease for which there is no cure. A response to the catastrophic change the clayark invasion brings is for a group of humans called the Missionaries to leave Earth and invade another planet, where, as the nonnatives, they become the invading alien force. However, the human colonists do not view themselves as aliens or invaders. Paralleling some aspects of human history, the Kohn people represent the native missionaries who went to places in Africa and India where the inhabitants were viewed as heathens in need of religious conversion. Rather than converting the Kohn people to their religion, the Missionaries in *Survivor* find themselves in an ironic Edenic space where they become addicted to the tempting alien fruit called *meklah*.

Meklah addiction as cultural and mental inflexibility takes shape in an ironic allusion to the biblical Garden of Eden. In *Blacks in Eden: The African American Novel's First Century*, J. Lee Greene discusses the use of the Garden of Eden as a structuring device for many early African American novels:

> Building upon the image of America as a New Eden, Anglo-Americans from the colonial period onward appropriated, transformed, and conflated passages from the Judeo-Christian Bible to justify their exclusion of Africans and descendants of Africans from the American family. The biblical stories of the Garden of Eden and of Man's Fall provided the nucleus around which they formulated tropological images of American society and subjects—what I call the Eden trope. (1–2)

Although Greene does not discuss *Survivor* in his study, some aspects of his Edenic trope are useful for understanding Butler's historical allusion to the colonization of countries like Africa and India and the cultural conquest of new worlds in part through the transmission of religion.

In *Survivor* the Edenic story becomes problematized further by the introduction of an alien planet and its natives. In the novel, the Kohn planet becomes at best a questionable Eden. Instead of a biblical God creating a paradise and creating humans to be placed there, a group of humans who call themselves Missionaries travel to the Kohn planet to discover that it is occupied by huge furry aliens who can alter their coloring. However, in *Survivor* the Missionaries do not travel to the Kohn planet to convert the natives to their religion and culture; they colonize Kohn in order to preserve for themselves their own culture and religion. When they meet the Garkohn, the Missionaries are forced to revise their plans to make of the Kohn planet a new Earth, but they hold fast to their ultimate goal of preserving human culture and religion. Like the Anglo colonists to America who viewed the land as a paradise only for a specific group of morally worthy people, the Missionaries view the Kohn planet as a way to preserve their culture and religion. They have sacrificed everything to come to the Kohn planet and make a new start because they feel it is the ethical thing to do. Unlike the Missionaries, early American colonists could choose to leave America and return to their native lands or go elsewhere. Because there is no escape from the Kohn planet, the Missionaries work out an uneasy truce with the Garkohn, the first aliens they meet. In exchange for protection and noninterference in their religion and governance, they will coexist in the valley with the Garkohn people. It is the Garkohn who introduce the Missionaries to meklah, and they purposely addict the Missionaries to meklah in order to control them.

Meklah addiction and its resultant cultural, mental, and physical inflexibility create dis/ease among the Missionaries. The act of eating meklah marks the beginning of the Missionaries' "Fall" from Edenic innocence and represents their inability to see beyond the limits of their own prejudice against different cultures. The Missionaries make themselves vulnerable to the Garkohn through the meklah addiction because they underestimate the Garkohn as uneducated savages, and they see that the meklah is abundant and a main staple of the Garkohn diet. As time passes, the Missionaries begin to feel dis/ease with the meklah addiction, for they see how meklah addiction robs them of their freedom. They are physically and mentally bound to the alien fruit and to the Garkohn land and people who produce it. And culturally they are fast losing ground to the Garkohn. The culture the Missionaries have fought to preserve is threatened by their dependence on an alien substance (137–80). The Missionaries will not be able to escape the meklah addiction until they learn to become more tolerant of and communicate with other factions of the Kohn people. Butler demonstrates that the Missionaries' unwillingness to adapt their thinking and learn to respect and communicate with the different Kohn peoples is just as harmful as their addiction to meklah. Their speciesism, or prejudice against aliens, is an addiction that is just as tempting as the meklah and almost as difficult to break away from.

Greene's Edenic trope becomes less relevant to understanding *Survivor* when one explores how meklah addiction conveys cultural, mental, and physical inflexibility among the Garkohn. Meklah addiction and its resultant inflexibility also create dis/ease in the Garkohn tribe. Because they become addicted to meklah and continue the addiction for several generations, they are inextricably bound to meklah. The Garkohn structure their society based on an unquestioning acceptance of their addiction to meklah. They view meklah as natural and necessary to their identity as a people. When the Garkohn take prisoners in their skirmishes with other Kohn tribes, like the Tehkohn, they purposely addict their prisoners to meklah in order to control them with the goal of integrating them into the depleted Garkohn ranks. For the Garkohn, it is unthinkable to choose to withdraw from eating meklah. Because they have maintained such a lengthy addiction, the meklah has become part of their physical makeup. Whether or not it is some innate element in the meklah compelling them to think so, they view meklah as a sign of strength and pride. If they are captured by an enemy Kohn tribe and forced to withdraw from meklah, the Garkohn die (75–76, 172). The Garkohn are physically and mentally tied to meklah and the finite area that produces it, and any withdrawal from the alien fruit is anathema to their continued survival. Butler indicates that, like the Missionaries, the Garkohn people's unwillingness to adapt their thinking and learn to respect, communicate with, and learn from the different Kohn peoples is a result of their dependence on meklah. They have ceded control over their lives to a harmful substance they believe defines their superiority over all other Kohn people and over the Missionaries. Butler shows that their unwavering faith in a false power leads to their downfall. Both the Garkohn's and the Missionaries' speciesism serves as a cautionary note about the temptations of clinging to false and destructive ideologies.

In addition to physical and mental inflexibility, meklah addiction creates cultural dis/ease among the Garkohn. Their addiction to meklah brought about a radical restructuring of their caste system. In most of the other Kohn tribes, the caste system is structured around the leading caste of Hao, marked by dark blue fur (162–63). The next level of leadership is the judges, who are a lighter blue color, perhaps mixed with green: "Judges were, among other things, lawgivers, advisers to rulers, and sometimes, rulers themselves" (9). Below judges come the hunters, who are in the green color range, and below the hunters is the lowest caste of artisans and farmers, who are yellow in color (50–54). Meklah addiction contributed to the demise of the Hao and judge caste system in the Garkohn tribe; however, the Garkohn are still genetically compelled to respect the Hao and judge caste segments of other Kohn tribes. While they pride themselves on their meklah addiction, they still seek to regain a judge caste to regulate their increasingly self-destructive behavior (137–38). Although the Garkohn feel that meklah addiction is good for them, they realize the cultural toll or dis/ease it has taken on their tribe, and they try to adapt. Butler does investigate the complexity of the Garkohn's cultural differences, noting that while they try to change by creating a tribe centered around meklah addiction, they also try to retain established societal hierarchies that provide stability effectively. The Garkohn are aware that meklah addiction has disrupted the balance of their society. Butler is saying that to some degree it is easy to see how not all change is good, and once one recognizes that, it is prudent to adapt into a cultural mindset and practice that is beneficial to all.

Because meklah addiction contributed to the loss of the blue Hao and judge caste, the Garkohn leader from the hunter caste plans to appropriate the Missionaries to serve as judges and checks on the wilder Garkohn tendencies. While the plan devised by Natahk—the leader of the Garkohn—is innovative and shows he is willing to adapt a little, the plan causes dis/ease among both human and Garkohn factions. The Missionaries reject it because it goes against their plans to preserve Missionary culture and religion. On that point the human Missionaries are culturally inflexible. The Garkohn do not approve because the Missionaries lack the blue color and physical hunting prowess they are genetically encoded to respect. Although the Garkohn acknowledge they miss the lack of the Hao and judge caste, many are not easily persuaded to alter their tribal order in such a fashion. Butler adds yet another layer to the psychological complexity of Garkohn politics: They are ruthless and unethical in assuming that the human Missionaries will want to adapt to the Garkohn social order. While the Garkohn admit their weakened political state and try to take steps to amend it, many cannot learn to look past the physical differences between the human Missionaries and the Garkohn people. The Garkohn stand as a testament to other political regimes in human history who sought to prop up their weakened states by co-opting and coercing others into their folds. Usually, the result of co-opting and coercing people to accept a false order is further instability and cultural chaos.

Meklah addiction creates dis/ease within the human societal order. The Missionaries, marginally a part of the Garkohn people, do not wish to be assimilated so intricately into the Garkohn culture. The Missionaries are offended by the uninhibited sexual and social behavior displayed by clayark-infected humans. On Earth, while they wait for their ship to be prepared, they live in a commune separate from the clayarks and those "wild humans" (1) who remain uninfected but exist on their own unprotected from the clayark humans. In the clayarks and the "wild humans," the Missionaries see a threat to their moral and ethical standards. Butler pits humans, identified as Missionaries, with an alien race that divides itself into the Garkohn and Tehkohn factions. The primary distinction between the Garkohn and the Tehkohn is that the Garkohns are addicted to meklah, and the Tehkohns disdain the use of meklah. When humans colonize the Kohn planet, the Garkohns introduce them to meklah. In keeping with the Garden of Eden story, meklah becomes a parallel for the forbidden fruit. By eating it, humans unwittingly gain knowledge and experience of addiction. As their addiction grows and they have more interaction with the Tehkohn and Garkohn factions, humans begin to see how they have become pawns in a larger struggle for social and political domination from the aliens. They are in an untenable situation, for they cannot leave the Kohn planet for a new world. They must learn to work with both Kohn groups. Expulsion from the only place on the planet where meklah will grow in abundance comes to represent the humans' expulsion from the questionable paradise of ignorance.

Butler provides an ironic counter to the meklah addiction in the form of the clayark symbiont. Meklah and the clayark symbiont both represent extremes of change that humans try to control. The alien compulsion of the clayark symbiont is another agent that causes dis/ease among humans on Earth. Butler uses brief references to the clayark plague to compare and contrast the degree of change that humans must navigate. Meklah addiction conveys a level of agency and autonomy that the clayark symbiont does not. One can choose to become addicted to meklah and then to refrain from using it. Although the withdrawal is painful, humans whose wills are strong enough can live through the withdrawal phase. Once infected with the clayark symbiont, however, there is no escape. For humans and other factions of the Kohn, meklah addiction in this respect represents substances/ideas that one may ingest/adopt, evaluate the effectiveness of, and discard when they no longer serve. On the other hand, the clayark symbiont represents a substance/idea that controls human autonomy and that may destroy humans. While both meklah and the clayark symbiont are used to control actions, at least with meklah there is a possibility of regaining control of one's life. Meklah and the clayark symbiont show two extremes of alien control. They are catalysts for dis/ease transmission that can result in positive or negative reactions. Butler compares alien catalysts to an individual's agency to show hope. Even when the individual will is subjected to alien substances, if the individual's will is strong enough, the individual can overcome most addictions, or at the very least the individual can decide not to cede complete control of him- or herself to the alien substance. The individual's will is powerful. It can construct or destruct.

Another addiction that inspires dis/ease transmission that may lead to constructive or destructive acts is the Ina-human symbiosis/addiction in *Fledgling*. Some may view the Ina-human symbiosis as not much of an addiction, but Butler is exploring ranges of addiction and adaptation in the relationships. The Ina-human symbiosis is a type of addiction because the Ina need their human symbionts in order to survive, just as the Garkohn do in *Survivor*. However, the difference is that the Ina addiction for humans does not need to be harmful so long as the Ina treat the humans well and with respect. Butler shows instances where the Ina-human symbiosis/addiction is negative when the Ina mistreat their humans or look down at them, but *Fledgling* primarily focuses on the Ina-human symbiosis/addiction as a positive bond. Writing a vampire story gave Butler another type of alien to whom humans can become addicted. However, Butler moves away from vampires being viewed as just hypersexual and "interestingly sexy" or as demons and murderers, as Sandra Govan has noted (38). By taking the "supernatural" element away and giving her vampires a name; a matriarchal culture; a language; a history; a religion; superior strength, speed, hearing, and sight; longer life spans; and a societal structure with a moral code and rule of law (Govan 34–35), Butler, in conversation with recent popular vampire literature, elevates the vampire from demon to a different species of humans who share goals similar to humans—to find love, raise and provide for their families, and be productive citizens. The Ina people, as Butler terms them, differ from humans in that they need to drink blood to survive; they cannot survive exposure to the sun; and, like the Kohn people, they are more open about expressing their sexuality. The Ina-human bond is one that creates dis/ease transmission, for it ties two different species together to sustain life and to create new life, or, when the Ina exploit their human symbionts, the symbiosis leads to destruction. The Ina-human bond is a metaphor for those inexplicable constructive or deconstructive agents that attract and repel people. The bond is more mysterious than supernatural because for the Ina and human involved, the bond is predicated on love. To some degree it is chemical, based on the practical blood exchange between Ina and human. Without the chemical tie and without the love and respect that encourage the bond, the Ina and the human will die. The mystery is in how much the chemical tie influences the love the Ina and humans share.

There are different types of Ina-human bonds. In *Fledgling* Butler explores the potential of the Ina-human bond through the protagonist, Shori Matthews, who is from the Ina species, or what humans in the book term a *vampire*. Like Alanna in *Survivor*, Shori's core identity is predicated on internal referents so that she can rely on it to sustain her when all is lost. Some Ina and humans view her as a deviant because she is a genetically engineered Ina who can walk around during the day. In the novel Shori's family has been attacked and massacred, and she has amnesia due to trauma from the attack. She is the sole survivor of the paternal Petrescu line, and has yet to reestablish ties to the maternal Matthews line (316). Given that she has lost her memory, she acts on her instincts.

Without any knowledge of who she is or where she comes from, Shori sets about recruiting a family of human symbionts to provide her with sustenance (28). Shori is not ever ashamed of her symbiotic relationship with her chosen humans. Her determination to treat them well, to love them, and to share her body with them as she drinks blood from them reflects on her spiritual side. Although her memory is damaged, the core of her being that reveres the beauty of the symbiotic tie remains. For her to do less—to mistreat her human symbionts—would cause her own physical and mental death. Although they are addicted to Shori, what her human symbionts respond to is the honesty of true feeling. Shori shows them in myriad ways that though she is physically more powerful than they are and has the ability to control them through their bond, she operates by a code of ethics that disallows deception and depravity. She sincerely loves and accepts herself and her human symbionts.

Shori's relationship with her human symbionts represents a normal, healthy Ina-human bond. But there are some Ina who exploit human symbionts. Blake, one of Shori's future human symbionts, tells Shori about an immoral Ina named Radu.

> "[N]ot everyone treats symbionts as people. This man [Radu] liked to [. . .] amuse himself with other Ina's symbionts. He was very careful and protective of his own, but he liked sending them among us with instructions to start trouble, raise suspicions and jealousies, start fights. He liked to watch arguments and fights. His symbionts were so good, so subtle that we didn't realize what was happening at first. It excited the hell out of him when two of Radu's symbionts almost killed one another. He got something sexual out of watching. The symbionts would have died if they hadn't been symbionts—but then, they never would have been endangered if they hadn't been symbionts." (137)

In order to stress the constructive nature of Shori's Ina-human bond, Butler must show its antithesis. Shori's bond is constructive because she does not abuse its power. Radu's bond is destructive because he does abuse its power. Radu becomes addicted to his ability to exploit and hurt others, and his addiction warps himself and the humans he thinks he protects. Butler uses Radu to caution about the destructively addictive nature of manipulation and coercion. Radu's actions mark him as someone who uses the Ina-human symbiosis to destroy. Although he does not physically torture or bruise them, Radu abuses his bond with his symbionts, compelling them to compromise whatever ethical standards they may have to sow dissent. He toys with his and other Ina's symbionts for his sexual pleasure, but the pleasure he gains is not something that he could or would share with his symbionts. Radu's sadism does not sustain life, nor does it establish trust between himself and his symbionts. In fact, it probably teaches his symbionts not to trust him since it is based on dishonesty.

However immoral Radu is, Butler provides three other examples of Ina who use their Ina-human symbiotic addiction to kill: Milo and Russell Silk and Katharine Dahlman. Shori learns of Milo Silk's disdain for humans from Joan Braithwaite, one of her Ina relatives:

"It's extremely difficult for us to kill or injure our bound symbionts. It's hard, very hard, even to want to do such a thing.

"Even Milo hasn't been able to do it. He resents his need of them, sees it as a weakness, and yet he loves them. He would stand between his symbionts and any danger. He might shout at them, but even then, he would be careful. He would not order them to harm themselves or one another. And he would never harm one of them. I think it's an instinct for self-preservation on our part. We need our symbionts more than most of them know. We need not only their blood, but physical contact with them and emotional reassurance from them. Companionship. I've never known even one of us to survive through casual hunting.... [W]e sicken. We either weave ourselves a family of symbionts, or we die. Our bodies need theirs. But human beings who are not bound to us, who are bound to other Ina, or not bound at all [. . .] they have no protection against us except whatever decency, whatever morality we choose to live up to." (275–76)

Joan's comments reveal how conflicted Milo Silk is. Though he needs his human symbionts and even cares for them, he holds them at a distance. Milo acknowledges his human symbionts as a food supply, but he will not allow himself to truly feel the joining of his symbiotic bond. His repression of the pleasure of the Ina-human symbiotic tie does not sustain him in positive ways. Instead, it leads him to warp his family as well. Milo influences his son, Russell Silk, to use his power to compel humans to attack and murder Shori's family. They do this because they are afraid of modifying Ina genetics so that they can survive in the sun. They are also racist because they view the genetic structure of humans and Shori's blackness as inferior. They do not want any Ina bloodlines to have black blood in them. When he is found guilty of his crime and punished by having his family disbanded, Russell Silk shouts at Shori: "'Murdering black mongrel bitch' [. . .] and 'What will she give us all? Fur? Tails?'" (306). Russell Silk, just like Milo, allows his fear of Shori's difference that attracts others and the disdain of humans that he learned from Milo to warp his concept of himself. He builds his identity on external referents: the subjugation of others. He is so addicted to hate and fear in his relationships with humans that he has lost his own sense of ethics. He can view the destruction of Shori's family as necessary to preserve a misguided sense of Ina purity, when Shori represents a stronger, better version of Ina. Butler demonstrates how an unwavering addiction to the fear of change and hatred of genetic difference can lead to stagnancy and instability. In a world where people fear change and hate others because they are different, progress stultifies and people suffer needlessly.

Like Milo and Russell Silk, Katharine Dahlman uses the Ina-human symbiotic addiction to destroy. Although Katharine Dahlman is not part of the conspiracy to murder Shori's family, she does order one of her human symbionts to murder one of Shori's human symbionts. Dahlman is so wrapped up in her fear and hatred of Shori because she is black and a genetically engineered Ina that she abuses her bond with one of her symbionts to order him to kill another human symbiont. Dahlman's casual disregard for the feelings of her human symbiont, for the human who is murdered, and for Shori shows her warped ethics. Rather than respecting her bond with her human symbiont, she uses her symbiont's love, devotion, and dependence on her to destroy others, and when she is judged, she is unrepentant. She truly cannot understand the gravity of what she has done (309). Katharine's actions reflect her own warped sense of self-importance, and that warped sense leads to her destruction.

The need for blood is an apt metaphor for the intracultural strife the Ina have over Shori's right to exist. Shori's deviance, ironically, is a sign of strength in the face of great loss. What instigates the massacre of her family and causes her amnesia is what saves her from Ina and human attack: her ability to be awake and alert during the day. What also saves her is her amnesia brought about by trauma from the attack to her family. She cannot grieve for them because she cannot remember them or the fifty-plus years of her life that she spent with them. So she resolves to live her life as best she can and try to rebuild a new family to honor her lost family. Shori can rebuild her life because though she has lost her memories, she has not completely lost her core values and ethics, nor is she ever ashamed of who or what she is. She establishes healthy relationships with her human symbionts and with those Ina who accept her as the next stage in Ina development. In a human world that views the Ina people as deviant and that would destroy the Ina if they could, Shori represents the continued survival of her people.

In *Fledgling* Butler maintains that how we manage our addictions and the dis/ease transmissions of those addictions—treat the ones we love—is a reflection of our spirituality. Spirituality comes from the healthy relationships we have that bind us through the expression of physical and mental love. Without the symbiosis of mind and body, it is difficult to find and maintain one's spirituality. And without that spirituality, we can lose the self, we may dishonor the memory of our family and ancestors, and we can jeopardize our future. Shori is a powerful, spiritual person because she is happy and at peace with herself. In the face of great loss, she can trust her instincts and make decisions based on her feelings and her interactions with others with whom she has built relationships of trust and love. She can find the strength to share herself with others and treat others who are different from her with respect and this ultimately will allow her to survive and create new generations.

Unfortunately, *Fledgling* marks the end of Butler's distinguished career. While the novel goes on to investigate the themes of addiction, adaptation, and the dis/ease both concepts present, *Survivor* should be noted as a fledgling artist's first attempt to engage those concepts. *Survivor* is a flawed novel, but it is the flaws that make it fascinating, for they show the germination of themes for later works Butler began developing early in her career. What establishes dis/ease in Alanna, *Survivor*'s protagonist, is seeing humanity in Diut, an alien whose people look radically different from humans and structure their society along a caste system determined by color and physical prowess. The Kohn are light years away from Earth and humans, but they have some things in common with humans, like respect for the rule of law and family. Alanna is disturbed further by the genetic compatibility between humans and the Kohn. What establishes dis/ease in Butler as a writer and in her audience is the astronomical impossibility of such serendipitous genetic compatibility between humans and the alien Kohn. In a 1991 interview with Randall Kenan, Butler notes:

> One of the things that I was most embarrassed about in my novel *Survivor* is my human characters going off to another plan[e]t and finding other people they could immediately start having children with. Later I thought, oh well, you can't really erase embarrassing early work, but you don't have to repeat it. So I thought if I were going to bring people together from other worlds again, I was at least going to give them trouble. So I made sure they didn't have compatible sex organs, not to mention their other serious differences. And of course there are still a lot of biological problems that I ignore. (500)

It is a testament to the strength of Butler as a gifted storyteller that the reader can suspend disbelief because at its heart, *Survivor* is a flawed novel about human flaws. Humans are painted in their best and worst lights. They are inflexible, intolerant, and yet flexible in many respects. They have to learn how to be flexible, or "mental chameleons" (118) in order to survive the rigors of a new world. Butler creates a story where humans get on a spaceship to take a one-way trip to settle on a new planet and trust the navigator to take them to a planet where they can survive with the available flora and fauna. The irony of the novel is that they leave Earth to escape the clayark invasion—an alien microorganism has invaded Earth and infects humans, compelling them to modify their behavior. When a human becomes infected with the clayark symbiont, all that matters is the compulsion to spread the microorganism to new human hosts. They abandon the trappings of civilization to follow the clayark compulsion, and once infected by the symbiont, the only escape is death. Further irony in *Survivor* comes when the humans land on the Kohn planet and meet and interact with the alien Kohn tribes. In a reversal of the clayark invasion humans seek to escape, humans invade the Kohn planet, where they unwittingly find themselves under the alien compulsion of meklah. Butler asks us to believe in a string of serendipitous coincidences.

1. The alien Kohn accept humans immediately.
2. The alien Kohn planet's flora and fauna aren't deadly to humans.
3. The alien Kohn can successfully mate with humans, producing viable offspring.

In the midst of so many alien variables, constants of love, marriage, family, respect for law, and survival exist to unite the humans and the Kohn. Granted, humans struggle to maintain these constants on Earth, but since humans are caught off guard by the clayark invasion, it is uncertain if they will survive. However, despite the dis/ease transmitted by the clayark invasion, if Earth has the technology to get the humans to another planet, why can they not do something more to root out the clayark organism? Perhaps it is flaws in human natures that are daunted and perhaps defeated by the extreme alienness of a microscopic organism that is methodically revising the standards by which humans define civilization. So, what is it about the flaws in *Survivor* that speak to us and can create dis/ease or cognitive dissonance? Is it perhaps our fears of our own human nature that can guide us to be humane or inhumane?

Stephen Jay Gould, in "So Cleverly Kind an Animal," an essay in *Ever since Darwin*, writes:

> What we criticize in ourselves, we attribute to our animal past. These are the shackles of our apish ancestry—brutality, aggression, selfishness; in short, general nastiness. What we prize and strive for (with pitifully limited success), we consider as a unique overlay, conceived

by our rationality and imposed upon an unwilling body. Our hopes for a better future lie in reason and kindness—the mental transcendence of our biological limitations.... We seek a criterion for our uniqueness, settle (naturally) upon our minds, and define the noble results of human consciousness as something intrinsically apart from biology. But why? Why should our nastiness be the baggage of an apish past and our kinds uniquely human? Why should we not seek continuity with other animals for our 'noble' traits as well?

... Natural selection dictates that organisms act in their own self-interest. They know nothing of such abstract concepts as 'the good of the species.' They 'struggle' continuously to increase the representation of their genes at the expense of their fellows. And that, for all its baldness is all there is to it; we have discovered no higher principle in nature. Individual advantage, Darwin argues, is the only criterion of success in nature.

... Can an apparently altruistic act be 'selfish' in this Darwinian sense? Can an individual's sacrifice ever lead to the perpetuation of his own genes? ... 'yes.' ...

... Our selfish and aggressive urges may have evolved by the Darwinian route of individual advantage, but our altruistic tendencies need not represent a unique overlay imposed by the demands of civilization. These tendencies may have arisen by the same Darwinian route via kin selection. Basic human kindness may be as 'animal' as human nastiness.

... If kin selection marks another stage in this retreat, it will serve us well by nudging our thinking away from domination and toward a perception of respect and unity with other animals. (260–62, 265–66, 267)

This quotation is important because Gould's works on Darwin were a big influence on Butler. Gould's words tie into what Butler investigates in human behavior—to what extent can humans and aliens work together for the communal good? Even though it is human nature to want to be dominant, we do not have to be at the top of the hierarchy and abuse other humans or other species to do so. In fact, it is not in any species's best interest to do so. What Butler is getting at in *Survivor* with the union of Alanna and Diut, or human and Kohn alliances and in *Fledgling* with Shori and her human symbionts, or Ina-human bonding is that it is in species working together, not underestimating or seeking to control each other, that we can find our greatest chance to survive, progress, and create ever-expanding potential. Genuine caring about others should not be seen as a sign of weakness. What can weaken someone is the corrupting addictiveness of dominance. For Butler in her works, "individual advantage" can be gained and maintained through humane and ethical partnerships between species.

Even though Butler sometimes opts to "ignore biology," in her fiction—and she has that right because, after all, she is writing fiction—she does not dismiss Darwinian theories about human biology. Rather, she strives to expand the range of hypothetical situations where humans must interact and work together to overcome their sometimes inhumane and animalistic ways. Whether it is the alien Kohn peoples interacting with and marrying humans or it is the Ina pairing with humans, Butler tests the notions of "altruism" and "individual advantage" by positing situations where people gain life and freedom by the bonds they share. What is germane to a group is a shared goal that is flexible and that can benefit all. What is destructive to a group is to dismiss foreign concepts or people based on a false sense of genetic superiority. Butler's goal is to stress that individual survival can be based on humane practices and that if we keep our minds open and do not underestimate those alien concepts or organisms we encounter, we can adapt into an ever stronger and viable species.

Despite or because of the flaws in *Survivor*, Butler's "ignoring biology" and her having the humans and Kohn be genetically compatible lead the reader to question: From where do the Kohn come? And what does that say about the process of evolution as we understand it? If the Kohn are compatible with humans, then at some point in the evolutionary history of the universe when both Earth and Kohn were developing, the same seed that was sown on the developing Earth must also have been deposited on the Kohn planet and left to flourish under different conditions. *Survivor*, with its aliens who are not so alien after all, is a human story with aliens in it. But somehow we believe the story because of Alanna and Diut, Jules and Neila, and Natahk and Gehl. Theirs is a human struggle to exist somewhere between stability and change. They try to control change brought about by addiction to varying degrees of success. By the novel's end, Natahk and Gehl are too rigid in their ways being caught up in meklah addiction and cannot survive. Jules and Neila simultaneously accept and reject change and walk off to an uncertain future, but they are a little wiser because they have seen the dangers of meklah addiction, and, one can extrapolate, addiction in general. Alanna and Diut have learned to work with each other, adapting and adopting concepts/behavior from their respective experiences that will allow them to function and make progress. Alanna found that some of her experiences as a wild human on Earth, the first principle she knew, are readily adaptable to survival with the Kohn. Diut accepts his half-human offspring, Tien, as a way of continuing his people. Diut, as part of the rare Hao leading caste, finds it difficult to produce viable offspring. He had to be flexible enough to look beyond the limits of his culture and people to produce the next generation. Tien, as impossible hybrid of two seemingly alien people, represents the best of two people who have learned to adapt and accept difference, and as such, she becomes a symbol of hope and survival. Butler, through Alanna's struggle with meklah addiction and Diut's struggle with the Garkohn, who define their culture based on its meklah addiction, cautions the reader that being "a mental chameleon" is necessary to survival. Meklah addiction raises the questions: In the face of uncountable variables, what does one control? One controls the ability to make a conscious effort to break free of self-destructive behaviors and thinking and to adapt and adopt ideas/behaviors that work for, not against, the individual. Because of Alanna's and Diut's flexibility and refusal to be ruled by addiction or dis/ease, they will survive.

Bernard W. Bell, in *The Contemporary African American Novel: Its Folk Roots and Modern Literary Branches*, writes of Octavia Butler:

> Exploring the impact of race and gender on humans in the future on Earth and other planets, she [Butler] creates speculative fiction in which the rulers include women and nonwhites whose power is based on extrasensory abilities and egalitarianism rather than on racial, sexual, or national domination.... In her essay "Why I Write," Butler states: "I began to write consciously, deliberately, about people who were afraid and who functioned in spite of their fear. People who failed sometimes and were not destroyed.... Every story I write adds to me a little, forces me to reexamine an attitude or belief, causes me to research and learn, helps me to understand people and grow.... Every story I create creates me. I write to create myself."...
>
> In *Survivor*,... [r]ather than a static state of being in the world with others, the dynamic state of becoming is at the center of Butler's speculative vision of identity formation in the future. (344–45)

While she does argue for tolerance and freedom, Butler, in her work, explores the issues most germane to her reality as a human being and a writer—how does she survive and create in a world where people view her as inferior? And how does she survive and create viable stories about humanity and human-alien interaction in the competitive science fiction publishing arena? *Survivor* is Butler's third novel, and as an early work we can see some of her themes about the struggle for autonomy from, integrity to, and control over change take shape.

Survivor, flaws conceded, deserves more careful scrutiny because it sets the stage for alien-human interaction that circles around stasis versus conflict versus adaptability that Butler went on to develop in *Clay's Ark, Wild Seed, Dawn, Adulthood Rites, Imago, Parable of the Sower, Bloodchild and Other Stories, Parable of the Talents,* and her final novel, *Fledgling*. Had she lived longer, perhaps she would have revised and expanded on the queries she investigates throughout her fiction—what is humanity, and what is humane in the face of alien and alienating change.

Bibliography

Bell, Bernard W. *The Contemporary African American Novel: Its Folk Roots and Modern Literary Branches*. Boston: University of Massachusetts Press, 2004.
Butler, Octavia E. *Clay's Ark*. New York: Warner Books, 1984.
———. *Fledgling: A Novel*. New York: Seven Stories Press, 2005.
———. *Survivor*. New York: New American Library, 1978.
Gould, Stephen Jay. *Ever Since Darwin: Reflections in Natural History*. New York: Norton, 1977.
Govan, Sandra. "Going to See the Woman: A Visit with Octavia E. Butler." *Obsidian III* 6, no. 2/7, no. 1 (2005–2006): 14–39.
Greene, J. Lee. *Blacks in Eden: The African American Novel's First Century*. Charlottesville, VA: University of Virginia Press, 1996.
hooks, bell. "Growing Away from Addiction." In *Sisters of the Yam: Black Women and Self-Recovery*, 67–77. Boston: South End Press, 1993.
Kenan, Randall. "An Interview with Octavia E. Butler." *Callaloo* 14, no. 2 (Spring 1991): **495–504**.
Rowell, Charles H. "An Interview with Octavia E. Butler." *Callaloo* 20, no. 1 (1997): 47–66.
Rutledge. Gregory E. "Futurist Fiction & Fantasy: The *Racial* Establishment." *Callaloo* 24, no. 1 (2001): 236–52.
Salvaggio, Ruth. "Octavia Butler and the Black Science-Fiction Heroine." *Black American Literature Forum* 18, no. 2 (Summer 1984): 78–81.
Schell, Heather. "Outburst! A Chilling True Story about Emerging-Virus Narratives and Pandemic Social Change." *Configurations* 5, no. 1 (1997): 93–133.
Schell, Heather. "The Sexist Gene: Science Fiction and the Germ Theory of History." *American Literary History* 14, no. 4 (2002): 805–27.
Shinn, Thelma J. "The Wise Witches: Black Women Mentors in the Fiction of Octavia E. Butler." In *Conjuring: Black Women, Fiction, and Literary Tradition*. Eds. Marjorie Pryse and Hortense J. Spillers, 203–15. Bloomington: Indiana University Press, 1985.
Zaki, Hoda M. "Utopia, Dystopia, and Ideology in the Science Fiction of Octavia E. Butler." *Science Fiction Studies* 17, no. 2 (1990): 239–51.

4 "When the Women Tell Stories"

Healing in Edwidge Danticat's Breath, Eyes, Memory

TARA T. GREEN

> There is always a place where women live near trees that, blowing in the wind, sound like music. These women tell stories to their children both to frighten and delight them.
> — (*Breath, Eyes, Memory* 233)

Edwidge Danticat, though born in Haiti, has established a firm standing as a U.S. writer. Her first novel, *Breath, Eyes, Memory* received national attention when it was promoted by Oprah Winfrey as part of her Oprah's Book Club series. Since then, Danticat has been included in the second edition of *The Norton Anthology of African American Literature*. As a representative of a Caribbean experience, specifically a Haitian experience, Danticat focuses mostly on Haitians' and Haitian Americans' attempts to reconcile the effects of traumatic events. Through an inclusion of African diasporic techniques and common themes, Danticat challenges readers to expand their idea of African American or black to be inclusive of the multiplicity of the experiences and histories of all people of African descent rather than to restrict it to a U.S.-centered one.

Danticat's work reflects an amalgamation of the two cultures she occupies—the United States and Haiti. As a result of the tragic events that occurred during the reigns of François and Jean-Claude Duvalier, Danicat's parents relocated to the United States, settling in Brooklyn, New York, in 1973. She and her brother joined them eight years later. Though she lived in Haiti for twelve years and often returns to Haiti in her work, the author refers to East Flatbush, Brooklyn, where she was raised, and to Miami, where she currently resides, as home. Her work, therefore, reflects her upbringing in both Haiti and America, which results in a literary aesthetic that proposes a unique cultural "symbolism, mythology, critique, and iconology" (Neal 1960). By her own admission, in fact, Danticat uses the work of U.S.-born black women to aid her in her development of her own art: "[W]hen I was writing *The Farming of Bones*, I was stuck on the issue of time. I had this woman in 1937, and I wanted her to be in 1961. How do I do this? A book that was very helpful to me was Toni Morrison's *Sula*. Time is handled so beautifully in that book" (Danticat, "How I Write" 66). Danticat suggests that there are similarities that women of the African diaspora use to tell their stories and that these techniques—for example, the relationship between time, storytelling, and experience—are uniquely conveyed by women. Not only has Danticat admittedly been inspired by African American women writers, but her work also encompasses characteristics of the diaspora.

As Danticat asserts and as Emilia Ippolito discusses, there are characteristics that are present in the literature of Caribbean women in particular, but may be present in the work of black American women writers as well. Among these is the use of black women's voices. Ippolito surmises that Caribbean women writers "refuse to be bound by traditional forms and tend to make use of the significant autobiographical first person narrator" (8). She notes further that "the multiplicity of narrative voices and perspectives within a text ... facilitates the representations of a world of fluidity" (8). To support this assertion, Ippolito cites examples of works written by Alice Walker and Paule Marshall. A third characteristic is also one that is applicable to Danticat's literature: "Re-appropriation of devalued folk wisdom—the body of subterranean knowledge that is often associated with the silenced language of women and the 'primitiveness' of orally transmitted knowledge—is important to the recovery of identity for the female in these works" (8). Ippolito's characteristics describe the heart of Danticat's *Breath, Eyes, Memory*, my focus here, which uses the autobiographical first-person narrator while also encompassing other narrative voices as the narrator, Sophie, also makes use of other women's voices in her own effort to recover her identity. In agreement with Ippolito, Karla F. C. Holloway examines the literature of contemporary black women writers of Africa and America to argue that black women's literature "reflects its community—the cultural ways of knowing as well as ways of framing that knowledge in language" (20). She goes on to state:

> The reclamation of women's voices is the critical accomplishment of contemporary literature by black women writers in America and Africa.

> Their return to the word as a generatve source—a source of textual power that both structures story and absorbs its cultural legacy—is a return to the power of the word itself. (20)

Both Ippolito, in her assessment of Caribbean women's works, and Holloway, in her examination of African and African American women's work, address the significance of language and culture in relation to the self. Danticat herself seems to challenge the idea of literary strategies that are uniquely Caribbean in the statements above and seems, rather, to embrace—in practice—the idea that her art is inspired by telling history and relaying its relationship to the people. I define *voice* as a mode of communication that is empowering, for when it informs, it allows for the development of knowledge and understanding that can impact not only an individual but a group of persons. In the case of black women, voices tell stories, preserve culture, teach other women, uplift, tear down, and have the power to heal not only other women, but the speaker herself. Danticat integrates the spoken word with the written word to emphasize the significance of voice to black women.

It is from mothers, as we see in *Breath, Eyes, Memory*, that daughters learn the importance of voice, particularly in their attempt to understand the ways of their culture. In the novel, Danticat focuses on mother and daughter relationships, which, according to Carole Boyce Davies, is common in works by other black women, including novels by Alice Walker, Toni Cade Bambara, and Gloria Naylor. Davies observes:

> Mothering and healing are intricately connected.... Reflecting a distinctly black feminist point of view, these writers reveal that black women, at certain junctures in their lives, require healing and renewal and that black women themselves have to become the healers/mothers for each other when there is such a need. (41)

Davies goes on to argue that the "fiction by black women indicates, mother-healers take on the responsibility of nurturing when biological mothers are unable to sustain the emotional support of their daughters" (41). She sites examples of Shug Avery's mothering of Celie in *The Color Purple*, Mattie's mothering of Ciel in *The Women of Brewster Place*, and Rosalie Parvay's mothering of Avey Johnson in *Praisesong for the Widow*. Unlike the authors of these novels, however, Danticat emphasizes the importance of the biological mother-daughter relationships as being an important aspect of growth. By focusing on the mother and daughter relationship between Martine and Sophie, Danticat demonstrates how healing can be achieved in the face of traumatic events. Particularly important to Martine and Sophie is the significance of the abused women removing themselves from the location of sexual violation and both women's moves toward forgiveness (of self and their abusers) and acceptance. But what is central to their healing is voice. Through her use of voice, Sophie develops an understanding of cultural practices and becomes empowered through confrontation. Although Martine—impaired by her inability to use her voice—does not complete the process of healing, her presence is needed for her daughter to engage in the process fully, which will allow Sophie to achieve the liberation and renewal she desperately seeks.

The novel is a coming-of-age story told from Sophie's point of view. When she is twelve years old, she leaves Haiti to live with her mother, who left her in the care of her sister, Atie. Sophie becomes estranged from her mother when she, in an effort to stop testing (a process by which the mother checks her daughter's hymen to determine virginity), breaks her hymen. Her mother, thinking Sophie has had sex with her older love interest, casts Sophie out to live with the man, Joseph, whom she soon marries. Approximately two years later, the women reunite in Haiti, reconcile their relationship, and begin anew. *Breath, Eyes, Memory* focuses on women who strive to heal mother-and-daughter relationships that are marred by sexual abuse. Both women are the victims of sexual abuse. Not only has Martine been raped, but she was also tested by her mother. Martine later tests her own daughter. Their shared experience makes the need for healing central to their psychological and spiritual survival.

Martine's Journey

The tragic act of rape abruptly transforms the developing identity of a hopeful girl when Martine, at sixteen, is assaulted by "a man whose face she does not see," probably a member of the *tonton macoute*—volunteer military police. As a result of this trauma, Martine is plagued by nightmares that cause her to relive the rape every night. Her sister says of the rights of women, "'Your mother and I, when we were children we had no control over anything. Not even this body'" (21). This statement is a profound one, for Atie is not only speaking of the public act of rape, which occurred in a field, but also about the private act of being tested by one's mother. For Martine, Haiti is a place that represents not only a site of tragedy, but also a place where she cannot live her childhood dreams of being a professional. She laments to her daughter, "'We always dreamt of becoming important women. We were going to be the first woman doctors from my mother's village. We would not stop at being doctors either. We were going to be engineers too. Imagine our surprise when we found out there were limits'" (43). Moving to the United States promises to be a new beginning for her, but new beginnings cannot emerge, for she remains haunted by unresolved issues of her past.

Martine's move from Haiti is a desperate act of survival. In Haiti, Sophie reports, her mother was barely in the survival stage as she was so traumatized by the rape that she would awake at night biting off pieces of her own flesh (139). The government discourages women from reporting such abuses, and her lack of voice, or the male-centered government's disallowment of the opportunity to confront the patriarchal society that favors men's abuse of women, leaves Martine feeling disempowered her entire life. Her mother's act of sending her to work for a rich family in another city does not solve her mental and emotional problems, which are only exacerbated when Sophie, fathered by her mother's rapist, is born. Four years later, Martine leaves Haiti for New York. She returns only twice, to heal her relationship with her daughter and to be buried. Martine and her mother undoubtedly hope that she can begin a move toward renewal; unfortunately, she remains in the survival stage and remains marginalized.

Martine does attempt to heal herself through attempts to stop reliving the memory of the rape by having her estranged daughter relocate from Haiti to America. Her attempt to heal herself and her relationship with the child she left behind in Haiti compels her to look beyond her belief that her daughter looks like the rapist. However, it will become obvious that confrontation in the right way and of the properly identified problem is essential. Since Martine has not confronted the rape—in fact, will not talk about it—her body remains haunted, as Sophie witnesses the depth of her mother's "hauntings" the first night she is in America when her mother awakens her in the middle of the night, screaming. Every night she relives the rape by the man who covered his face. For her, healing seems unreachable. Talking about the rape with a therapist frightens her, for she is unable to confront the rapist. Clearly, Martine relocated to New York in search of a life that she knew she could not have in Haiti. While relocation could mean more than merely an opportunity for her to attain a certain economic status, it could also mean the possibility of achieving a level of spiritual freedom. Despite her efforts—moving to the United States, reuniting with her daughter, dating a man of the Haitian upper class, and providing her daughter with the best education she can—she cannot heal the wounds of the past.

Beyond Martine's nightmares is her reluctance—or sheer inability—to tell her own story. When they broach the subject of the rape and Sophie's conception, Martine's vague retelling of the event speaks volumes about her inability to confront it. Sophie can tell "from the sadness in her voice" the impact of the event on her mother. Martine leads with the words, "the details are too much." In brief, a man grabbed her from the side of the road and put her daughter in her body. She goes on to say, "'A child out of wedlock always looks like its father'" (61). According to her daughter, her mother does not sound hurt or angry. The story of Sophie's conception contrasts with the story Aunt Atie tells her and that she remembers before her mother tells her story without details. According to Atie's version, Sophie "'was born out of the petals of roses, water freedom the stream, and chunk of the sky'" (47). While Atie may have been using this story to deflect from the truth, Donette A. Francis reads Martine's account as a sign that she has still not fully dealt with her trauma. Through Sophie's retelling of her mother's inability to provide details and her lack of emotion, Francis surmises, "Martine's disassociation is a faint attempt to deal with a trauma that has irrevocably altered her subjectivity and has literally rendered her speechless.... Martine believes she has no power to construct an alternative narrative that would enable her to integrate this trauma into her life" (80). The story she tells Sophie proves to be significant. On the one hand, she provides the child with a truth about her own personal history that she previously did not have. However, Martine also unconsciously passes the trauma of her past onto her child. Sophie's birth is no longer a natural occurrence; it becomes one that was not only unwanted but also contrived by the "boogeyman," a haunting figure—an unnatural entity. While she was once a product of beauty, she is now the product and center of her mother's suffering. On the other hand, the daughter is able to discern, if not then in retrospect, the importance of telling as a step toward spiritual wholeness.

Their conversation is arguably the most significant passage of the novel. Not only does Martine tell her daughter the truth about her conception—and, without consciously doing so, share with her the mental effects of the tragedy on her—she also tells Sophie about testing. She explains to her daughter that testing was a practice that was commonly performed by women of her mother's generation: "'The way my mother was raised, a mother is supposed to do that to her daughter until the daughter is married. It is her responsibility to keep her pure'" (61). Martine's feelings about the practice are ambivalent. On one hand, she seems to excuse her mother, Ife', for causing her sister to "scream like a pig," because this was typical behavior of women of her generation who were charged with the responsibility of keeping their daughters pure. On the other hand, she acknowledges that the practice did nothing to protect them. While the women are concerned with being pure, which suggests that certain rights have to be in place to make a decision to actually stay pure, the government does not recognize these rights. Men can take the women's purity as and when they please. As a result of Martine's *purity being taken,* her mother stops testing her. In a tragic way, Ife' has failed this aspect of her motherly duty, and Martine is destined to follow in her footsteps. In one conversation, Sophie learns significant lessons about what will be the crux of their mother-and-daughter relationship. The conversation ends with an observation from Sophie in retrospect: "'It took me twelve years to piece together my mother's entire story'" (61). As we see in Sophie's retelling of her mother's story, their stories are bound one to another.

Since Martine has not confronted the assaults on her body—rape and testing—she remains incapable of committing to her longtime lover, Marc. Although she has achieved what would have been impossible in Haiti—being able to marry a man of a class higher than hers and a chance to transform another aspect of her identity—she will not marry him, even though they have been dating for at least ten years. Martine is a woman who shuns intimacy. Before her second pregnancy, Martine expresses her reluctance about marrying Marc, implying that her relationship with Marc is an unclean one. When twelve-year-old Sophie asks her if she is going to marry Marc, Martine proceeds to engage in a conversation regarding her intention that her daughter remain a "good girl." Later, when Sophie and Martine return from Haiti, Sophie asks her mother if she has someone she can call to pick them up from the airport, to which Martine replies, "'The only person you have to count on is yourself'" (180). This is a significant comment from a woman from a communal society—from which she has just returned—but it is clear that she has adopted a way of thinking that prioritizes independence as a means of survival. Martine's emotional separation from Marc can be read as her desire to claim and maintain control of her physical and emotional life, as she attempts to do when she leaves Haiti, a country that she says still makes her ill. (On the plane Martine tells her daughter she only wants to return there to be buried.) Yet her attempt fails, for her problems with Marc go beyond a need for control. Unfortunately, Martine is ashamed of openly being loved by him. Her adult daughter notices this when they return to her mother's home and she witnesses her mother blocking the answering machine while listening to him state his love for her. She notes that it is "as though he was there in the flesh and she was standing with him and they were naked together" (180). It's precisely this idea of being naked together in view of others—that is, emotionally naked—that Martine wants to prevent. Confrontation of public acts—in this instance, a consensual one—is too much for her to bear, as she has not been able to confront the public act of her rape.

Later, Martine suggests that her reasons for being with Marc are the result not of love but of fear of being alone. She needs him to feel safe. She says that she sleeps with him so that he can wake her during the night when she has nightmares. Martine's pregnancy brings all her insecurities to the surface. Not only does she hear the baby speaking to her, she also openly questions her worth as a woman. She tells her daughter: "'I am a fat woman trying to pass for thin. A dark woman trying to pass for light. And I have no breasts. I don't know when this cancer will come back. I am not an ideal woman'" (189). This abusive self-loathing is yet another effect of the rape. Martine further questions her ability: "'And repeat my great miracle of being a super mother with you? Some things one should not repeat'" (189). Martine's low self-esteem also shows her inability to create an identity that is hers alone or to define herself beyond the trauma.

Martine's inability to engage fully in the healing process—by speaking to a therapist about her mother's testing her and her childhood rape—makes her body a haunted space. As such, the voice that she identifies as her unborn baby reveals the feelings she harbors, but will not confront, regarding her traumatic past. Significantly, hearing a male voice coming from within her own body not only usurps her own voice but simultaneously recalls her sister Atie's observation that they had no control over their bodies, not only through the threat of rape by men, but also by the need that mothers feel to monitor their daughters' sexuality as a result of men's desire to define the worth of women based on their sexual purity. The baby's voice suggests to her that she is not pure. Martine's feelings about herself as a "defiled" woman are stated and affirmed by this pregnancy, which is the result of her having sex with a man who is not her husband. Of course, it is not clear whether or not she consciously stabs herself in the stomach to commit suicide or whether she is in a sleeplike stupor, but in any case, Martine is clearly trying to attain control of her body by ridding herself of the voice within and the feelings and memories associated with that voice. Ultimately, her inability to forgive herself for her treatment of her daughter (even when her daughter has forgiven her) and her inability to love herself and Marc contribute to the only other form of healing Martine can embrace—death.[1]

Although Martine seems to want to heal, as demonstrated through the act of bringing her daughter to the United States (even though Sophie is a constant reminder of the rape), engaging in a sexual relationship with a man, and going to Haiti to reconcile with her estranged daughter, ultimately her inability to fully confront the rape renders her paralyzed. Martine's greatest achievement as a woman and as a mother is leaving her daughter with her story, by demonstrating to her the dangers of not telling the story. Though the consequences of this story yield tragic experiences for both daughter and mother, the fact that Martine cannot confront the story itself leaves Sophie with the knowledge and strength to tell the story to others. Ultimately, Sophie learns from her mother's example that removing oneself from the trauma is only a first step in the healing process. In order to heal, one must choose to move beyond mental, physical, and psychological scars. Voice—speaking one's own story—is essential in achieving this.

Sophie's Journey

As stated earlier, Martine's act of summoning Sophie to New York reflects her desire to be healed. Sophie, however, perceives her relocation as a disruption to her life. Her understanding of her culture, because of her youth and lack of experience, gives her a perspective about Haiti that differs significantly from her mother's. When Sophie arrives in New York, she sees a strange place that contrasts drastically with Haiti. She describes a place that seems overwhelmed by activity and that has an overtone of sadness. Her description follows that of the revelation Martine has about discovering limits in Haiti: "'All the streets were suddenly gone. The streets we drove down were dim and lazy'" (43). While her mother speaks of limits in Haiti, her daughter appears to discern limits in the United States. Immediately, Danticat shows the space that exists between these two generations of women. Though both women are from Haiti, they perceive the new location for home quite differently.

When Martine begins to test her daughter, the relationship she had hoped to heal is severed once again. Literally, severance becomes the catalyst that separates mother from daughter. Within this context is Martine's desire to maintain a bond of closeness with her daughter. When Martine tests Sophie the first time, she tells her a story from Haitian folklore:

"The Marassas were two inseparable lovers. They were the same person, duplicated in two. They looked the same, talked the same, walked the same. When they laughed the same and when they cried, their tears were identical [. . . .] When you love someone, you want him to be closer than your Marassa.[. . .] You want him to be your soul.[. . .] The love between a mother and a daughter is deeper than the sea.[. . .] You and I we could be like Marassas. You are giving up a lifetime with me." (84–85)

Martine's comparison of the mother-daughter relationship with that of the relationship between a man and a woman says much about her position as a parent at this point. Her decision to test her daughter is an act of incest, according to E. S. Blume, who defines incest as "the imposition of sexually inappropriate acts, or acts with sexual overtones, by—or any use of a minor child to meet the sexual or sexual/emotional needs of—one or more persons who derive authority through ongoing emotional bonding with that child" (qtd. in Robinson, par. 7). She states further, "If the act prevents a woman from being close to herself and other people, makes her scared, depressed, or has devastated her life, then what matters is that it happened, even if only once, and therefore falls under the definition of incest" (par. 17). Martine has not only resolved herself to being the protector that her mother was—the tester—even though firsthand experience has shown her that testing does not protect a daughter from having consensual or nonconsensual intercourse. She also transmits the verbal, though not written, folklore as a lesson with the hope that she is empowering her position as her daughter's mother. Martine's words, however, are an attempt to justify her actions while simultaneously serving as a distraction from the reality of the abuse, not just for Sophie, but for herself. Again, Martine cannot confront the act of sexual violation, even as she engages in it. Her words rather serve to disempower both her and her daughter who now share a legacy of violation and parental betrayal.

Sophie rejects the legacy by removing herself from the place of abuse when she chooses to break her own hymen through the insertion of a pestle. The fact that she chooses to dislocate sets her on a path much different from the one Martine took when she left Haiti. The decision, in Sophie's case, is one that she makes of her own free will. She spends the rest of the novel trying to reconcile the repercussions of this decision. Not only does she lose contact with her mother for several years, but she cannot have a healthy relationship with her husband, and she fears that she may, in turn, pass the trauma of her and her mother's lives onto her own daughter.

Though Sophie makes a move in the right direction, going to Joseph and leaving her mother does not heal the wounds of testing. In fact, it seems as though she relives the event each time she has intercourse with him. Their sexual relationship echoes too loudly the sexual abuse Sophie suffered from her mother. This is likely because she has removed herself from the place of trauma, but she has not yet engaged in confronting the trauma by verbal confrontation. According to Robinson, "Prior to beginning healing work, marriage is not recommended, even between loving partners. The intimacy of marriage intensifies any existing problems a single person may have" (par. 37). Sophie is still in the beginning stages of healing not only psychologically as she does by her act of breaking her hymen and freeing herself from her mother, but the physical healing from the stitches has hardly begun when she gives in to performing her "duty" as a wife to Joseph. At this time and at all others, during sex with her husband Sophie practices doubling, as she did when her mother tested her. She shares no enjoyment from the event, and Joseph seems oblivious of the pain that his wife suffers from their interactions. Although Sophie is honest with Joseph when she asks him for understanding, upon her return from Haiti, he responds, "'I do understand. You are usually reluctant to start, but after a while you give in. You seem to enjoy it'" (196). Clearly Sophie's husband does not understand the depths of her problem.

Sophie is clearly searching for wholeness, which is why she sees Joseph as a surrogate father. Not only is he the same age as her mother, he is also of a similar or at least familiar background; he is a New Orleans Creole who speaks Creole. Michel S. Laguerre defines Creole as "a language evolved from communicational interaction between French colonialists, administrators and missionaries, the African slaves and free people of color, and to a lesser degree, Native Indians" (27). New Orleans has a history similar to Haiti's, as it also was colonized by the French and was home to people of African descent, both slave and free. As early as the Haitian independence, New Orleans became a home to Haitian immigrants. According to Laguerre, "the Haitian American population in Louisiana was the largest settlement of the St. Domingue refugees in the United States." He further states, "Attracted by New Orleans' heavy Creole population, émigrés from New York, Philadelphia, Baltimore and Charleston also migrated in small numbers—either to join relatives, to seek employment, or for personal reasons" (65). Danticat appears to be demonstrating the importance of the diapsora in the woman's journey by joining together a Haitian woman with an American-born man of mixed ancestry similar to his wife's. Further, Sophie has wanted to see her mother as the Virgin Mother Erzulie. Like the Virgin Mother, Sophie was, without her permission, impregnated with a child. Joseph becomes the father to that child. After self-mutilation, Sophie leaves her mother and seeks refuge in the next logical place—the home of her surrogate father. She can only hope that he can provide her with the safety and security she needs, but Sophie will find that she alone is responsible for healing those wounds.

Healing is a process that takes time, as is evident in Sophie's struggles over a period of two years (from the time she leaves her mother, gives birth to Brigitte, and reconciles with her mother in Haiti). Before Sophie confronts her abuse and her abuser, she finds subconscious ways to express her desire to control her body through bulimia. As such, food becomes a catalyst to access the effects of abuse. Ultimately, bulimia is a means to control. According to Susan Bordo, "the bulimic is [thus] not so unreasonable in thinking that total control over food is required in order for any control to be maintained" (59). While there is little evidence that substantiates the idea that there is a link between eating disorders and sexuality, Michael W. Wiederman determines that "at least for some individuals with eating disorders, history of traumatic sexual events plays a crucial role in their current sexual avoidance and dysfunction" (308). Clearly, Sophie's inability to enjoy sex with her husband is, Danticat suggests, the result of sexual abuse at the hands of her mother and her attempt to reconcile this history by controlling her body. Bulimia represents Sophie's struggle to heal the sexual assaults of her past.

Bulimia also serves as a way to cleanse herself and to make herself into a "good girl." Valerie Loichot, in her article about the importance of food in this novel, notes that "[f]ood also acts as a connecting balm because of its healing properties inseparable from its nutritional functions. It serves to cure a body or a mind struck by illness" (96). The first time we see food acting as an agent to heal the body or mind struck by illness is the first night Sophie is in America and her mother wakes from her nightmares. Not understanding the nightmares but realizing that a sort of sickness was plaguing her mother, Sophie offers to make Martine a cup of tea, which she refuses. This is the first sign that Martine is unable to take the necessary steps toward healing. Sophie also does not know that her grandmother gave her mother tea to induce an abortion. While tea becomes an agent for cleansing the body of what haunts it—an unwanted child and unwanted nightmares—it also represents the consistent need to heal the relationship between mother and daughter that is bound by tragedy. Sophie's bout with bulimia is her struggle to heal.

Unlike her mother, when Sophie becomes a mother she attempts to heal herself of the history that plagues her body and mind through exercises in confrontation. Her return to Haiti is a major part of the confrontation process. Only there can she ask and try to answer the question surrounding the lack of control that women have over their own bodies, which is one that, as a wife and as a mother to a daughter, Sophie must answer in order to construct a healthy identity for both her and her daughter. For the most part, Sophie seeks to know why testing is part of the culture of Haitian parenting. Her grandmother, as the oldest woman in the family, is the only one who can give her some insight to this issue. She tries to explain the impact that the daughter's actions have on the family: "'If the child dies, you do not die. But if your child is disgraced, you are disgraced'" (156). The community's perception of a woman takes precedence over the woman's bodily rights. As such, Sophie demonstrates that her grandmother's explanation is not hers alone, for within the culture stories are told that serve to govern behavior of women and to empower men. Sophie classifies these stories as part of a virginity cult that compels mothers to "protect" their daughters by "keeping them pure." One such story is about the marriage of a rich man who chooses to marry a poor girl "because she was untouched." On their wedding night, the girl did not bleed. Since he did not have a blood-stained sheet to hang in the courtyard the next morning, the man feared that his honor and reputation would be damaged. To defend his honor he took a knife and cut his wife between the legs, but the blood kept flowing. The girl died defending her husband's honor. This story is one of the best examples of how folk stories can devalue the rights and voices of women. The only means that women have to reclaim any semblance of power is to use their voices, as Sophie does, by not only retelling the story, but critiquing it. Her critique is part of the confrontation that brings her to Haiti, her place of origin. Through the exchange with her grandmother, Sophie is able to confront the issue in the location where it is "justifiable" practice.

The meeting of mother and daughter is a critical part of the healing process for Sophie. It is imperative that she express her disdain for the pain the practice causes, a sentiment she has not yet shared with her mother, who is directly responsible for inflicting the pain that testing brings. As Sophie confronts not only testing but also the women who have participated in the practice, she is able to also confront her mother as abuser. According to Sophie, she herself blurts out the question: "'Why did you put me through those tests?'" When her mother tells her that she will answer Sophie, but asks her to never ask again, Sophie thinks that she should have the right to ask as many times as she needs to because she needs to understand. The daughter's right to confront her own violation conflicts with her mother's decision *not* to confront her violation. Her response supports this as she states, "'The testing and the rape. I live both everyday'" (170). It is obvious here that Martine can help her daughter to heal, but she is not able to help herself. Sophie's return to Haiti and to the source of her personal problems is an important step in healing the wounds of her past. As a mother, daughter, and wife mending the severed bond between herself and her mother by attempting to understand Martine, confronting her abusive actions, and forgiving her for the decisions she made, Sophie will be better equipped to be healed and to not repeat the practices of the mothers in her family. By releasing the burden of her abuse she can find the peace her grandmother advises her to find: "'You cannot always carry the pain. You must liberate yourself'" (157). Sophie's grandmother is the best source for this advice, since she herself has undergone the same pain as her granddaughter.

Sophie's movement toward healing is not one that she takes alone. The sexual phobia group she joins—comprised of women from all over the world who are coping with the effects of sexual abuse—is another step in the healing process. There she is able to move "a little closer to being free" when she burns her mother's name, after naming her as her abuser, without guilt. Robinson articulates the meaning of healing as "being at a place of peace, acknowledgement, and acceptance, knowing that one's entire life has intrinsic worth and purpose independent of the survivor's past with childhood" (par. 8). Sophie appears to have found acceptance and acknowledgment through group therapy, counseling, and confrontation. She is now moving toward finding a peaceful space independent of her childhood.

Independence of the childhood does not necessitate independence from the diaspora, suggests Danticat. Sophie also sees a therapist, a "black woman," who is a Santeria priestess who lived in the Dominican Republic. Danticat's use of this woman is an example of her interest in women of the diaspora, for this therapist employs a healing strategy that is diasporic and is not Western. Francis notes, "The therapist's geographical and spiritual routes are meant to signal that she brings an alternative Afro-diasporic cosmology to her therapy practice that weds therapy with religion as necessary to Sophie's healing process" (85). Sophie's relationship with this therapist helps her to answer questions about her feelings regarding her mother. Sophie admits that she does not hate her mother and she "has met her" for the first time (207–8).

Sophie is echoing the statement of her mother who, upon seeing her daughter for the first time after Sophie abruptly left home, says, "'You are now a woman, with your own house. We are allowed to start again" (162). Sophie's idea of "meeting her mother for the first time" suggests a movement toward renewal. She undoubtedly has moved past her pain and has reached a level of understanding that maturity and her status as a mother have given her. Sophie's journey toward healing has resulted in forgiving her mother for the practice of testing. Forgiveness of one's abuser is the last stage of the process.

Forgiveness and understanding emerge as prominent components of healing. Acceptance emerges as yet another. Danticat allows for the emergence of cultural togetherness in this novel in order to bring together mother and daughter and the daughter's husband, who until shortly before Martine's death was merely an old man who came between them. Martine embraces him as a kindred spirit. While Marc acknowledges that "we are all African," Martine corrects him with specifics. She states that she began to feel like a Southern African American and begins to sing, "'Sometimes I feel like a motherless child ... A long way from home'" (215). Martine's words are fitting, for this is the last time she and her daughter will be together. Martine's death will be a beginning and an end for her and Sophie; both women will be free.

While Sophie confronted the issue of testing during her first visit, she confronts the issue of rape and its meaning on the day she buries her mother. Her move toward the cane fields as her grandmother and aunt ask her a question that serves to mark a moment of rebirth for her is pivotal: "'Are you free, my daughter?'" (233). We can assume here that Sophie will be a better person as a result of having confronted her problems with her mother, reconciling their relationship, and returning to the "place" of her conception. We must recall the words of Sophie's therapist in this process: "'Even if you can never face the man who is your father, there are things that you can say to the spot where it happened. I think you'll be free once you have your confrontation. There will be no more ghosts'" (211). Healing can come only through confrontation, but it is Sophie's realization about her mother and her rape that will prove to be freeing. She concludes that her mother was brave and, more revealing, "'my mother was like me'" (234). If one is brave, then so is the other. With this knowledge, she is indeed free.

Sophie has moved toward achieving spiritual healing by engaging in therapy with a woman who is a priestess and in group therapy that focuses on attaining "peace, acknowledgement and acceptance." Confrontation of the oral word and through the written word, forgiveness, and understanding are essential parts of healing. Through this process, relationships between mothers and daughters, Robinson defines spiritual healing as "moving from a place of brokenness, emptiness, and feelings of separation from oneself and others, to awareness of one's infinite connection with a loving and caring Spirit or higher power, however the woman defines that power" (par. 8). Notably, the therapy strategies that Robinson describes regarding the use of candles and the recitation of affirmations are central to the therapy sessions described by Sophie. Secondly, psychological healing means "embracing one's life—not hiding from it or denying what has happened. It also refers to an ability to acknowledge one's damaged psyche and construct out of it a self that is free, self-aware, and healthy" (par. 9). Martine achieves neither spiritual nor psychological healing. Still residing in a space of marginalization, she is unable to move beyond the rape, and her suicide is the route she chooses to achieve liberation. However, through confrontation and therapy, Sophie is well on her way to achieving psychological healing and self-empowerment.

In this novel, a daughter heals while a mother does not. Sophie's movement toward liberation is demonstrated as she uses a first-person perspective to tell her own story that is interwoven with those of other women. This mode, similar to that used by Alice Walker in *The Color Purple*, results in the empowerment of the narrator who tells the story and of the other women of the community whose stories are also told. As Holloway argues, reclamation of voice is essential for women, and their voices can at once confront culture and result in self-empowerment. In *Breath, Eyes, Memory,* not only does Sophie liberate herself, but others who are in need of healing learn how to liberate themselves as well. Healing and voice, Danticat proves, are inextricably bound.

Note

1. The first kind of healing would have been of her body from breast cancer. Danticat mentions it, but she does not give details. We might surmise, however, that this form of healing was also a form of survival.

Works Cited

Bordo, Susan. *Unbearable Weight: Feminism, Western Culture, and the Body.* Berkeley and Los Angeles: University of California Press, 1993.
Danticat, Edwidge. *Breath, Eyes, Memory: A Novel.* New York: Vintage Books, 1994.
———. "How I Write." *Writer* 12 (2004): 66.
Davies, Carol Boyce. "Mothering and Healing in Recent Black Women's Fiction." *Sage* 1 (1985): 41–43.
Francis, Donnette A. "'Silences Too Horrific to Disturb': Writing Sexual Histories in Edwidge Danticat's *Breath, Eyes, Memory.*" *Research in African Literatures* 2 (2004): 75–91, http://web3.infotrac.galenet.com.
Holloway, Karla F. C. *Moorings and Metaphors: Figures of Culture and Gender in Black Women's Literature.* New Brunswick, NJ: Rutgers University Press, 1992.
Ippolito, **Emilia.** *Caribbean Women Writers: Identity and Gender.* Rochester, NY: Camden House, 2000.
Laguerre, Michel S. *Diasporic Citizenship: Haitian Americans in Transnational America.* New York: St. Martin's Press, 1998.
Loichot, Valerie. "Edwidge Danticat's Kitchen History." *Meridians: Feminism, Race. Transnationalism* 5 (October 2004): 92–116.
Neal, Larry. "The Black Arts Movement." In *Norton Anthology of African American Literature.* Ed. Henry Louis Gates Jr. and Nellie Mc Kay, 1960–72. New York: Norton, 1997.
Robinson, Tracy L. "Making the Hurt Go Away: Psychological and Spiritual Healing for African American Survivors of Childhood Incest." *Journal of Multicultural Counseling and Development* 3 (July 2000): 160–76. Acadenuc Search Premier. North Arizona University, Flagstaff, AZ, 2 February 2005. http://search.epnet.com.
Wiederman, Michael W. "Women, Sex, and Food: A Review of Research on Eating Disorders and Sexuality." *Journal of Sex Research* 4 (1996): 301–11.

5

The Coming-of-Age of the Contemporary African American Novel

Olympia Vernon's Eden, Logic, and A Killing in This Town

DANA A. WILLIAMS

A signal characteristic of the contemporary coming-of-age story involves a protagonist and her companion experiencing oneness with nature before encountering an event that jolts them out of childhood innocence and initiates their journey toward maturity.[1] Representative texts illustrating this point abound, but Toni Morrison's *Sula* is exemplary in this regard. In the scene just before Chicken Little slips from Sula's grip and is flung to his death into the water, Sula and Nel are innocently experiencing oneness with nature in an impromptu ritual the narration refers to simply as "grass play" (58). In concert, both girls stroke the blades of grass. Then Nel finds a thick twig and strips its bark to reveal its smoothness. Sula does the same. After Nel uproots the grass to create a clearing, Sula begins to trace patterns in the grass with her twig. Quickly bored and ultimately unappeased by the tracings of their intricate patterns, Nel begins rhythmically to dig deeper and wider into the earth. Eventually, the girls' two holes become one. Nel's twig breaks, and, out of disgust, she throws her twig into what is now one hole. They look around and find other "small defiling things" to drop in. Finally, they carefully replace the soil and cover their makeshift grave of unusable things. All of this they do intuitively, for they never speak a word.

This scene, for me, reads as a wonderfully poetic metaphor for the African American novel "come-of-age." What began in 1853 with William Wells Brown's *Clotel* has evolved in this new millennium into the contemporary African American novel, which actively and effectively alters the discourse of American literature and culture. Like *Sula* and *Nel*, the writer strokes blades of grass (the imagination) to find her twig (the genre or the medium). She tears away the twig's layer (its excessive conventions) until it is smooth enough to use. She clears a path of her own and begins to trace patterns (the "tradition"). More prone toward innovation than replication, she uses her twig to dig deeper and wider. But, alas, the inflexible twig—the genre itself—breaks. So it must be modified if the "grass play" is to continue. If the genre is going to be useful, the limitations must be abandoned. Small defiling things, unusable traditions and conventions, must be put in a hole and covered. In the end, the "grass play," in its attempt to sustain itself, literally changes that which was and creates a thing anew.

"Grass play," at its finest, is at work in Olympia Vernon's novels—*Eden* (2003), *Logic* (2004), and *A Killing in This Town* (2006)—as she intuitively (and unwittingly) constructs three coming-of-age narratives that first employ and then expand American literary traditions.[2] This essay observes Vernon's engagement with the female pastoral, the Southern gothic, and lynching as trope as three of the crucial conventions of American literature that enable her novels to redirect the traditional coming-of-age narrative and, consequently, to posit these novels as exemplars of how the African American novel continues to enhance its characterization as discourse altering.[3]

That African American literature engages genre as discourse and intuitively alters it to accommodate the challenges of modernity is evidenced in texts as early as Frederick Douglass's *Narrative of the Life of Frederick Douglass* (1845) and Harriet Jacobs's *Incidents in the Life of a Slave Girl* (1861), where both authors manipulate select conventions of the spiritual autobiography to create their own narratives of emancipation. This discourse-altering project continues throughout the tradition, from James Weldon Johnson's management of the autobiography as form to create *The Autobiography of an Ex-Colored Man* (1912) as fiction to Jean Toomer's handling of genre to produce *Cane* (1923) to Ntozake Shange and Audre Lorde's creation of new forms to fashion *for colored girls* (1975) and *Zami: A New Spelling of My Name* (1982).[4] Genre modification as a discourse-altering act is, of course, reminiscent of Signifyin(g), which, according to Henry L. Gates Jr., is the process of "repetition and revision, or repetition with a signal difference" (xxix). As Gates aptly suggests, recognition of Signifyin(g) as a literary process helps us observe that which is "black about American literature." What his theory of Signifyin(g) fails to reveal, however, is how African American writers initiate discourse-altering processes that move beyond repetition and "tropological revision" to *redirect* rather than simply *revise* American literary tropes and traditions. Gates's failing can perhaps be explained by African American literature's intrinsic resistance to the limitations of the language of theory to read its texts. Morrison's oft-quoted statement about her resistance to traditional theory as a lens through which to read her novels bears repeating here:

> My general disappointment in some of the criticism that my work has received has nothing to do with approval. It has something to do with the vocabulary used in order to describe these things. I don't like to find my books condemned as bad or praised as good, when that condemnation or that praise is based on criteria from other paradigms. I would much prefer that they were dismissed or embraced on the success of their accomplishment within the culture out of which I write. ("Rootedness" 342)

Bearing in mind the limitations of theory as evidenced by Gates's failing and Morrison's protest, this essay attempts to negotiate the age-old "race for theory"[5] dilemma by simply observing the ways in which Vernon's texts participate in "grass play" to alter crucial American literary discourses.

One such discourse can be located in the construction of the coming-of-age narrative. As one of America's oldest narrative forms, the coming-of-age narrative was initially foremost concerned with America's creation myth. As R. W. B. Lewis suggests in *The American Adam: Innocence, Tragedy, and Tradition in the 19th Century*, the protagonist in the earliest narratives was male, and he was portrayed as an archetypal Adam. Because the American Adam myth was so concerned with delineating America's creation and innocence as a nation, the coming-of-age protagonist was rendered apart from civilization and as the start of history. This separation and new beginning was represented by the journey that posited him as independent and innocent. As the genre matured, writers continued to render their protagonists as rugged individuals, but his detachment from civilization became more symbolic as the protagonist's life began to be portrayed against the background of social history. In short, the traditional coming-of-age narrative (consider James Fenimore Cooper's, Mark Twain's, or Herman Melville's narratives, for example) was most often represented with three primary constants: a young, innocent protagonist; a journey that shows this protagonist's transformation from youth to maturity; and the protagonist's privileging of individualism and self-determination over community and socialization.[6]

Long before Vernon ventured to write, African American authors had begun to modify the form to accommodate race as a factor that informed the African American protagonist's coming-of-age. As Claudine Raynaud argues in "Coming-of-age in the African American Novel," it is the "discovery of American society's racism" that is, in fact, the "major event in the protagonist's development and in his 'education'" in the African American narrative. From W. E. B. DuBois's rendering of his awakening to blackness-as-difference in *The Souls of Black Folk* (1903) to Janie's inability to find herself in the class picture in Zora Neale Hurston's *Their Eyes Were Watching God* (1937) to the realization that the introduction of Whiteness destroys the innocence of blackness in Richard Wright's "Big Boy Leaves Home" (1937), race/racism serves as the major factor in the premature onset of maturity in the early African American coming-of-age narrative. Race, then, complicates one of the most basic frameworks for the American coming-of-age narrative—the idea of American innocence. Not only does the reality of slavery negate this myth of innocence, but it also challenges the myth's corresponding depiction of the black male as an object who is not afforded the liberty of maturing.[7] Thus, a signal departure the African American coming-of-age narrative makes from the traditional American form is the former's willingness to forgo the concept of rugged individualism and to replace it with a concept of belonging that affords the protagonist a community to sustain him and that allows his coming-of-age to serve as a metaphor for the formation of black subjectivity in America.[8]

Vernon's narratives, then, have the benefit of a modified form in antecedent texts; yet the "grass play" must continue. Like other African American coming-of-age narratives, *Eden, Logic,* and *A Killing in This Town* are wisely aware of the relationship race has to maturity and subjectivity. The narratives are similarly aware of the modified form's tendency to preserve the protagonist's relationship with the community and his or her willingness to learn from elders and ancestors. What Vernon's novels reject immediately, however, is the straightforward narration that most often characterizes the form. Instead, Vernon's narratives are experimental and overtly more concerned with the language available to her characters to move the plot forward than simply with the plot itself. As a consequence, her writing is often compared to Morrison's and Faulkner's. Even as Vernon rejects these comparisons outright, suggesting that her novels are "called to her by angels," both the style and the content of her novels are reminiscent of Morrison and of

Faulkner and any number of other Southern writers.[9] The experiences she writes about uniquely—a young girl assigned the task of caring for an ailing relative, another young girl struggling to manage the tragedy of being repeatedly raped by her father, and young White males daring to transcend their racist pasts—are culturally layered experiences that render her prone to the occurrence of what Sethe refers to in *Beloved* simply as "rememory." She tells Denver that even after a thing is gone, it still exists, and not just as a rememory of the one who owned the experience, but out there in the world for all to see: "'Someday you be walking down the road and you hear something or see something going on. So clear. And you think it's you thinking it up.... But no. It's when you bump into a rememory that belongs to somebody else'" (Morrison, *Beloved* 36). Vernon's comments about the independence of her writing, ironically, seem to support the reality of rememory:

> I've got words stocked from the womb and I am about 30 years late in executing them. With all these years of waiting, all this buildup of words, I don't need to imitate. The words have been there and belong only to the characters in my mind. They are late coming, but they are emerging and they carry no blue print to push them along. (Stewart n.p.)

Vernon does, indeed, forgo traditional blueprints to guide the style of her writing, even as some of this writing conveys the energy of rememoried experiences, and allows the characters' dexterity with language to push their narratives along instead.

It is the young Maddy's command of language in *Eden*, in fact, that renders her so effective as a narrator. More important than her command of language, however, is Maddy's command of her *self*. The story Maddy tells is of her own coming-of-age, which, like many coming-of-age stories, is precipitated by death. After embarrassing her mother, Faye, by drawing a picture of a naked woman on the first page of Genesis with red lipstick during Sunday Bible study, Maddy is banished to the bedside of her Aunt Pip, who is dying of breast cancer. Pip is Faye's sister, but their relationship is strained because Pip had slept with Faye's husband and Maddy's father, Chevrolet. As punishment for his adultery and for taking Faye's pride, Faye's and Pip's mother cuts off Chevrolet's arm and feeds it to a pig, but this does not stop him from creating gambling debts that Faye must work herself nearly to death to pay off to keep the town loan shark, Jesus, from killing him. Maddy is joined at Pip's bedside by her aunt's best friend, Fat, who becomes a widow after her husband, Justice, is lynched by White men for allegedly raping a White woman. All this and more Maddy narrates with the intelligence and awareness of a young girl who astutely observes human behavior and who reads encyclopedias to pass time.[10]

Like the earliest coming-of-age narratives, *Eden*, as suggested by its title, is concerned with beginnings. Unlike the traditional coming-of-age narrative, however, the novel does not set out to show the precivilization innocence that informs the American Adam myth. Instead, *Eden* uses conventions of the pastoral (some of which it adopts, some of which it critiques) to manipulate the traditional coming-of-age narrative to better accommodate Maddy's experience. As a contemporary Southerner concerned more with investigating *truth* than with positing the South as an "*improved* paradise or cultivated garden in order to expiate its guilt over chattel slavery" (Harrison 2; emphasis added), Vernon rejects tendencies of old pastorals that idealize the rural world and that imagine the South "as a kind of new Eden, an unspoiled garden" represented by White Southern womanhood (3). Maddy's Eden is, instead, the black female community of rural Pyke County, Mississippi, and she overtly rejects the myth of its purity and innocence in the novel's first line: "'One Sunday morning, during Bible study, I took a tube of Aunt Pip's fire-engine-red lipstick and drew a naked lady over the first page of Genesis'" (Vernon, *Eden* 3). Clearly, Maddy is more interested in reality than in myth. Real womanhood, to her, is better represented by the sexually free Aunt Pip (and the implications of Pip's red lipstick) than by the notion of White southern womanhood as emblematic of Eve that gets Fat's husband, Justice, lynched.

As a contemporary pastoral, *Eden* critiques the more traditional form, particularly its use of Southern White womanhood to represent the new South as virginal land. Thus, it also critiques White patriarchy's cavalier behavior of lynching black men allegedly to protect its recreated Eden and her pure and innocent inhabitants. This critique aligns the novel with other alternative female pastorals, which, as Elizabeth Jane Harrison notes, create female protagonists who draw their identities from the land rather than becoming symbolic of it. In the sense that it works against prevailing literary models, the alternative female pastoral is also a visionary genre that allows its liberated women to challenge traditional roles and definitions of woman. Once the new society is imagined and the female hero learns to move beyond the southern garden representation, she is able to develop her own autonomy.[11] And this is the characteristic of the woman's pastoral most relevant here to our reading of *Eden* as a coming-of-age novel.

Significantly, Maddy enters the narrative with a sense of her own autonomy. This is why Vernon's choice to have her narrate the text is so vital to the novel's success,[12] because, through her narration, we come to know just how self-defined she really is. Despite the fact that many of the people in Maddy's community think "something" is wrong with her, that she is not "normal" for a fourteen-year-old (14), she does not accept their notion of her as deviant. She acknowledges that she is different—she is, after all, an avid encyclopedia and dictionary reader—but she sees that difference as a corollary of the courage and independence she desires. Her self-awareness is so broad that she openly acknowledges her limitations, both in terms of her experiences and her expected behavior. She confesses:

> "At fourteen, I had never kissed a boy or let him stroke my pubic hair. I had seen a penis only when I had walked in on my daddy using the john. I knew very little about myself. I knew little because there were things I was not supposed to do as a Negro child, questions I was not supposed to ask. I knew one thing and wore it alone. I knew to act Negro when other Negroes were around, not to talk about the bones I studied in the encyclopedia, the different species of animals, the words the Negroes in Pyke County never used. I was not to know why my ideas, my thoughts, my body were often too much for me." (17)

Even as she knows that something about her is extraordinary, Maddy is unsure exactly what that thing is and why or how it has come to be. And while it is clear here that Maddy's coming-of-age is racially informed (the one thing she knows is how to be Negro), she is not limited by race. Because she reads "everything," she is as aware of how White scientists, people in general, and animals alike are conditioned to a "used to" type of living (10) as she is of herself. But she refuses to accept this type of living as her fate. Instead, she is reasonably rebellious.

Maddy's teacher, Miss Diamond, for example, is one of those people conditioned to a "used to" type of living. But Maddy, as student, challenges this conditioning. Surely Miss Diamond is not "used to" students who determine for themselves what historical figures are worthy of study. But Maddy is not the typical student. Again, her self-determination is made obvious through her narration. She refuses to take a test on Hitler, because she knew "about how he'd killed Jews, the babies and mamas and papas and grandmas and grandpas and sisters and brothers and uncles and aunts and cousins and future presidents and so on and so forth" (61). So she cuts his picture out of her encyclopedia and burns it with her father's lighter. She serves three days of detention willingly until she decides that she is "tired of being silent" (62) and resolves that the worst thing that could happen to her is that someone would tell her mother. But, as Maddy learns later in the narrative, her mother, too, appreciates her self-determination.

In one of the few instances where Maddy's mother stands up for herself, Faye tells her husband that she scrubs floors and serves White people to ensure that Maddy has the life she wants and deserves: "'[A]s long as I see a book in her hand and she's standing up to that Miss Diamond up there in that school yard, I'm gone keep on scrubbing them floors and saying 'yes, ma'am and 'no, ma'am and cleaning them floors so tough that I can see my child's glory in 'em'" (98). Learning that her mother understands her desires for autonomy moves Maddy that much closer to maturity. She relates her thoughts in the narration:

> "She [Maddy's mother] had never mentioned one word about my back-talking Miss Diamond.[. . .] Or the many times I'd been in detention for having my own beliefs. She never talked about it. Just a mother, a strong woman who carried her pride in her hands, working hard so I wouldn't have to ever go through life without my own self-learned education. I loved her." (98)

It is, in fact, her mother's understanding, along with the nurturing of the community of women, both real and imagined, that ultimately helps to affirm Maddy's autonomy and helps to ensure that she understands the difference between being a subject and an object.

In addition to the wisdom she gains from the remembered conversations she had with her grandmother and from her mother's few courageous moments, Maddy's maturity benefits greatly from her interaction with Fat and Pip. Both women, unlike her mother, are confident in their sexuality, and they encourage Maddy to be similarly confident and aware. Fat exposes her to the power of love by refusing to stop loving Justice and to stop communicating with him, despite the fact he has been lynched and hung from a tree outside of their home. Pip teaches Maddy about her period and how to distinguish men as diarrhea from men as shit. Pip also reinforces Maddy's uncertainty about Adam's dominance over Eve and, subsequently, Maddy's intuitive resistance to being dominated. Pip asks Maddy, "'You think Eve told Adam what to do?'" Before Maddy can answer, Pip laughs and then adds: "'I had a dream I swallowed the bastard'" (131). But Pip understands that there are consequences to "eating her father," as she describes it, and she conveys this to Maddy. So Maddy must find a way to resist being dominated without suffering Pip's fate.

Since none of the women she knows has been able to escape the tragedy that plagues them, Maddy imagines a community of women who gather around her to usher her safely into maturity, which the narrative represents, at least in part, as awareness of herself as a sexual *being* rather than as an object. Determining that no man would rape her and that no cancer would enter her breasts and take her voice, she shaves her head and begins to dance with "the women and grandmothers and daughters of breast cancer" who lead her to the forest, where she sees all things (236). Ultimately, she gains enough awareness of her most intimate self that, in the moments before Pip dies and Fat resolves to join her, she can dream in the forest naked and unashamed, creating her own, very real land of Eden.

Liberating herself and the traditional pastoral as genre, Maddy recreates Eden as something greater than a reimagined South interested primarily in protecting its limited idea of innocence and purity. By the end of her narrative, she has renegotiated the representation of Eden to accommodate a broader definition of womanhood. She is able to do so by rejecting the myth of stereotypes and by insisting, instead, upon fashioning autonomous individuality. None of the characters in *Logic*, Vernon's second novel, is as providential as Maddy in their quest for reimagining the self. As representations of the South's terror, their individuality as characters is more or less denied.

This representative characterization undergirds the novel's engagement with the Southern gothic, thereby allowing the novel to adopt this form's critique of the ahistorical myth of American innocence and purity. As Lewis P. Simpson suggests in his introduction to *3 by 3: Masterworks of the Southern Gothic*, early American Southern writers developed a unique version of literary gothicism, which he argues could be appropriately called *pastoral Gothic* and which, by the twentieth century, found its Southern writers envisioning the "image of the South as a symbol of the disorder and depravity of the modern age at its worst, filling their stories with a complete catalogue of the bizarre and the horrible: rape and incest, murder and suicide, lynching (by fire or rope), castration, miscegenation, idiocy and insanity" (xiii). Thus, the characters' failed attempts at recovering the "self" become a metaphor for the South's flailing attempt to do the same.

Vernon's portrayal of her protagonist, Logic, as a sacrificial lamb highlights the fact that the very idea of innocence and purity is flawed, even before it becomes a myth. The novel is the story of a young girl who, by most standards, could indeed be considered innocent and pure. She is too young to have done any harm in the world. Yet even she must suffer. She falls from a tree one day, and her mother, Too, the town's midwife, takes a needle, fishing twine, alcohol, fresh cotton, and a leech and closes the flesh of Logic's scalp. Too is able to save her life, but Logic no longer lives a "normal" life. Her words are limited, and her father, David, rapes her repeatedly. Too knows that David is raping Logic, but Too feels too disempowered to stop it. Logic's lone friend is a sexually confused neighbor whom she calls "the tallest," but even his empathy is not enough to prevent her death at the end of the novel.

In the tradition of the Southern gothic, the two characters who struggle to come-of-age are "abnormal" by most standards. Logic, brain-damaged from the fall, is inarticulate more often than she is not. And the tallest, the only person she speaks to regularly, cannot decide if he would prefer to be male or female. At night he wears his mother's clothes and makeup. Both characters of the gothic-influenced text are also obsessed with body parts. The tallest draws detailed illustrations of the human body, including its veins, glands, and organs, while Logic obsesses over these "body maps." It is a drawing of pituitary glands, in fact, that she stares at to distract her mind as her father rapes her on the "operating table." Ironically, both children are probably more "normal" and alive than any of the adults living in Valsin County. Logic, for instance, realizes that her mother and father, though alive, are dead. So she prays that "Jesus would walk through the doors of [her] house, after she ha[s] left the world, and wake the hell out of the living" (Vernon, *Logic* 230). The ex-con who fixes the family's fence would even rather go back to jail, where he, too, is repeatedly raped, than to stay in the oppressiveness of death that is Valsin County, Mississippi.

By the end of the novel, the lessons the narrative offers us about coming-of-age, as it relates to innocence and purity, become fairly clear. As Vernon notes in an interview with Dee Stewart, Logic is "an innocent child, a lamb, born into the world where lambs are called to be slaughtered" (n.p.). Yet she cannot remain innocent, thus highlighting the notion that innocence as long-lasting is a myth. Innocence is fleeting, at best. Logic seems to have some sense of this, so she intends to make herself some wings to fly away. But before she does, she becomes as destructive as the forces that try to destroy her. When she realizes she is pregnant with her father's child—she never admits this; instead, she makes a birth certificate for her doll Celesta, naming herself the mother and her father Celesta's father—she prepares the supplies for an abortion and asks the tallest to perform it. The attempt fails because the tallest is afraid that Logic might bleed to death, as his mother almost did when she aborted her baby. Logic, then, refuses to eat, so the baby dies. It is only after she realizes that the baby has stopped moving that she admits that she should have eaten something other than berries to keep the baby alive.

She continues down this path of destruction until the end of the novel, when she kills her father and then herself. The narrative suggests all along, though somewhat ambiguously, that Logic intends either to kill herself to get to heaven or simply to fly away to a better life. She constantly asks questions about death, and she finds out from a woman selling life insurance how to spell heaven. Over the course of the narrative, she carves the words "I will see you again in," one by one, on her stomach, and she works diligently on her wings. Once her wings are complete and she learns how to spell *heaven*, thus enabling her to complete her inscribed message, she intends to fly away from her life of horror. She tells her father she finally knows how to spell the word, but he laughs at her and tells her that she cannot spell it because she is retarded. She then recalls a conversation she had with the tallest, where he wrote on the ground what she should do the next time someone called her *retarded: Blow their brains out* (242). With little hesitation, she takes her father's gun from the window and shoots him. Then, with blood on her wings, she goes to the roof of the house, puts around her shoulders the metal chain her father had hung from the roof (which Too suspects he does with the intention of death), and jumps. Her final words remind us of her sacrificial status: "'In His will is my peace.'" But even as the sacrificial lamb, Logic is not wholly innocent. Inevitably, she adopts the destructive spirit that surrounds her. Thus, the novel makes it clear that permanent innocence, whether it is Logic's or the South's, which she and the narrative represent, is ultimately impossible.

The myth of purity is similarly impossible, and this we learn from the tallest's attempts to come-of-age innocently. Like so many of the characters in the novel, the tallest is overwhelmingly challenged by his sexuality. The son of a prostitute named George, the tallest knows he should have a man's desire for a woman. So, on occasion, he humps his half-sister. But at night he wears his mother's dresses and shoes and puts on her makeup, and at the "circle-of-me," his secret outdoor safe haven, he feels free to explore his ambiguous sexuality. While his mother and Logic accept him for who he is, the tallest knows that he unnerves the rest of the world, both with his sexuality and his physical manifestation of abnormality. Enlarged since birth, his forehead bones protrude from his skull, so he refers to himself as "the son of an elephant." He takes vitamins in hopes of making the bones go down, but this, of course, is to no avail. Interestingly, however, he does not consider himself a victim. Instead, he simply hates totalitarianism. The tallest's challenge, then, becomes finding a way to navigate it without succumbing to it.

When Logic and the tallest go to the "other side," within Valsin's city limits, it is apparent that the tallest can indeed navigate his way through life successfully as a nonpurist. We also see this command of himself when he interacts with the Missis, the White woman Too works for. When she tells him that her only ailment is sadness, he laughs and tells her: "'All right to be sad, white woman. Jesus was sad. But He damn sure wasn't depressed'" (225). He then makes it clear to her that he will not be visiting her again, because she too has stopped eating and given up on life, while he has "shoes to stuff" (he puts tissue in his mother's shoes so they will fit him). The tallest has learned to deal with the hand he has been dealt, and he tries to convince others to do the same. His mother dies, the government takes his siblings, and he cross-dresses, yet he knows that he must continue on. Even after Logic, his only friend, kills herself, he cannot bring himself to cry again. Instead, he picks up from the ground the blue purse he had asked Logic to bring to see if it "fit him" and declares that since he has no more lives to save, "no one would stop him from living" (248). In short, he accepts his "otherness." He refuses to adopt a myth of purity, so he, unlike the gothic South he critiques, can simply be himself and avoid imposing a totalitarian way of thinking and being on others.

The consequence of such an imposition, one based on the myth of supremacy—White supremacy, to be specific—is the very idea Vernon investigates in her third novel, *A Killing in this Town*, where she further complicates the coming-of-age narrative by reintroducing a major trope in both African American and American literature: ritualistic lynching.[13] She first invokes lynching as trope in *Eden*, but it is in *A Killing in this Town* that she uses the trope aggressively to critique the tradition of young White boys' coming-of-age in a racist Mississippi. African American fictionists like Richard Wright and James Baldwin, among others, had paired lynching as trope with the coming-of-age narrative in earlier texts with great effectiveness.[14] What sets Vernon's narrative apart and renders it a discourse-altering text, however, is that her coming-of-age protagonist is a young White boy who reverses the lynching ritual by replacing a black body with a White body.

A Killing in this Town is the story of Adam Pickens's coming-of-age as it relates to the mixed-race town of Bullock, Mississippi. The narrative centers upon the tension that exists between the black and white citizens of the town and the ritual that exacerbates this tension. Vernon hones in on the height of the conflict almost immediately:

> It was a ritual in the town of Bullock, Mississippi. On the eve of a boy's manhood, thirteen, he must become a member. He must go to a nigger's house and call him out of it. He's got to tell the others, abed his horse, to hitch the nigger up to the pulley, hands tied. Feet tied. And drag him, drag the nigger through the woods, until his torso is bloody and his head and body are bloody.
> Until he loses an eye. (7)

This particular section of the narration is focalized through Earl Thomas, the town's only preacher and the black man whose turn it is to be "called out." Thirteen years earlier, Earl had received a letter from the government addressed *To the Men of the Pauer Plant, Courtesy of the Pastor*, indicating that others who had worked at similar power plants were dying mysteriously of an unknown lung disease. Because Earl was the only pastor in town, the responsibility to warn the White men—Klansmen led by Hoover Pickens—was his. Despite his inhibitions of daring to speak to White men, to act as their savior before their lungs burst, Earl recognizes that his responsibility to men who dragged black men for the sake of ritual "had sprung forth out of duty to God, to the public" (5). So he attempts to give the letter to Hoover Pickens, only to be pinned down, called a nigger, and tossed about by White men until he begged for mercy. Thirteen years later, "Hoover Pickens's boy, Adam, was now coming-of-age. He'd have to find him a nigger to drag" (7). Earl knows that "nigger" is himself.

In the narrative present, Hoover's lungs ache; he is dying of the lung disease Earl had tried to warn him of. And young Adam is being fitted by the Klansmen seamstress, the orphaned Lenora Bullock, for his hood and robe. Even as it is not yet clear to Adam, it is clear to his mother, D.D., from birth that Adam is special. He had been born sick and weak, and he was saved by a mutt named Midnight. To displace Adam's sickness, Midnight breathed Adam's air: "the vitamins of the tongue . . . shifted the bad blood out of the boy, until it slept . . . in Midnight's own body and came out in his feces" (14).[15] D.D. claims that she could tell by the positioning of his feet that "wisdom was what had brought him into the world" (24). So she tolerates Adam's curiosity when he asks questions she cannot answer: What is the difference between a bird and a nigger? Where does a bird go when it falls to the ground? What's God busy doing? But no one is prepared for

Adam's willingness to forsake the mythology of his American Adam namesake as set apart from history in favor of the mythology of his biblical namesake, who is charged with forging a new beginning. Yet this is exactly what he does.

With the help and encouragement of a remorseful Gill Mender, the now-eighteen-year-old young man who, five years ago, "called out" Curtis Willow, the town's last victim, Adam sets out to redeem the race from its past sins. In order to do so, he must subvert the mythology of the Klan's declaration, which is posted in Hoover Pickens's barn:

> *We are white men, born unto the earth*
> *And land, which is ours and belongs to us, as*
> *Free and automatic white men.*
> *All niggers must be obedient.*
> *They are not a part of the human thread.*
> *But are animals and must be dragged from*
> *Their properties and stricken from the*
> *Blood of the nation.*
> *The same thing goes for hypocrites.* (51)

Gill understands the inherent falsity of the myth and is finally moved to resist it, and he finds in Adam a willing spirit of rebellion against his father and the other Klansmen. Gill knows that the men act in the spirit of the American Adam mythology and, correspondingly, out of a need to establish tradition in order to compensate for their lack of an authentic familial legacy of which they can be proud. Most of the men either were abandoned as children or they father children with women who have been abandoned. So they re-create their own notions of history and of the nature of mankind as they see it. What they fail to realize, however, is that the natural order of the world is cyclical, not linear. The violence they initiate and inflict on black men over the years must ultimately return to its place of origin—to them. Thus, not only does Hoover Pickens come to realize that it is Hurry Bullock, a fellow Klansmen, not Earl Thomas, that he has kicked to death and then dragged. He must also finally read the letter that initiated this particular "calling out" in the first place:

> *To the Men of the Pauer Plant. Courtesy of the Pastor;* it told and warned, each of the symptoms striking him intimately, of an invisible, needle-like pang in the lungs, a bloody cough, the body shutting down, and the final warning, the Pauer Plant of Bullock, Mississippi. [. . .] Earl

Thomas had simply come to save them. (232)

The novel, then, is ultimately about salvation and redemption—a black man's attempt to save a community of White men, despite their racist past, and a young White man's attempt to redeem his namesake from the legacy of his forebears. The attempt to rewrite the trope of lynching as one of redemption and of hope requires "grass play" indeed. As Trudier Harris notes in *Exorcising Blackness: Historical and Literary Lynching and Burning Rituals,* the history of the phenomenon of ritualistic lynching "as it defined relationships between blacks and whites is one which has influenced the literary output of every generation of black writers in this country" (5). So the challenge of finding new ways to utilize the trope is heightened for the contemporary writer. Rememory-ing and redirecting antecedent texts, Vernon makes both subtle and aggressive plays on the trope. The first lynching, which has already taken place before the narrative present of *A Killing,* for instance, follows the trope's traditional design. The death of a black man is justifiable because a White woman's purity is allegedly in jeopardy, which the novel narrates thusly:

> Lenora Bullock [. . .] thought of Curtis Willow: he had come from the river—naked and alarming—the emaciated, hungry stream of the Mississippi dripped down the lead of his penis. His head turned with detachment away from her. . . .
> A strict, staggering muscle pulsated in his face: his breath yet withheld, his eye wept and blended into the waters of the Mississippi.
> He had simply gone for a swim. (Vernon, *A Killing,* 165)

The narrative moment here, of course, rememories Wright's "Big Boy Leaves Home," where Big Boy and his friends, after finishing what they thought would be an innocent swim, find themselves naked in front of a White woman who screams for help as soon as she sees them. The narrative then redirects Wright's scene by having the White woman admit to her desires for the black man.

> With her bare hand, Lenora Bullock unbuttoned her blouse, the nipple erect and protruding, and touched him . . . and she forced Curtis Willow's involuntary hand into her mouth and swallowed the river.
> . . . His arm swung from the shoulder and he could smell the powder of Caucasia—a catastrophic, infinite mutation that led him to pause.
> Lenora Bullock yelled out: Nigger, you're dead. (166)

More aggressive than this subtle redirection is Vernon's overall approach to rewriting the trope, which is to create a reversal of sorts. Notably, this approach, too, rememories an antecedent text. John Edgar Wideman uses the idea of a reversal in his appropriately titled novel *The Lynchers* (1973), where four black men hopelessly plot the public lynching of a White police officer. They fail to execute their plan for a number of reasons, one of which Harris argues is because Wideman ensures their failure in order to show that even as it is natural for black people to want revenge, it is "not within their will or within their sense of community to effect that revenge" (141). Harris continues: "[B]y showing the mental breakdown of these imitators of white lynchers, Wideman may be suggesting that insanity is precisely the condition of society which . . . continued to kill other human beings in such a violent way" (142). Thus, *A Killing* need not embark on a similar attempt at simply reversing the seat of power from white to black. Instead, the novel beckons back, consciously or unconsciously, to one of the earliest forms of ceremonial exorcism—scapegoat rituals—to offer a sophisticated critique of America's early obsession with ceremony at the expense of the very *authentic* civilization it so desperately craved and falsely claimed to preserve.

As Harris notes, "Peoples of cultures of classical antiquity and still earlier saw their scapegoat ritual, the expulsion of evil, as a periodic part of their lives. They had holidays, and they had sacrifices. For white Americans, there was no regular ritual cycle" (13). In some instances, White Americans compensated for this lack through the creation of rites of passage for their young men. Participants in the ritual did not necessarily have to believe in the sanctity of the ritual. They could simply be socialized into the roles they were to play either until they cooperated with the ritual or were cast out because of their failure to adopt it willingly or begrudgingly. To validate further its myth of America as a paradise, an Eden of sorts, the White worldview of the universe had to be maintained at all costs. When that worldview is upset, "in order to exorcise the evil and restore the topsy-turvy world to its rightful position, the violator must be symbolically punished. If the guilty party is not found, a substitute, or scapegoat, will do" (12). Notably, in early scapegoat rituals, "many of the victims . . . were allowed as long as a year to prepare for their inevitable deaths" (12). *A Killing* adopts the tenets of this practice almost effortlessly. The traditionless White men of Bullock create for themselves a ritual cycle, one that upholds the notions they believe in most firmly, that White supremacy is the natural law and that black people must realize and accept their powerlessness. To ensure its continuation, they socialize young boys into the roles they are to play, even before they become the focal point of the ritual. Adam participates peripherally in Gill's initiation before he navigates his own. When the White world begins to fall apart—all of the men are dying of the lung disease—Earl Thomas, ironically, becomes the scapegoat for the White world gone astray,[16] only he has thirteen years to prepare for what all believe to be his inevitable death.

The ultimate irony is that, in the end, the ritual works, once it is executed in the tradition in which it was initially conceived (by so-called "undeveloped societies" as opposed to "civilized" early Americans). With the well-being of the entire community at stake, not just the White community where the men are dying and the women are walking-dead and not just the black community where women can only love their men "as if they were already dead," Gill and Adam are more than willing to offer the dying Hurry Bullock as a sacrifice of atonement to purge the town of evil and to restore the hope of Eden, even if none of the *authentic* ritual's participants (Adam; Gill; Curtis's widow, Sonny; and Earl and his wife, Emma New) can live there to see its fulfillment. "They were no longer included," the narration tells us—"willed out of the Garden at once, out of Bullock and into the aboriginal liturgy of the condition they had been born into" (Vernon, *A Killing*, 237). Thus, they escape to their own garden, one more ancient than Eden.

The African American novel has long concerned itself with broadening the American literary tradition to accommodate and to reflect broader American experiences. Thus, discourse-altering has inevitably become one of the novel's most rewarding enterprises. In this regard, Olympia Vernon's novels are no exception. More concerned with exploration than with abiding by simple categorizations, they engage a range of traditions, from the cautionary tale to the coming-of-age narrative. Then, like Sula and Nel, Vernon begins her "grass play." Drawing upon the models of the female pastoral, the Southern gothic, and ancient scapegoat rituals, among others, and discarding those traditions and myths she deems unusable, she creates a style of her own that simultaneously remembers its antecedent texts and forges new pathways that reveal the beauty and the horror alike of the human condition. From Maddy in *Eden*, from Logic and the tallest in *Logic*, and from Gill and Adam in *A Killing in This Town*, we learn the many ways race and gender complicate coming-of-age, but, more importantly, we learn the many ways to execute our own "grass play" not only to come of age and to survive but to thrive.

Notes

1. In the young girl's coming-of-age narrative, the young girl is less likely to have a companion than in the young boy's coming-of-age narrative. In most instances, however, the presence or absence of a companion in the narrative does not impact the story tremendously.

2. Vernon consistently denies in interviews that she attempts to write in a particular tradition or that she is influenced by any particular writer. She claims never to have read Toni Morrison's novels, excepting excerpts from one text, even as *Logic* is reminiscent of *The Bluest Eye* and even as there are obvious similarities in the two writers' inventive use of language to advance their texts. She similarly claims that she did not read Faulkner, whom she is often compared to as a Southern writer, until after her books were written.

3. *Discourse-altering* is the term Eleanor W. Traylor uses to refer to the way African American literature redirects literary traditions, thus encouraging new ways of reading and writing that better accommodate what she refers to as *contemporaneity*. The latter term, she contends, is a more appropriate coinage of the concept that is traditionally referred to as *postmodern*. The argument, then, is that African American texts change contemporary American literature in a manner similar to the way the Africanist presence changed modern American literature. Morrison highlights the latter in detail in *Playing in the Dark*. See also Angelyn Mitchell's interpretation of Traylor's notion of *commemoration* as *rememory* in *The Freedom to Remember*.

4. One of the strengths of *Cane* is the way Toomer handles genre. The text cannot be definitively categorized because of its blending of genres—Toomer uses poetry, sketches, drama, vignettes, and short fiction as narrative forms. Shange's manipulation of form some years later in *for colored girls* does not blend genres as much as it creates a new one—the choreopoem, which choreographs movements within poetry as a fictionalized narrative that is concurrently coherent and independent. Lorde's *Zami* blurs genres as it adopts the features of the autobiography, of fiction, of poetry, and of the coming-of-age narrative to create what she refers to as her "biomythography."

5. See Barbara Christian's essay "The Race for Theory," which debates the feasibility of creating a theory that is specific to an African American literary sensibility. Inherent in her argument is the notion that theorizing is a limiting enterprise, in terms of the way texts can be read.

6. Notably, these constants are equally true for the traditional coming-of-age narrative that adopts a White female protagonist.

7. For an excellent commentary on how the black male as companion fails to gain subjectivity in the coming-of-age narrative or *Bildungsroman* by white (especially Mark Twain) and black writers alike and how Henry Dumas's fiction responds to and transforms this failure, see Tabitha N. Smith's "'Ark of Bones': (Re)Piloting the American *Bildungsroman*," chap. 1.

8. See Raynaud, 110.

9. Vernon's style is perhaps most akin to Morrison and Faulkner. Her content, however, might remind readers of Southern women writers Eudora Welty, Flannery O'Connor, Alice Walker, or Toni Cade Bambara.

10. Maddy's command of her self and of language reminds readers of antecedent female narrators such as Frankie in Carson McCullers's *Member of the Wedding*, Claudia in Morrison's *The Bluest Eye*, and Hazel in Toni Cade Bambara's *Gorilla, My Love*.

11. See Harrison, 10–12. Maddy's achievement of autonomy is so crucial to an accurate characterization of the text as discourse-altering because she is one of few young girls who come of age with such autonomy. Black women writers like Morrison and Alice Walker create female characters who achieve autonomy ultimately, but few of these women do so as young girls. Even as Celie in *The Color Purple* begins her story as a young girl, she is an older adult by the time she achieves autonomy. The same is the case for Sula in *Sula*. Claudia is relatively autonomous in *The Bluest Eye*, but the narrative is not her own. It is Pecola's, and Pecola, of course, fails to achieve autonomy.

12. Maddy's reliability as a narrator is, at times, questionable in those instances when she makes observations that are too mature even for her.

13. I am using the term *lynch* here as it came to be used after 1840: to put to death. Prior to 1840 the term was used to refer broadly to the act of being punished without a court hearing or fair trial. Over the course of the years, it has also come to include death by hanging or burning and is often accompanied with genital castration as punishment for black males' sexual offenses against White women.

14. Consider Wright's "Big Boy Leaves Home" and James Baldwin's "Going to Meet the Man" in particular.

15. Here, again, we find an instance where a black presence (in this case, Midnight) is used to change an otherwise White (Adam) situation. See Smith's reading of Jim and Huck Finn and Morrison's *Playing in the Dark* for further commentary.

16. Midnight is also a scapegoat. He is taken to sit with Hurry Bullock to save him. But he cannot or will not. Hoover eventually shoots Midnight in the leg to convince Adam of Hoover's ruthlessness. The shooting makes Adam more willing to participate in the reversal.

Works Cited

Christian, Barbara. "The Race for Theory." In *Within the Circle: An Anthology of African American Literary Criticism from the Harlem Renaissance to the Present*. Ed. Angelyn Mitchell, 348–59. Durham: Duke University Press, 1994.

Gates, Henry L., Jr. *The Signifying Monkey: A Theory of African-American Literary Criticism*. Oxford: Oxford University Press, 1988.

Harris, Trudier. *Exorcising Blackness: Historical and Literary Lynching and Burning Rituals*. Bloomington: Indiana University Press, 1984.

Harrison, Elizabeth Jane. *Female Pastoral: Women Writers Re-Visioning the American South*. Knoxville: University of Tennessee Press, 1991.

Lewis, R. W. B. *The American Adam: Innocence, Tragedy, and Tradition in the 19th Century*. Chicago: University of Chicago Press, 1955.

Mitchell, Angelyn. *The Freedom to Remember: Narrative, Slavery, and Gender in Contemporary Black Women's Fiction*. New Brunswick, NJ: Rutgers University Press, 2002.

Morrison, Toni. *Beloved*. 1987. New York: Plume, 1988.

———. *Playing in the Dark: Whiteness and the Literary Imagination*. Cambridge: Harvard University Press, 1992.

———. "Rootedness: The Ancestor as Foundation." In *Black Women Writers (1959–1980): A Critical Evaluation*. Ed. Mari Evans, 339–45. Garden City, NY: Anchor-Doubleday, 1984.

———. *Sula*. 1973. New York: Plume, 1982.

Raynaud, Claudine. "Coming-of-age in the African American Novel." In *Cambridge Companion to the African American Novel*. Ed. Maryemma Graham, 106–21. Cambridge: Cambridge University Press, 2004.

Simpson, Lewis P. Introduction. In *3 by 3: Masterworks of the Southern Gothic*, vii–xiv. Atlanta: Peachtree Publishers, 1985.

Smith, Tabitha N. "'Ark of Bones': (Re)Piloting the American *Bildungsroman*." Ph.D. dissertation, Howard University, 2006.

Stewart, Dee. "Finding Logic: An Interview with Olympia Vernon." July 21, 2004. http://www.suite101.com/article.cfm/african_american_women_writers/109979.

Vernon, Olympia. *Eden*. New York: Grove, 2003.

———. *A Killing in this Town*. New York: Grove, 2006.

———. *Logic*. New York: Grove, 2004.

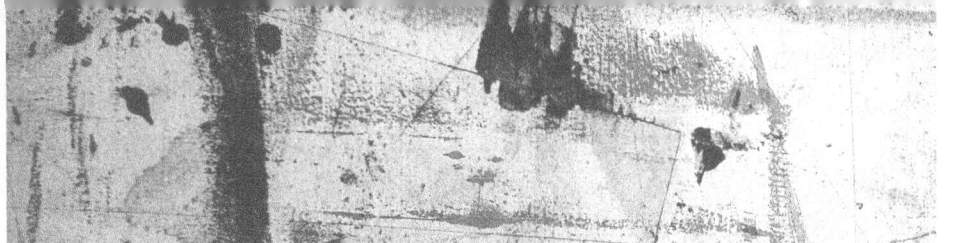

6 Another Night, Another Story

The Frame Narrative in Toni Morrison's Paradise and Alf Laylah Wa Laylah [The Arabian Nights]

MAJDA R. ATIEH

This essay utilizes and applies the recurrent and pervasive taxonomic characteristics of the frame to the narrative of Toni Morrison's *Paradise* (1998), the third novel in her trilogy: *Beloved* (1987), *Jazz* (1992), and *Paradise*. This critical approach avoids exploring the features of *Paradise* as a frame narrative by exclusively comparing it to another frame narrative. The frame structure in *Paradise* does not develop through its similarity to some construction or specific frame narrative that belongs to a certain culture or period. Determining the frame structure in *Paradise* by its resemblance to another frame narrative would suggest that the sample frame narrative is a hierarchical and hegemonic model. To the contrary, my analysis illustrates how *Paradise* emerges as an innovative frame narrative and how it adopts and adapts the taxonomic characteristics of the frame by employing inventive techniques. Concurrently, this study links *Paradise* to the heritage of the life-giving frame narratives and accentuates its significant reproduction of the celebrated Arabic story cycle of *Alf Laylah Wa Laylah*.

My exploration of the frame elements in *Paradise* relies on the interdisciplinary theories that David Ullrich integrates in "'Organic Harps Diversely Frame'd': A Theory of the Frame and the Frame Narrative." Ullrich uses both a literary and an extraliterary approach that originates from fields related to narrative literature, such as narratology and discourse theory. Through this interdisciplinary approach, Ullrich synthesizes the following characteristics of the frame:

> [A] frame occurs in various disciplines and recurrent circumstances. These situations can be summarized as follows: (1) a fundamental shift in a perception-determining belief occurs; (2) an extraordinary incident or "world" intrudes into the ordinary, "flow" of day-to-day experience; (3) an abrupt change in method of communication occurs; (4) a metacommunicative message is sent; (5) a distinction is made between "ordinary" conversation and story. (iv–v)

Through integrating these taxonomies of the frame and the frame narrative, this essay shows how the narrative of *Paradise* exhibits new frame techniques and emerges as an innovative version of the universal frame narrative.

In *Paradise*, the first applicable pervasive taxonomy in the literary and extraliterary analyses of the frame is the intrusion of an unconventional world into a predictive world. In literary narrative, the framing world is the stereotypic world that exhibits conventional situations, while the framed world is the extraordinary realm. In *Paradise*, the Convent is presented as a framed world, for it intrudes on and violates Ruby men's static and closed world of "disallowing" (189). The criteria of adjacency and dissimilarity are constitutive elements and prerequisites in the presentation of *Paradise*'s different worlds. Ruby is isolated from the rest of the world and "has ninety miles between it and any other" (3). This distance implies isolation and rejection of foreigners. Ultimately, any person who does not belong, in color, race, and "cult" (11), is a stranger and an outcast in Ruby. The antithesis of Ruby's racialized criterion of acceptance is the adjacent Convent, which, like an African home, welcomes strangers. The tension between the two worlds of *Paradise* distinguishes this novel from earlier frame narratives. In previous frame narratives, tension evolves between the frame and tale (as in *King Cheops*) and between the commonplace world and the fantastic or supernatural world (as in *Heart of Darkness*). In *Paradise*, tension evolves between the world of allowing and "disallowing." The framed world's principles are constructed through the eyes of the nine men who have not gone deep into the Convent. Through their eyes, the world of the Convent is the world of "revolting sex, deceit and the sly torture of children" (8) where "graven idols" are "worshipped" (9). For the nine attackers, Ruby is the redeemed world, for "God [is] at their side" (18), while the Convent is the world of the women who are "unredeemed by Mary" (18) because it is the "devil's" (17) world that is disconnected from God's earth (18). Thus, the Convent and Ruby become the symbols of two opposing moralities in the novel.

In *Paradise*, traveling in space and time appropriates and facilitates the transference of reality between the two worlds of the frame. In several early frame narratives, such as *King Cheops* and *Panchatantra, Canterbury Tales*, and *Decameron*, telling a story is one major technique that prepares the protagonists in the framing story to enter the framed world. Narrating a story is one way of traveling through time: Protagonists may listen to stories from the past. The entrance into the framed world may also occur through traveling in space, meditation, or dreaming. Ullrich observes that "it is not simply a quirk of coincidence that several frame narratives have as a characteristic the protagonist's falling asleep and dreaming a dream or traveling from a conventional to an unconventional world" (48). *Paradise* involves a distinctive form of intrusion or transference: physical movement along with reverie. The nine men who enter the Convent at the beginning of the narrative are already travelers in space. Now they will make another movement. This travel will be in time for they will enter the memories of the Convent, which they do not know or comprehend because they see through the eyes of their myth. They will be the spectators or viewers of an unconventional world because they are a group of stubborn "travelers" (Morrison, *Paradise* 189) who have carried their "stubbornness" (the Oven) to any place. They enter the kitchen, which even contrasts with their "cook oven" or "community kitchen" (99). This kitchen is a reminder of the kitchen of the embezzler where all his parties are held (71). This kitchen also evokes in their minds the white kitchen that signifies rape and humiliation (99). So they are travelers with, as Morrison observes, "preformed" views, which they do not want to renounce (Verdelle, "Paradise Found" par. 5). Clinging to their casting myth explains, nine attackers cannot intrude into the framed world through dreaming. According to frame theory, the dreamer does not recognize his values: "[W]ithin dream or fantasy the dreamer does not operate with the concept 'untrue'" (Bateson 185). Since the dreamer is unconscious of all values he holds in real life, the nine men cannot be dreaming because they are aware of their myth. Morrison even highlights the absence of dreaming in the framing story: the young man, K.D. "thinks he is dreaming" (Morrison, *Paradise* 4). K.D. does not have his "dream of his choice" (55) because he follows the myth of the old generation. Thus, physical movement and reverie distinctively facilitate the contact with the framed world in Morrison's novel.

In *Paradise*, Morrison uses innovative frame discourse markers and metacommunicative devices to suggest for the readers that the intruding world into the framing world is ideologically different. In "Edgework," Katharine Young—like Gregory Bateson—demonstrates how the frame helps the audience to differentiate between disparate levels of reality and to show that what follows is of a different ontological status from what has just preceded it (277). In previous frame narratives, the keys employed to facilitate the transference of reality signify difference in terms of period and distance. In *Paradise*, Morrison employs novel keys with regard to the nine men's entrance to the Convent. The first key is the display of mocked difference that they do not know what is in the cellar of the Convent:

> They have never been this deep in the Convent. Some of them have parked Chevrolets near its porch to pick up a string of peppers or have gone into the kitchen for a gallon of barbecue sauce; but only a few have seen the halls, the chapel, the schoolroom, the bedrooms. Now they all will see the cellar and expose its filth to the light that is soon to scour the Oklahoma sky. (Morrison, *Paradise* 3)

It is important to mention that Morrison elaborates on the description of the Convent's entrance. The driveway does not lead to the front door; it leads to the southern door: the kitchen door (37). The fact that Ruby men have always entered through the back door (the kitchen door) means they will find a world that is different from the world of their expectations and stereotypical views. Another technique that Morrison uses is highlighting the coldness of the Convent. The first note signifying the difference of the world of the Convent women is the chill the nine men feel when they enter it in July: "For at the dawn of a July day how could they have guessed the cold that is inside this place?" (3). This chill is in contrast with the heat of Ruby men's anger. The sudden warmth that these men feel afterward does not denote a change in the temperature of the Convent. Instead, it signifies their heightened anger and desire to control and destroy the strange world of the Convent. After the killing begins, "the chill they first encountered is gone; so is the mist. They are animated—warm with perspiration and the nocturnal odor of righteousness. The view is clear" (18). This change implies that they want to enforce their own heat of revenge into the cold world of the Convent. The change in the nine men's feelings from coldness into warmth forewarns the listeners and readers that the tension intensifies.

Along with the metacommunicative devices, a contact between the internal and external audience is established in *Paradise*. A reading of this narrative in light of frame theory reveals so many shifts and breaks in the frame that one cannot think but purposeful. The omniscient narrator prepares his internal listeners, and ultimately the readers, to expect a shift in the frame world. In this way, the readers are drawn into the framed world along with the nine Ruby men. These frame breaks and boundary markers function as metastatements that indicate a shift in topic. For instance, "Now they all will" (3) and "they see" (17) are boundary markers, which prepare the reader to recognize that a different world is intruding on the world of Ruby. Also, these shifts imply that Ruby men will be like viewers of a different world. So a contact is established between the readers, the internal listeners, and the Convent viewers who enter the memories of the framed world.

The frame in *Paradise* is explicitly metacommunicative. This technique implies that the author attempts "to comment on the story directly or indirectly (through a character who is 'outside' the enframed narrative)" (Ullrich 109). In *Paradise*, the metacommunicative aspect is obvious through the use of the medium of the external narrator who is not a character. Morrison's external narrator directly and indirectly comments on the events in the novel along with other speakers or outsiders: Patricia, Reverend Misner, and Lone. All of them do not belong to Ruby's world—by opinion, by color, and by kinship. So they are outsiders because of Ruby's racist principles.

Accentuating *Paradise*'s incorporation of innovative frame techniques does not underplay its reproduction of certain classical paradigms of the frame narrative, particularly *Alf Laylah Wa Laylah*. The criteria of this formal and thematic comparison between Morrison's *Paradise* and *Alf Laylah Wa Laylah* reflect and are considerably based on the affinity between the Arabic and African American modes of narration and organization. As will be later construed in this essay, the kinship between these two modes is established through certain shared Arabic and African American traditions and cultural perspectives and through their oral art of storytelling that relies on individual and collective memory as a structure for narration.

The comparison between the framing stories of *Paradise* and *Alf Laylah Wa Laylah* centers on the primary narrative of both works in terms of theme and content. Both works start with primary narratives that focus on the threat of killing and the motivations behind this threat. While *Alf Laylah Wa Laylah* starts with the primary narrative of "King Shahrayar," *Paradise* starts with "Ruby." Both King Shahrayar and King Shahzaman in *Alf Laylah Wa Laylah* and the Ruby men in *Paradise* are abiding by a mesmerizing myth. They are the travelers in space and time, whose travel does not invoke a new framework of meaning and life. They all invoke the old law of an eye for an eye. In *Paradise*, the fathers' past exclusion and rejection by white and all-black towns mesmerize

Ruby men: "[T]hey have never forgotten the message or the specifics of any story, especially the controlling one told to them by their grandfather—the man who put the words in the Oven's black mouth. A story that explained why neither the founders of Haven nor their descendants could tolerate anybody but themselves" (13). In the same way, both Shahrayar and Shahzaman are moved by a rigid message that they do not want to change. Both have chosen to leave their lands, but upon hearing the story of the Genie they decide to return and take their revenge. In "Infidelity and Fiction: The Discovery of Women's Subjectivity in *Arabian Nights*," Judith Grossman observes that King Shahrayar "fixed his world in the image of that event [his wife's betrayal], and over and over again enacted the ritual of killing the 'evil wife'" (126). Similarly, the inscription on the Oven fixes Ruby men. They are "haunted" (Morrison, *Paradise* 266). While King Shahrayar does not want his wife's betrayal to be repeated, Ruby men do not want the plight of their grandfathers to be repeated: "Freedmen who stood tall in 1889 dropped to their knees in 1934 and were stomach-crawling by1948. That is why they are here in this Convent. To make sure it never happens again" (5). In the same way, the king is going to kill his wife so that the unfaithfulness of his first wife will not be repeated. In both works, King Shahrayar and the Ruby men are obsessed with past incidents that explain their desire to exclude and to eliminate. Finally, in both works, transfixing history harms more than helps its perpetuator and upholder. In *Alf Laylah Wa Laylah*, King Shahrayar's myth excludes him from his people, jeopardizes his justice, and closes his line. In *Paradise*, Ruby's male-driven myth closes the community. Thus, both King Shahrayar and Ruby men have excluded themselves and ended their line.

Another taxonomic characteristic of the frame that links *Paradise* to the classical frame narrative of *Alf Laylah* is the "Chinese box" or "story-within-a-story" technique. In this context, Ullrich explains that "there are two basic kinds of frame narratives, the so-called 'Chinese box' or 'story-within-a-story' frame narrative [. . .] and the 'picture-frame' frame narrative" (109). In *Paradise*, this Chinese box technique entails "interior stories [that] are likely to be fully-developed tales, usually completely separate from one another" (Murfin and Supryia 134), but they are connected by the narrative frame. The framed world of *Paradise* consists of stories of rejected women. Each story is linked to the other through the appearance of a new character. In *The Poetics of Prose*, Tzvetan Todorov accentuates the importance of characterization in wielding narration: "[T]he appearance of a new character invariably involves the interruption of the preceding story, so that a new story, the one which explains the 'now I am here' of the new character, may be told to us. A second story is enclosed within the first; this device is called *embedding*" (70). Thus, the motivation of embedding is characterization. In the same way, characterization in *Paradise* generates embedded stories.

"Mavis" is the first framed narrative that triggers the chain of Chinese boxes. This story is about the rejected runaway Mavis, who heads from the North to the South and finds protection at the Convent. However, this story is not finished because it introduces another story through the characters of Connie and the Mother, who are not explained. By introducing the character of Connie, the narrator links the narratives "Mavis" and "Consolata." So the external narrator of *Paradise* introduces a new character with aspects that drive the reader to wonder about the new character. Who is Connie? Why does she wear glasses all the time? Who is Mrs. Morgan? Who is the Mother? In a way, "Mavis" has an open and incomplete aspect. Also, the preview that "Mavis Albright left the Convent off and on, but she always returned, so she was there in 1976" (49) implies that the narrative is not completed yet.

The second framed narrative in the chain of Chinese boxes is "Grace." This heading indicates that a new central figure will appear in this narrative. This narrative is about another traveler who arrives at the Convent. The "Grace" narrative is connected to "Consolata" through Connie's mysterious eyes. Connie's eyes are still a secret, and the story is not finished. This narrative is linked to the previous narrative "Mavis" through the encounter between Mavis and Gigi. Also, this narrative is linked to the coming narrative through the reference it gives in the end: "They did everything but slap each other, and finally they did that. What postponed the inevitable were loves forlorn and a very young girl in too tight clothes tapping on the screen door. 'You have to help me,' she said. 'You have to. I've been raped and it's almost August'" (77). This story ends with the arrival of a new figure at the Convent. The introduction of the new character implies that the narrative is incomplete and that a new story will begin. In the same way, "Seneca" is linked to "Mavis," "Grace," and "Consolata" through Seneca's arrival at the Convent. Also, Pallas is the last traveler whose story is separate but linked to the other framed stories. "Divine" introduces the character of Patricia and eventually her narrative. Likewise, the "Patricia" narrative introduces the character of Lone. So the frame links all the separate narratives together through characterization. In this way, all of these narratives are not "self-sufficient" (Todorov 76). The appearance of a new character is a potential story, which provides an explanation to the gaps in the previous narrative. And, as Todorov concludes, "every new character signifies a new plot. We are in the realm of narrative-men" (70). This "realm" signifies the realm of framing in *Paradise*.

In *Alf Laylah Wa Laylah*, the frame also generates stories through characterization. In the framed collection of tales, the appearance of a new character leads to the narration of another tale. The introduction of characters occurs through two ways: the external narrator, Shahrazade, and the characters in the framed tales. In the first case, Shahrazade presents new characters with new stories. She "suspends" the narration and links the story being told with the coming one through a "preview" (Murfin 134) of its main characters:

فقال الملك لشهريار لزوجته شهرزاد: إن حكاية أبي قير و أبي صير، فيه موعظة و عبرة
لكل كبير و صغير. إني جدير لذلك أن تكتب و تحفظ و تروى. قالت شهرزاد: هل اذا
لوقت إذن يا مولاي لو أنا سمعت حكاية عبد الله البري و عبد الله البحري؟

Then King Shahrayar told his wife Shahrazade: "The tale of Abi Kayr and Abi Sayr is both a sermon and a lesson for the old and the young. Therefore, this narrative is worth writing, memorizing, and retelling." Then Shahrazade said: "'O Mawlayi, so what would you say if you heard the tale of Abdullah, the Seaman, and Abdullah, the Landsman?'" (*Alf Laylah* 3: 95)

So Shahrazade chains the tales together through presenting new fictional characters. Alternatively, the fictional characters themselves present new stories that are related to the situation in which they find themselves. For instance, in the tale "The Fisherman and the Genie," the appearance of a young crying man, whose legs are petrified, motivates the king to wonder about this mystery. The king's questions lead to the narration of the embedded story of the young man:

فقال الملك: أيها الشاب أخبرني عن هذه البركة و سمكها الملون، و عن هذا القصر و سبب
حدتك فيه، وسبب بكائك، فلما سمع الشاب هذا الكلام نزلت دموعه على خديه و بكى
بكاء شديدا.

The King said: "O young man, tell me about the secret of this pond and its colored fish, and about this castle and the reason for your weeping and loneliness." When the young man heard his speech, his tears ran down his cheeks and he cried out in anguish. (1: 42)

Both *Alf Laylah Wa Laylah* and *Paradise* present a structural similarity related to their circular and nonlinear narration that reflects an affinity in their cultural perspective of time. Morrison "treats time not chronologically, but as a divided, multilayered dimension. Flashbacks and 'flashforwards' abound, and a multiplicity of times are narrated. Time is more like circular African time than linear European time, as each novel proceeds in both a chronological direction and a circular or spiral redoubling" (Page 33). This type of narration relates to Morrison's view of life, as she points out: "People's anticipation now more than ever for linear, chronological stories is intense because that's the way narrative is revealed in TV and movies. But we experience life as the present moment, the anticipation of the future, and a lot of slices of the past" (Mulrine par. 7). In *Paradise,* the lack of chronological order in the framed narratives reflects the process of memory that guides and structures Morrison's narration and serves to stress continuity in the face of dissolution and death. The novel starts with the present threat of death, jumps into the past in the framed collection, then goes back to the present moment of attack. Also, the order of the framed narratives does not follow the conventional time. If they follow, they should have begun with "Consolata," for its protagonist is older than the protagonists in the other framed narratives. Moreover, even the narration of each framed narrative is not linear. For instance, "Divine" begins with the wedding that Pallas attends, then goes back to recount Pallas's arrival at the Convent. In the same way, the narration of *Alf Laylah Wa Laylah* is nonlinear and time is circular. In the Arabic tradition, time is circular. This feature is reflected in the "arbitrary arrangement" (Gittes 60) of the Arabic *qasida,* which is not static, lacks "logical cohesion" (Nicholson 134), and follows the memories of its reciter. Likewise, the structure of *Alf Laylah Wa Laylah* is arbitrary and circular. Beginnings are endings as in the tale "The Fisherman and the Genie":

قال الفريت: افتح لي حتى احسن اليك، فقال له الصياد: تكذبت اي علم انن مثلي
و مثلك كمثل وزير الملك يونان و الحكيم رويان. قال العفريت: و ما صدق امر وزير الملك
يونان و الحكيم رويان؟

The Genie said: "Open for me and I will be good to you." Then the Fisherman said: "You are lying Wicked! Our case is like the case of Yunan, the King's Vizier, and Ruyan, the Philosopher." Then the genie said: "And what is the tale of Yunan, the King's Vizier, and Ruyan, the Philosopher?"(*Alf Laylah* 1: 18)

Also, the tale "Muslim bin al-Waleed and the Bondwoman, the Poet," begins with the verse that Doubol al-Khozay recites at the end of his story with Muslim bin Al-Waleed. So, the beginning of this tale is its end:

حكى أيها الملك السعيد، أن الخليفة هرون الرشيد، دعا يوما بعض
الشعراء و الندماء و الظرفاء، و قال لهم: أريد أن أعرف من قائل هذا البيت.

> It has been told, O Happy King, that the Caliph Harun al-Rasheed summoned one day some of the poets, drinking companions, and wits. Then he said to them: "I want to know who recited this bayt." (3: 236)

So, through the workings of their memories, the characters themselves wield the narration to the realm of the past and begin their recounting with the ends of their tales. This nonlinear narration relates to the circular time in the Arabic mode of storytelling, which reflects the individual and collective memories that do not follow the order of "conservative" time (Ledbetter 161).

The framed stories in *Alf Laylah Wa Laylah* and *Paradise* signify the world of possibility and change, the opposite of the framing world of myth and closure. Grossman points out the enormous scope of possibility in the framed stories of *Alf Laylah Wa Laylah*: "Shahrazade's first story shows the King that in a world of variable circumstances, in which evil and good women are both to be found, the [. . .] task is to make discriminating choices and decisions; and further, that since evil springs from sorrow, justice should be tempered with compassion" (123). Tales like "The Fisherman and the Genie," "Ali, the Egyptian Merchant," and "Nur al-Deen and Shams al-Deen" present different female subjectivities (bad and good) and show that evil is not an instinctive vice in women.

In *Paradise*, the framed narratives also present possibility and change. "Mavis" is the first story that prepares for the world of the possible and contrasts with the world of the Oven. This story ends with a note about Mavis's departure from the Convent and her last return in 1976 (49). Mavis's return to the Convent implies that this world of allowing induces change in its refugees. The Convent as a place of conversion is implied and predicted in its structure. Before it becomes a convent, it has been a world of fear that expects attack from outside. The "cartridge"-shaped place gets rid of its fear from the outside when the nuns arrive: "The closed-off, protected 'back,' the poised and watchful 'tip,' an entrance door guarded by the remaining claws of some monstrous statuary, which the sisters had removed at once. A rickety, ill-hanging kitchen door the only vulnerability" (71). This vulnerability implies that this fear from outside is defeated. What is left is the fear from inside. This fear is highlighted in Connie's comment when Mavis asks, "'You all ain't scared out here by yourselves? Don't seem like there's nothing for miles outside.' Connie laughed. 'Scary things not always outside. Most scary things is inside'" (39). The change in the structure of the Convent is the first step toward the defeat of death. The Convent will be attacked again, but this attack is not dangerous because it is not significant. The evidence is the door, which "has never been locked" (285). And as Mavis decides to stay, Grace chooses to remain in the place in which she finds love. "Seneca" is the third framed narrative, and it ends with a note about the care she finds at the Convent: "Downstairs, someone was calling her name. 'Seneca? Seneca? Come on, baby. We're waiting for you'" (138). Likewise, "Divine" concludes with a scene of harmony between Mavis and Pallas: "When they were in front of Mavis' bedroom door she didn't open it. She froze. 'Hear that? They're happy,' she said, covering her laughing lips. She turned to Pallas. 'They like you too. They think you're divine'" (182). "Consolata" is another story that shows how change is an aspect of the Convent. Consolata longs for death because of her depressing relationship with the "living man": her "thirty years of surrender to the living God cracked like a pullet's egg when she met the living man" (225). Like the stubborn Rubyists, Consolata is a "hardhead" (246). She becomes haunted by her affair with the "living man" and loses her sight as an indication of her blindness by this past: "a sunshot seared her right eye, announcing the beginning of her bat vision, and she began to see best in the dark" (241). Lone teaches Consolata to step into the world of the dead man, which is different from the world of the "living man." There she can pull up the "receding" "pinpoint of light" (245). Then she gets out of her framing body and life. Consolata's change is reflected in the way she introduces herself: "'people call me Connie'" (38) changes into "'I call myself Consolata Sosa'" (262). Consolata is the old and strange traveler in time who heals herself and stands in contrast to Ruby's ancestral travelers in space who petrify and close their community.

In light of its framed world of possibility, *Alf Laylah Wa Laylah* shows how narration, retelling, and dreaming can redeem and heal a human life. In "1001 Words: Fiction against Death," Wendy B. Faris demonstrates how "Scheherazadian narrators fight bravely, if uselessly, against the end which figures their own deaths" (812). In "The Fisherman and the Genie" the fisherman relates a tale to save himself, while in "The Merchant and the Genie" the three sheikhs have to relate their stories in order to save the merchant from the genie's threat. Each sheikh has to relate his story and save one-third of the merchant's blood (*Alf Laylah* 20). Also, in the tale "The King and the Peasant's Wife," the wife's family retells the story of the peasant's punishment of his wife in order to convince the king to clarify the real story to the peasant:

احتالوا لقصد حكاية زوجة اهل عليه، فقالوا له: أيها الملك العادل، ان لنا قريبا استأجر منا ارضاً ليزرعها، و بعد ان زرعها سنين، ترك عند زراعها فان لم يكن يريد زرعها، فليردها الينا.

> They conspired to narrate the peasant's story to the king, so they told the king: "O Just King, we have a relative who borrowed our land in order to cultivate it. After planting it for several years, he left it without cultivation. So, if he does not want to sow it let him return it." (3: 230–31)

The king retells the story of his encounter with the wife to the peasant, and saves the wife from punishment. Shared dreams also lead *Alf Laylah*'s dreamers to their path of redemption. In the tale "The Wonders of Coincidences," a poor Baghdadian man dreams about a house, which is located in Egypt and full of treasure. He travels to Egypt in order to find this fortune. However, when he arrives there, al-Waly informs him that he has dreamed about the same house, but its location is different—it is in Baghdad. The poor man returns to Baghdad and finds the treasure that saves him (2: 233). Thus, the first dream leads the poor man to al-Waly, whose dream reveals the exact location of the gold. Dreams signify a different world into which the dreamers step, realize better visions, suspend misery, and redeem hearts from grudge. In *Alf Laylah Wa Laylah*, dreaming not only involves stepping into a better world, but it also recovers all bad memories only to suspend them in the end. In the Egyptian tale "Nur al-Deen and Shams al-Deen," dreaming is a sign of redemption because it obliterates all memories of hardships and ordeals. The vizier Shams al-Deen locks his nephew Hassan Badr al-Deen inside a casket so that Hassan sleeps and thinks that all the travails and perils he had suffered have only happened in a dream. This aspiration for redemption is intensified when Hassan thanks God for this dream:

فالحمد لله الذي جعل ذلك كله قي المنام و لم يجعله في اليقظة

> "I thank Allah who made all of this in a dream not in reality." (1: 152)

Hassan is resurrected through sleeping and dreaming in the casket. So dreaming retrieves then ends disturbing memories, and it also redeems and heals afflicted souls.

In the same way, *Paradise* exemplifies how dreaming, remembering, and retelling bring about healing processes that allow the central characters to become full members of their community. Consolata is a central character whose dreaming heals her and the Convent women. If Hassan of *Alf Laylah* resurrects from a casket, Consolata also resurrects from a coffin: "[A]lready in a space tight enough for a coffin, already devoted to the dark, long removed from appetites, craving only oblivion, she struggled to understand the delay" (Morrison, *Paradise* 221). Consolata steps into the world of dreams when she heads to the garden: "As she rose to replenish her vice, a grand weariness took her, forcing her back to the seat, tipping her chin on her chest. She slept herself into sobriety. Headachy, sandymouthed, she woke in quick need of a toilet [. . .] she decided to catch a little air and shuffled into the kitchen and out the door" (250–51). The world of dreams helps her remember her encounter with the "living man" in a different way. Rememory helps her recognize the blindness of the strange traveler and see herself (252). By healing herself, Consolata is able to lead the Convent women into the world of dreams that heals them. The epitome of this healing is realized through telling stories at the Convent: "This is how the loud dreaming began. How the stories rose in that place. Half-tales and the never-dreamed escaped from their lips to soar high above guttering candles, shifting dust from crates and bottles [. . .]. In spite of or because their bodies ache, they step easily into the dreamer's tale" (264). Consolata rids the women's afflicted bodies of their memories and introduces them to the spiritual world: "'My child body, hurt and soil, leaps into the arms of a woman who teach me my body is nothing my spirit is everything'" (263). By rendering their hurting memories into dreams and tales, the Convent women are able to heal and save themselves from inner suffering. As Consolata reflects, "unlike some people in Ruby, the Convent women were no longer haunted" (266). The healing of the Convent women highlights the difference of the Convent as a world of possibility and change.

As the framed narratives in *Paradise* and *Alf Laylah Wa Laylah* proceed, the apocalypse of death gradually vanishes, and its threat is not mentioned anymore. In *Paradise*, a reference to the catastrophe brought by the intruding nine men appears in the first framed narrative—"Mavis." But the scene of their intrusion does not appear in "Grace," "Seneca,"

"Divine," and "Patricia." This absence signifies that the threat of death begins to lose its magnitude as the narrative progresses. In *Alf Laylah Wa Laylah*, the apocalypse of death also fades with Shahrazade's narration. For the first two nights, Shahrazade asks the king's permission to spare her in order to narrate her tales. In these two nights, Shahrazade breaks off when the morning comes. Her sister asks her for more tales, but Shahrazade answers that this continuation depends on the king's permission. However, the haunting threat of death does not last. Shahrayar even reconsiders and commutes his intention of executing Shahrazade on the first night. The fact that her narration is permitted reveals that the threat of death is forgotten. In *Narratology*, Mieke Bal argues: "In case of the *Arabian Nights*, this forgetting is a sign that Scheherazade's goal has been accomplished. As long as we forget that her life is at stake, the king will too, and that was her purpose" (51). So the defeat of the threat of death starts by forgetting its presence.

In both narratives, postponement and suspension are two crucial narratological techniques that effectively contribute to the defeat of death. In *Paradise*, the "Lone" narrative shows how suspension in narration becomes an act of self-reconstruction. "Lone" goes back to the primary narrative of invading the Convent. It picks up from where a previous narrative stopped and resumes the suspended threat of killing. However, the threat of the framing world has no effect on the framed world. When Lone heads to the Convent to warn the women of danger, they do not believe her. The healing has had its effect on them: "None of them would listen. Said Connie was busy, refused to call her and didn't believe a word Lone said. After driving out there in the middle of the night to tell them, warn them, she watched in helpless fury as they yawned and smiled" (Morrison, *Paradise* 269). Harmony and redemption prevail at the Convent. Its refugees have learned to avoid the drift that Consolata warns against (222). Though Ruby men do not change their perceptions or intention to kill the Convent women, the act of narration has defeated the threat of death. By the time the narrator goes back to the framing narrative and retells the massacre, the women have gained their healing. As Morrison explains, "It's interesting and important to me that once the women are coherent and strong and clean in their interior lives, they feel saved. They feel impenetrable. So that when they are warned of the attack on the Convent, they don't believe it" (Marcus par. 23). The evil of Ruby men's plan of attack is overcome by the Convent women's solace. Similarly, *Alf Laylah Wa Laylah* overcomes death through suspension and postponement and stimulates individual and communal redemption. Shahrazade's tales force Shahrayar to postpone the trial and to listen till the end. This postponement is, of course, the effect of narration. Faris illustrates how by postponing death night after night through telling stories to the king, Shahrazade simulates the postponement of human death through the prolongation of fictional life (816). After Shahrazade finishes the narration of the tales, Shahrayar (unlike Ruby men) abandons his myth about the inherent evil in women and decides to spare Shahrazade (*Alf Laylah* 3: 318). In this way, Shahrazade's narration saves her life, liberates the community, and redeems Shahrayar from his myth. Thus, the framed world of tales has had its effect.

In both narratives, narration breeds renewal and rebirth. In *Alf Laylah Wa Laylah,* the framing story's open-endedness reflects a renewal and rebirth theme. Shahrazade's narration breeds life: "During the time Shahrazade narrated her tales, she had delivered three sons for the King" (*Alf Laylah* 3: 318). The birth of these children stands in opposition to Shahrayar's myth, which has closed his line before. So Shahrayar's history breeds closure and death, while Shahrazade's narrative breeds life and renewal. It is interesting to note that the birth of Shahrazade's children parallels the "progressive structure" (Faris 71) of *Alf Laylah Wa Laylah* because, in each case, from one story is born another. As in *Alf Laylah Wa Laylah,* narration breeds rebirth and renewal in *Paradise.* The theme of defeating death and creating life is apparent in the number of the narratives, including the framing story: "Ruby," "Mavis," "Grace," "Seneca," "Divine," "Patricia," "Consolata," "Lone," and "Save-Marie." The number nine signifies birth and life (the number of months the fetus remains in the mother's womb). Pallas's baby, Divine, also symbolizes birth in the framed world of change (the Convent). This birth contrasts with Ruby's closure generated by its myth of exclusion—the death of the Fleetwoods' baby girl, Save-Marie. As in *Alf Laylah Wa Laylah,* the progressive structure of the novel reflects birth.

In this way, both narratives are open-ended and favor communal narration. Both the framing and framed stories in *Alf Laylah Wa Laylah* are open-ended and unfinished, though the inserted tales come to an end. The open-endedness of the framed stories lies in the possibility of retelling them. Numerous examples of retelling these stories appear when the internal listeners in the inserted tales decide to write these tales and add them to the historical records. Also, the possibility of retelling both the framing story and the framed tales is a prominent feature of *Alf Laylah Wa Laylah*. After Shahrazade finishes narrating her tales, Shahrayar orders his chroniclers to write and to memorize both the legendary tales and his experience with Shahrazade. Writing and retelling these stories imply that new listeners and readers will hear and read them. Thus, the writers, the narrators, the listeners, and the readers will help recover these tales and defeat the haunting threat of death again and again. So writing, retelling, and reading these tales contribute to the open-ended aspect of their narration. The open-ended narration in *Paradise* involves two aspects: multiplicity of interpretation and possibility of retelling. In *Paradise,* both the framing and the framed stories are unfinished. The framing story depends on the framed stories to explain its unspecified characters (their names are not given in "Ruby") and to show whether the demise of the Convent women is the resolution. In "Unspeakable Things Unspoken," Morrison mentions that "the indeterminate ending [. . .] follows from the untrustworthy beginning" (31). The uncertain beginning and ending would complete, as Morrison accentuates, the "outlaw quality of the book" (24). In *Paradise,* the end is not clear. After the attack on the Convent, Roger Best, the undertaker, does not find any signs of murder. He "opened one door that revealed a coal bin. Behind another a small bed and a pair of shiny shoes on the dresser. No bodies. Nothing. Even the Cadillac was gone" (Morrison, *Paradise* 292). Also, the readers do not know what happened because the story of the attack has different versions of narration. Besides Lone's and Pat's versions, each member in Ruby narrates the story of the attack in a way that suits his/her family. The presence of different versions of the incident implies that it has different interpretations, so it is indeterminate.

Throughout this frame-narrative analysis of *Alf Laylah Wa Laylah* and *Paradise,* similar methods of narration and organization evolve: the participation of the readers and listeners in the narration, the favor for open-endedness, and rebirth/survival strategies. All these elements sustain the orality of these two narratives and reflect affinity in their cultural perspectives.

Works Cited

Alf Laylah Wa Laylah. 3 vols. N.p.: Dar Al-Hilal, 1958.
Bal, Mieke. *Narratology: Introduction to the Theory of Narrative.* Toronto: University of Toronto Press, 1997.
Bateson, Gregory. "A Theory of Play and Fantasy." In *Steps to an Ecology of Mind: Collected Essays in Anthropology, Psychiatry, Evolution, and Epistemology,* 177–93. Northvale, NJ: Aronson, 1987.
Faris, Wendy B. "1001 Words: Fiction against Death." *Georgia Review* 36 (1982): 811–30.
Gittes, Katharine Slater. "The Frame Narrative: History and Theory (Arabian, European)." Ph.D. dissertation, University of California, San Diego, 1983.
Grossman, Judith. "Infidelity and Fiction: the Discovery of Women's Subjectivity in *Arabian Nights.*" *Georgia Review* 34 (1980): 113–27.
Ledbetter, Mark. "An Apocalypse of Race and Gender: Body Violence and Forming Identity in Toni Morrison's *Beloved.*" In *Picturing Cultural Values in Postmodern America.* Ed. William G. Doty, 58–72. Tuscaloosa: University of Alabama Press, 1995.
Marcus, James. "This Side of Paradise." Interview with Toni Morrison. December 5, 2003. http://www.amazon.com/exec/obidos/tg/feature/-/7651/002-2462573-3719256.
Morrison, Toni. *Paradise.* New York: Knopf, 1998.
———. "Unspeakable Things Unspoken: The Afro-American Presence in American Literature." *Michigan Quarterly Review* 28 (1989): 1–34.
Mulrine, Anna. "This Side of Paradise." *U.S. News & World Report,* January 19, 1999. http://www.usnews.com/culture/articles/980119/archive 003034.htm July 1, 2004.
Murfin, Ross, and Supryia M. Ray. *The Bedford Glossary of Critical and Literary Terms.* Boston: Bedford/St. Martin's, 1998.
Nicholson, Reynold A. *A Literary History of the Arabs.* New York: Scribner's, 1907.
Page, Philip. *Dangerous Freedom: Fusion and Fragmentation in Toni Morrison's Novels.* Jackson: University Press of Mississippi, 1995.
Todorov, Tzvetan. "Narrative Men." In *The Poetics of Prose.* Trans. Richard Howard, 66–79. Ithaca, NY: Cornell University Press, 1977.
Ullrich, David. "'Organic Harps Diversity Framed': A Theory of the Frame and the Frame Narrative, Including a Taxonomy and Its Application to Nineteenth-Century British Literature (Coleridge, Conrad, Shelley, Wordsworth)." Ph.D. dissertation, University of Wisconsin, 1987.
Verdelle, A. J. "Paradise Found: A Talk with Toni Morrison about Her New Novel." *Essence* February 1998. July 1, 2004. http://www.findarticles.com/p/articles/mi_m1264/is_n10_v28/ai_20187690.
Young, Katharine. "Edgework: Frame and Boundary in the Phenomenology of Narrative Communication." *Semiotica* 41, no. 1–4 (1982): 277–315.

A Stranger on the Bus

Reginald McKnight's I Get on the Bus *as Complex Journey*

SANDRA Y. GOVAN

> I opened myself to the gentle indifference of the world.
> —*Albert Camus*
>
> Africa? A book one thumbs / Listlessly till slumber comes.
> —*Countee Cullen*

Reginald McKnight's *I Get on the Bus* (1990) is a first novel (it is also the first novel in a projected trilogy) that became a provocative cult classic when it first appeared. In terms of plot, the novel follows Evan Norris, a young African American, back to Africa. Tracing Evan's physical and psychological dissolution, McKnight takes his protagonist on a journey through an Africa tourists seldom see. Readers watch as Evan struggles with his disaffection from the Peace Corps; we see him attempt to juggle the peculiar advice of black American expatriate Africa Mamadou Ford; we are engaged onlookers as the stories and riddles of West African folklore enfold him. And, we witness a troubled doubled-consciousness as an existential fate, one that interweaves and blends together a West African literary sensibility with that of French novelist Albert Camus, and overwhelms him. Be warned. McKnight provides no happy ending.

Set in Senegal, West Africa, *I Get on the Bus* follows the fortunes of an African American Peace Corps volunteer who has gone actually "back to Africa," just as Marcus Garvey once implored all American Negroes to do, in search of his identity. *Bus* is a compelling, some say hallucinatory, tale that takes readers on a fascinating journey, although not always in the direction(s) readers might anticipate. David Bradley's comments on the book jacket—"Anybody who wants to feel what it means for an American black to confront Africa [. . .]"—might lead readers to expect that the novel's sole focus is the relationship to and connections between Africa and African Americans. And because Senegal, a former French colony, appears more mysterious, more alluring or exotic in our imaginations, as readers we might also anticipate finding in the novel some answers to the poignant multilayered inquiry Countee Cullen posed back in 1925, during the midst of the Harlem Renaissance. Note the opening stanza of Cullen's evocative poem, "Heritage":

> What is Africa to me:
> Copper sun or scarlet sea,
> Jungle star or jungle track,
> Strong bronzed men, or regal black.
> Women from whose loins I sprang
> When the birds of Eden sang?
> *One three centuries removed*
> *From the scenes his fathers loved,*
> *Spicy grove, cinnamon tree,*
> What is Africa to me?

Although we may ponder the novel's setting, the opening lines immediately arrest our attention; we are caught by the voice and the puzzling predicament of Evan Norris, McKnight's protagonist and the book's narrator. Evan's very name is ironic. In Celtic myth, his name means well born or young warrior/fighter. Yet from the moment we meet him, Evan is not fighting. Instead, he is adrift, disconnected, dislocated; he has apparently surrendered to the atmosphere about him, having lost the will to act on his own volition while in Africa yet inexplicably vowing to remain, to let "this hot sun and these strange people have their ineffable effect" on him (3). The first words Evan utters are rendered as a series of short, precise declarative sentences. McKnight employs a staccato rhythm that, through balanced evocative images, vividly conveys a sweltering, stifling, suffocating atmosphere, simultaneously revealing through an intransitive, yet cadenced, sentence structure a character beset by an inexplicable lassitude and a deepening sense of ennui.

> "The bus stops. I get on. It is crowded and hot. There is no air and the skin feels like chicken fat. No one will make way for me. It is well past midday and everyone is tired and irritable; I cannot blame them. It is

always hot here. The Senegalese sun has no mercy. It is colorless, cruel. I have been here only three months; a desert of twenty-one months stretches before me. Sometimes I get very tired. I think I am coming down with something." (3)

The rhythmic texture of McKnight's prose arouses our sense of sound as surely as a freshly baked chiffon cake with lemon glaze arouses our sense of taste. Precisely as Carolyn E. Megan suggests (in one of the very few essays about this novel), McKnight relies upon "rhythm and sound as a way into the text." Megan asserts further that McKnight actually directs our attention toward what she identifies as "the textual reality of a piece,[. . .] the rhythm, meter, and sound" (56). To her assessment I would add that in linguistic terms, this particular passage juxtaposes an energetic inviting rhythm against the absolute lethargy apparent in the speaker's voice and attitude. The passage shows no agency in its syntactic structure. In other words, it is replete with simple intransitive sentences, and transitive linking sentences, with no agents as their subjects. This syntactic structure mirrors the mindset of McKnight's narrator as consistently, throughout the text, Evan shows no active force.[1]

Given this beautifully crafted introduction to the novel's protagonist, to his malaise and what seems early on his disaffected consciousness, we might also logically anticipate that McKnight would take as his subtext an exploration of the psychological phenomenon of double-consciousness, a concept first articulated by W. E. B. Du Bois in his classic *The Souls of Black Folk* (1903). An examination of double-consciousness through analysis of Evan Norris would make a fascinating study. In a passage familiar to all who study African American literature and culture Du Bois pronounced, "[T]he Negro is a sort of seventh son, born with a veil and gifted with second-sight in this American world,—a world which yields him no true self-consciousness but only lets him see himself through the revelation of the other world. It is a peculiar sensation, this double-consciousness, this sense of always looking at one's self through the eyes of others" (8). Not only does the specter of Du Boisian doubling seemingly haunt Evan throughout *Bus* ("One ever feels his two-ness,—an American, a Negro; two souls, two thoughts, two unreconciled strivings; two warring ideals in one dark body" [8]), but in his behavior throughout the novel, in the dilemmas he faces or avoids, in the situations with which he must cope, it is through Evan Norris that McKnight ingeniously dramatizes a highly disturbing double-consciousness. Throughout the novel, for instance, Evan repeatedly demonstrates the unwitting ability to not only *see* himself through the eyes of others, but in several instances he unaccountably finds that his consciousness has *shifted* and he has fused with another person, actually *becoming* the other. This transit of souls, so to speak, affectively illustrates Du Bois's "two souls, two thoughts, two unreconciled strivings; two warring ideals in one dark body" in a manner quite distinctive.

During these transmigratory instances, or hallucinations, Evan is simultaneously conscious of himself *as* himself and as "other." The first of these "Du Boisian moments" occurs early in the text. Following a long-distance telephone conversation with his mother, who is at home in America while he is alone in a Dakar hotel room, Evan slams down the receiver. That act initiates a shattering burst of pain. After cradling his head and closing his eyes, Evan opens them to find himself once "again on the bus. I am the driver. My hands are on the wheels. My left foot rides the clutch. My right foot is poised over the brake. I cannot see the road very well, but it is as if I know where I am. *It is a peculiar sensation*"(23). Although the passage continues ("I am half-lost, half-bemused, half-terrified, half-aghast—"), I have emphasized Evan's phrasing, "a peculiar sensation," to direct attention to the identical phrase so resonant in *Souls*.

During another moment of super-heightened consciousness Evan makes a more startling discovery. Once again he finds himself on the bus, this time embarking upon a more extraordinary transmigratory journey:

> I am on the bus. Not my hair, not my clothes. I have breasts. I am a woman. I am tired because I have been working all day for the rust-skinned American. *How can it be that I can be a woman and myself and not myself at the same time?* (193; emphasis in original)

This passage may elicit reflection on several levels. First, it seems to illustrate quite literally the seemingly self-evident conceptual framework that Du Bois's theory of double-consciousness provides the novel. Then, too, the passage could also be read as a metaphysical moment, a point where McKnight, through Evan's experience, offers a muted or an oblique critique of the exploitation of the African working woman, a woman who is just as exploited by her African American employer as she would have been had she been the house servant for some French colonial agency. Curiously, while McKnight recognizes Du Bois's work as "profoundly important to [his] development as a thinker and a writer," Du Bois, he posits, had no "conscious or witting effect" on his novel.[2] Perhaps, as McKnight contends, the reinscribing of Du Bois upon his text was accidental and thus neither conscious nor intentional. Wittingly or not, however, the fact of double-consciousness remains as an inescapable trope of *I Get on the Bus*.

Moreover, given the unambiguous allusion to Joseph Conrad's *Heart of Darkness*, deftly inserted amid a string of revealing declarative details operative in the novel's second paragraph ("I teach a little English here and there, but mainly I do nothing. I sit in my bungalow, get high, and pretend *I am Kurtz waiting for Marlow*. I kill flies. I read books" [emphasis added]), the astute reader might expect to find not only that the novel examines questions of personal identity but that same reader also might assume that *Bus* examines questions of racial identity (what it means to be black); what it means to be a black American "home" again; or perhaps readers might focus upon the nature of evil at the "heart of darkness," which Conrad depicted as Africa. In truth, many of these expectations are satisfied. Without question, some of the mysteries inherent in Cullen's pensive question, "What is Africa to me?" are plumbed as McKnight's novel takes us deep into the village life and folk culture of Senegal. He clearly enjoyed creating the folkloristic aspects of his novel—its stories of powerful magical marabous, of mysterious jinni and demm.[3] McKnight also clearly revels in the dialect and idiolect created for his characters, their particular speech patterns, cultural idiosyncrasies, and community habits.

Evan gets his opportunity to experience village life as a result of his falling ill near the village of N'Gor. Actually, he has been ill for quite some time, but has obstinately avoided medical treatment for his malaria, relying solely upon cigarettes or marijuana. Evan claims to find something "enriching" and "intriguing" about his acute pain; he is "fascinated" by it. In his own perverse way Evan could be said to relish his intense pain because, as he recognizes, "It is doing something to me. I am not prepared to say that it is making me stronger . . . [but] I do not doubt this illness is leading me some place literal, real." He cannot imagine his "journey occurring in any other way" (27). In fact, Evan's illness, his pain and resulting discomfort serve as catalysts to initiate his personal odyssey into village life and into himself. The journey commences shortly after a bout with particularly acute pain, an episode which occurs soon after Evan has had a confrontation with his Peace Corps supervisor. He recalls a similarly wrenching moment generated by a remembered conversation he once held with his parents. Evan then balances his perceptions of the Senegalese people—"beautiful, dignified, unknowable"—against the cynical diatribes of his father and the more noble values of his mother. From his middle-class father comes the belief that "people are people[,] the same everywhere you go." But while he will admit that "'some are saints, [. . .] most of 'em ain't worth a dog's goddamn. Don't ever forget that you are in this world to look out for number one. Num-ro-uno. Number one. That's all you got.'" By contrast, Evan's mother has tried to teach him "to be: kind, generous, adaptable, patient." Evan acknowledges that the adverse teachings his parents provide become a "source for [his] discomfort" (27–28).

Arguably, while Evan's discomfort may stem from the conflicting parental advice repeated until all becomes codified dogma, that discomfort must be magnified by both his present physical condition and his psychological distress. The former may well be induced by his untreated malaria, with its resulting intense headaches. The latter, however, is surely exacerbated by the novel's several surrealistic moments—Evan is on the bus, he's not; he's dreaming and unconscious, he is awake but no one is aware of his presence—coupled with his own certainty that he has committed a heinous crime. Once, while in the grip of one of these dissociative moments, when he has "floated for an indeterminable length of time," believing he is being mugged, Evan kills a crippled African beggar. The man he believes he kills is a double amputee with no legs. In his mind's eye Evan sees himself repeatedly smashing the cripple's head into the ground with a cement slab that he has torn from the broken sidewalk (16). There are, however, no apparent witnesses to this alleged murder except a dog. And as savage as the crime would seem to be, no such crime report is ever made to the police, the press, or the public. The reader probing for deeper meaning or symbolic intent might pause at this juncture to speculate about the viciousness of the scene McKnight has sketched. It is possible to read Evan's discomfort, his guilt for ostensibly killing the beggar, a man who cannot stand independently upon his own legs, as both metaphor for and symbol of Evan's mental health. We must ask whether the violence of his supposed act suggests an unarticulated internalized psychological trauma, perhaps a mirroring signifying Evan's inability to stand independently and face his life. Perhaps this alleged violent murder is his visceral reaction to that inability.

It is in this condition that Evan is rescued, or so we are led to believe, and brought to N'Gor village. Under the ministrations of Aminata Gueye and her father, the local marabou, he regains some sense of himself. Monsieur Gueye watches him and prepares healing teas for him to drink; Aminata shares a wealth of African folklore with him while he recuperates. Yet Evan fears Aminata's father because the penetrating glare from the marabou's single eye discomforts him, leaving Evan with a "crushing airless feeling," and because the old man's glance pushes him inward, making him "sense something" about himself. He values Aminata for her comforting teasing presence, her easy way of taking him far deeper inside a culture he has only seen as an observer (45). To borrow once again from Du Bois, McKnight seems to cast Aminata almost as a spirit guide, the figure who takes Evan behind the Veil so that he is permitted to see the true souls of black Africa, a soul few visitors are permitted to see. Though Aminata may deride Evan for being a spoiled "américain noir," she nonetheless tells him "stories, beautiful, funny, strange, sad or any combination of the four." Although he knows the stories are children's tales, he finds he must "listen to them as if they were as vital to me as air." Aminata's tale of Aida and the two suitors who must vie for her hand by training a hare to kill a lion really intrigues him. When at a climatic moment Aida's father exclaims, "'Ayy! Ayy! He has done it! Wyyy!'" Aminata turns to Evan to say, "'Oh, it was something American man. There was this hare, pulling the dead lion on the ground.'" The sound of her voice lulls him, makes his head hum—"her voice was a pillow, soft and deep," yet as Evan says, "'her story was kola nut, keeping me alert'" (46).

Without question, McKnight probes the vortex of complex identity issues engulfing Evan Norris. Without question, by locating this intriguing protagonist where he is physically and psychologically, that is to say, by situating him as a paradoxical character, a curiously listless young man with no discernable roots—no ties to family, friends, or faith; lonely, alienated; no firm cultural or intellectual mooring in anything and so he "believe[s] in everything" yet understands very little, McKnight not only tackles questions of identity but also explores questions of belief, of culture, of community, of self, and of romantic relationships, as well as questions of evil (286).

In this multitiered reading, Evan Norris seems to be one of the earliest literary "cultural mulattos," a term used by both Trey Ellis and McKnight to signify a hybrid African American character. While not necessarily biracial or of "mixed-blood"—half white or half Negro—by virtue of his experiences in the world this character becomes essentially deracinated, losing his "blackness," his distinct connection to African American cultural norms through the overpowering influence of "a variety of sub-cultural streams."[4] Cast as the cultural mulatto figure, Evan Norris becomes one of the key hooks that secures *I Get on the Bus* to an Afrocentric perspective, to the African American literary canon. In a subversive, indeed, almost transgressive manner, through both word and deed McKnight's perverse hero recalls several iconic characters from the pages of canonical texts. He is, like James Weldon Johnson's narrator in *Autobiography of an Ex-Colored Man* (1912) and Ralph Ellison's protagonist in *Invisible Man* (1952), oftentimes a passive young man whom readers want to shake, to "knock some sense into," as the old folks say, precisely because of his perverse passivity. Just as Johnson and Ellison present us with articulate first-person narrators who are educated and intelligent yet simultaneously incredibly naive and easily manipulated, so, too, does McKnight present readers with a similarly articulate and intelligent yet ambivalent, alienated, and unwary hero. Furthermore, just as their respective narrators are pushed by circumstances into the journey or quest in the search for self, the quest for a viable identity, so, too, is McKnight's protagonist pushed into his quest.

Arguably, however, two key differences separate the canonical texts from McKnight's brash and unanticipated addition to the canon. First, both Johnson and Ellison employ *nameless* narrators to signal the identity crisis at the center of each novel. Second, as noted above, the young male protagonists Johnson and Ellison employ are forced by external pressures to embark upon their quest for self-determination. The death of a mother in Johnson's novel radically alters his narrator's course, while being dismissed from his insular college community dramatically alters the fate of Ellison's naive narrator. Both protagonists are forced to leave safe havens; they must each then negotiate the complexities of a suddenly much larger world—a world that is black and white and culturally mysterious.[5] By contrast, Evan should be much more capable of negotiating the broader world. He completes his university training and shortly thereafter joins the navy. His separation from his parents is voluntary. Unlike either Johnson's or Ellison's protagonist, Evan even has a black woman, a professional woman, as his girlfriend. (The fact that she is also his psychologist is problematic—a relationship I will address later.) Yet despite a seemingly strong grounding in familial and social relationships, including a loosely knit friendship network of largely white hippie types, Evan remains the ungrounded decentered character. His quest for self begins with retreat. He does not turn to a mythical North-as-haven but instead runs all the way to Africa. Once there, he apparently loses more of himself, becoming submersed in an unanchored identity, rather than being able to rise into a more viable one.

Given these solid linkages to the African American canon, what readers may not anticipate is a contemporary African American novel wherein a French writer figures prominently. Yet Albert Camus's post–World War II existentialist classic, *The Stranger* (1944), functions almost as a mimetic structural organizer, the Eurocentric subtext for this ostensibly Afrocentric text. Thus, although McKnight does indeed subtly signify upon several major touchstones from the African American literary canon, his first novel is something of, to borrow terminology from contemporary music, an African American "cover." That is, *I Get on the Bus* is almost a virtual rewriting, under the guise of blackness, of *The Stranger*. McKnight readily concedes the relationship, acknowledging that "the book's chief influence had been Camus's *The Stranger*."[6] Because such clear correspondences exist between the two texts, I would posit that in large part what we find in McKnight's first novel is a deliberate, elaborate, yet nuanced literary pun. In contemporary critical parlance, *Bus* smacks of intertextual signification.

As noted previously, even a cursory reading of *Bus* reveals Evan Norris as a strange, amoral character whose actions are frequently inexplicable. He is a Peace Corp teacher who does little teaching ("'[M]ainly I do nothing. I may not do my job—nobody cares or notices what you do here anyway'" [3]). He is a man who refuses to see a doctor for recurrent pain and rejects the necessary precautions to prevent malaria, thus inviting often excruciating suffering. Early in the novel Evan tells us, "[S]o far I have refused to take my quinine tablets. They think I am nuts. But really, I am not." He believes his pain is "enriching"; he believes it is "very, very intriguing." He knows it is "doing something" to him. And yet he refuses to take his medicine "until [he] find[s] out precisely what it is" (15). Self-absorbed and solipsistic, Evan Norris is a disaffected "stranger" to Africa, to himself and to his family, to all who care about him, continually boarding, riding, and getting on, or off, the bus. His journey to the end of his road is as complex, as complicated, as that of Camus's mysterious protagonist, the unfathomable Meursault.

Scholars examining *The Stranger* frequently have been puzzled about how to receive Camus's novel. Victor Brombert asks, "Is it a novel of ideas, does it contain a thesis, and what has the author set out to prove? Should it be judged a psychological study of a pathological case [. . .]? Is it a 'philosophical' novel, and if so, does Camus propose any solutions?" (119). In his "Camus's *The Stranger*," Arthur Scherr notes widely diverging critical responses to the novel and its protagonist. "Many readers and critics conclude that its protagonist is either a fool, a madman, or a callous boor." Some assert that Meursault is a character with "diminished [. . .] self-esteem and thwarted ambition"; others argue that he "permits others to define his reactions and to create a social identity for him." Scherr quotes René Girard, who "labels Meursault an irrational, unintelligent child" suffering from an "egotistical martyrdom" and an "ultra-romantic conception of the self." He further notes that Wyndham Lewis, among several others, perceives Camus's protagonist as "a symbol of the alienation pervading a modern, urbanized society devoid of religious faith" (Scherr 151). Actually, several of the questions critics ask about *The Stranger* could as well be asked of *Bus*—to wit, is the novel "a psychological study of a pathological case?" Does McKnight "propose any solutions" to the dilemmas created for Evan Norris? If Evan merely permits others to define his reality, the larger question becomes why? What motivates him? Why does he refuse to respond in a "constructive" or "meaningful" way to the chaos surrounding him? What is the source of his sense of futility, of his resignation? Why is he so seemingly content on the margins of society and what, if anything, does his acquiescence apparently signify? This kind of interrogation provides us food for thought. A closer look at the relationship between the two protagonists, one African American, the other European, both living in Africa, may provide some answers.

Jean-Paul Sartre evidently read *The Stranger*, a novel set in Algeria, as Camus's method of giving readers the "feeling" of the absurd rather than the "notion" of it. Brombert quotes from Sartre, who, in defining the idea, argues, "The absurd is a condition as well as the lucid consciousness some people have of the condition." He continues, "[N]either man nor the universe, if taken separately, is absurd; but since it is the essential nature of man to exist-in-the-world, the absurd becomes one and the same with the human condition." Brombert then extrapolates from Sartre's comments that "man realizes the futility of all his efforts," and further that "man is not only a stranger facing the world but also a stranger in relation to himself. Sometimes the stranger sees himself in a mirror but does not recognize his own features. Such a realization of the absurdity of man's fate inevitably leads to rebellion. If God does not exist, if nothing makes sense, then everything is permitted" (120). For a preface to a later English edition of his novel Camus wrote, "[T]he hero of the book is condemned because he doesn't play the game. In this sense he is a stranger to the society in which he lives; he drifts in the margin, in the suburb of private, solitary, sensual life." Camus further stipulates this additional characteristic of his hero: "He refuses to lie. Lying is not only saying what is not true. It is also and especially saying more than is true, and as far as the human heart is concerned, saying more than one feels" (C. O'Brien 19).

I share these observations and assessments about *The Stranger* in support of my contention that despite his whiteness, Camus's Meursault is the ancestral doppelganger for McKnight's Evan. There are fundamental similarities between the moral attitudes and philosophical stances of these two characters. Just as Meursault lives removed and thus is a figurative stranger to the culture he lives within, so too is Evan Norris. He has drifted to the margins of society in America; in Africa his status remains that of outsider. The illness he will not treat further guarantees that he exist on the margins, in a very "private, solitary," and strangely "sensual life" with either Wanda, his American girlfriend, or his African love interest, the marabou's daughter, Aminata.

Clearly, multiple parallels link these two novels. But the first and most obvious parallel to catch both eye and ear is Camus's introduction to Meursault, an introduction that in its brevity and emotional spareness seems to present to us a dispassionate and utterly indifferent individual. The novel begins:

> "Maman died today. Or yesterday maybe, I don't know. I got a telegram from the home: "Mother deceased. Funeral tomorrow. Faithfully yours." That doesn't mean anything. Maybe it was yesterday." (3)

While the rhythm of Camus's prose may be affected by the American translation, the precision of his syntactic strategy remains. Linking McKnight's prose to Camus's passage is the crispness. Again we see the simple intransitive sentences, the shocking "punch" of the diction, juxtaposed against the detached tone and the declarative abruptness that suggests an apparent lassitude in Meursault, just as McKnight's introduction to Evan subtly indicates his passivity. However, unlike the scant critical attention directed toward McKnight's rhetorical style in presenting Evan Norris, Meursault's terse response to the news of his mother's death has over time generated a fairly rancorous debate among critics. Some speculate that Meursault's language suggests that the death of his mother means nothing to him. Others, like Colin Wilson, argue that he is a "brainless idiot" (Scherr 150) for making such a comment. Some see him as a "dim, rather unsatisfactory" (Thrody, *Macmillan Modern Novelist* 19) protagonist; still others link him to the moronic. In his study for the Modern Novelists series, Philip Thrody quotes from an astute 1962 study of *The Stranger* which describes Meursault as a "forlorn, dispirited, *isolato* who seeks with his own indifference to match the indifference of the world" (Thrody, *Macmillan Modern Novelist* 19).

Certainly these characters are similar; they both suffer from indifference, ennui, and detachment. Each man stands on the periphery of the dominant social realm swirling about him, yet neither fits well into his immediate environment. Both, for instance, have supervisors who accuse them of lacking ambition. Meursault's boss discusses with him the opening of a new Paris office; he then suggests that Meursault might want to accept the new position because it offers something different; it offers Paris as inducement for a new life, a departure from life in Algiers. Paris would mean change. Meursault's reply, "'people never change their lives [. . .] in any case, one life is as good as another,'" startles the supervisor; who then accuses Meursault of having "no ambition" (Camus 41). Similarly, following a confrontation with his boss over the classroom techniques of a fellow teacher whom Evan insists is "cruel" and mean to her African students, Evan's boss tells him that he lacks the experience to judge the teacher in question and that in any event, Evan is "not the most ambitious guy" he has ever met (McKnight, *Bus* 32).[7]

Neither protagonist has the comfort of a close-knit family—presumably Meursault's father is dead; his mother has just died, as we learn in the infamous opening sentence. Camus gives us no information about any siblings. By contrast, we gradually learn that Evan is estranged from his family and quite removed from them, as he resides in Africa and his family lives in America. During the telephone call that afterward initiates one of his surrealistic transmigratory moments, Evan's mother conversationally admits that his father is "disappointed" in his brother for having dropped out of college again. Evan's response to her, "He is always disappointed," reveals an underlying tension between the father and his sons. Evan adds that given their respective ages as young men (his brother is twenty-four and he is twenty-nine), their father's repeated disappointment with his sons' decisions, whether to go to school or to enlist in the Peace Corps, is not their problem but his. When his mother protests that their father is motivated by love—"'Daddy loves you both, darlin'. He just—,'" Evan cuts her off, shouting back, "'Funny how you've always said that, Mom. I've never heard him say it myself'" (19).[8]

While both men have girlfriends or significant relationships with women in their lives, these relationships are ambiguous or, at best, problematical. Meursault establishes a sexual relationship with Marie Cardona, a young woman who used to work as a secretary in the same office. Although he has always felt attracted to Marie, he has not acted on any desire until he meets Marie on the beach, the day following his mother's funeral. On that day, he casually initiates sexual contact with her as they play in the water; that evening they go to a movie. He kisses her once and then, as he says, "'She came back to my place'" (20). His desire for Marie intensifies; much of their sensual foreplay involves the beach, swimming, then returning to his apartment and jumping into bed together. Marie can arouse Meursault with her laughter. He appreciates her style, her beauty, and her sexual initiative; but the moment she asks the crucial question—whether or not he loves her—he says without hesitation, "'I told her it didn't mean anything but that I didn't think so.'" To assuage Marie's pain at learning this unexpected revelation (she "looked sad"), he kisses her again as they prepare lunch (35). It is this dislocation from the social norm, this unseemly failure to articulate supposedly normal feelings (grief or love) in a normal manner or to attach any "meaning" to intimacy, that makes Meursault appear dimwitted or moronic to some, and a detached, dispirited isolato to others. While Meursault's connection to Marie is both mutual and sensual, barring his inability to perceive any deeper meaning to their relationship and his callous failure to question or to think about what their relationship signifies to her (whether love "means anything"), the sexual partnership he has formed with Marie apparently satisfies them both. Though he later concedes that he "probably didn't love her," Marie nonetheless asks Meursault if he wants to marry her. When he is again noncommittal but obliging—apparently neither love nor marriage carries any value for him, but they can get married if she wants to—after mumbling to herself that he is "peculiar," for no apparent reason beyond sexual gratification Marie still decides she wants to marry Meursault (41–42). Despite being kept at a distance, despite the absence of any concrete signal of emotional connection from Meursault, Marie *chooses* to accept him, peculiarities and all, while Meursault is simply willing to accede. Subsequently, she stands by her man through his arrest, trial, and imprisonment for murder. Later, the courts deny her visiting privileges because of her lack of marital status.

Granted that Meursault's relationship with Marie is curious and somewhat disturbing, Evan Norris's relationship with women involves an even more complicated and complex set of gender dynamics because Evan is intimately involved with two distinctly different women—one African American, the other African. His relationship with Wanda, his American girlfriend and the woman his mother expects him to marry, is dubious from the start. Although his mother thinks Wanda is "perfect" for him, Evan admits to himself early on that Wanda's willingness to accept him (as Marie accepts Meursault) is unfathomable to him. Therefore, unlike Meursault, he will not simply acquiesce to her wishes (or to his mother's): "I cannot marry a woman who loves me for no reason I can perceive, who forgives and forgives and forgives" (28). However, rather than clearly communicate the one decision he makes, Evan enlists in the Peace Corps and leaves.[9] His cowardly departure reflects his passivity, his disengagement, and yet an ambivalence as well: "'I left not knowing, not particularly caring, what happens between Wanda and me.

This bothers me because I love her'" (29). Evan's admission of ambivalence shows some modicum of reflection, some questioning of internal stresses, that we do not see in Meursault.

Wanda is an interesting character. She is far more vocal, far more a presence in *Bus* than Marie is in *The Stranger*. A licensed psychologist, Wanda nonetheless breaks a cardinal rule of her profession by maintaining an intimate relationship with Evan, her client. She not only sleeps with him, she continues to counsel and assess him. Evan believes that he must serve as some kind of talisman for Wanda ("'I am her Galatea'") who is honest and "does not lie." He concedes that she is his "moral touchstone," and thus good for him; he admits that she sees "potential" in him as a future mate; and yet, though she is ostensibly wiser and a mature, seasoned woman, Evan does not see the merit she sees in him, why he would be worth her time and energy. Repeatedly he professes that he "cannot marry a woman who loves [him] for no good reason that [he] can perceive," and, in that same vein, announces, "'I cannot see why she loves me'" and that he "'come[s] away [from her] seeing the streaks of my unworthiness'" (28–29). Having placed Wanda upon a pedestal, Evan concludes his assessment of their relationship by convincing himself that because Wanda is a "finished, complete [person] with or without [him]," he is useless to her; she, therefore, does not need him in her life as he is merely her someone she can smooth and perfect through "lovemaking and conversation." Yet moments later, Evan finally concedes that his unilateral severing of their relationship is selfishly driven, based upon his "need for something of [his] own." His interior observations become broader based, moving from romantic entanglement to a more abstract existential analysis that posits, "Life is not as she and my mother would have it. It is not a gift. Life is hard. It is stupid. One must earn it" (29). The observations Evan makes about his lover, his mother, and life are telling because they illustrate how McKnight has expanded the development of this African American Meursault. In such moments, though his comments may serve solely to point up his growing sense of futility, Evan still appears to be more self-reflexive, more expansively self-expressive than Camus's existentialist character.

In Camus's tale we see a character whose narrative reveals far more of his actions than his thoughts. Consider the evening following the funeral of his mother when Meursault takes Marie to see a comedy. He reports: "'The movie was funny in parts, but otherwise it was just stupid. She had her leg pressed against mine. I was fondling her breasts. Toward the end of the show, I gave her a kiss, but not a good one. She came back to my place'" (*The Stranger* 20). By contrast, when Evan reflects upon his relationship with Wanda, he begins with a striking summation ("She is older, smarter, more human"), followed immediately by a deeper assessment of the mutuality in their relationship, seeming more aware of her as a person and showing far more perceptive ability than Meursault evinces.

> "Not only do her big eyes look into the very core of my eyes, but unabashedly reveal the inner workings of her own character. But I cannot see why she loves me. It is like watching some subtle mechanism tick and shift behind smoked glass. My mother is right. Wanda does not lie. She is good for me, my spiritual, physical, and moral touchstone." (29)

At best, Evan's relationship with Wanda is guilt-ridden and doomed from the start—by their seventh counseling session they are intimate, thereby in violation of professional ethics. But they are exceedingly mismatched. From afar Evan can concede their differences, and analyze the distinctive habits that will always, despite a professed love, keep them apart: "'I am a perpetual student, a perpetual wanderer, an habitual quitter. She is terminally middle-class, hopelessly careful and controlled, professional. A professional human being'" (95). But as irresponsible as his affair with Wanda becomes, Evan's relationship with Aminata is far more complex, even dangerous, for she is not some working-class secretary or any ordinary African woman, but the marabou's daughter. Yet when the two are together, Evan is beset by conflicting impulses. He recognizes her purity: "'[S]he has not been debauched,'" and "'She is a good Muslima. She is a good daughter, a good human being.'" He understands that given his status as both guest and stranger in her father's house, sexual intimacy should be the furthermost thing from his mind. Yet Evan is so attracted to Aminata that the two are engulfed by a sexual tension suffusing what I think is one of the most surrealistic (and explicit) moments in literature, a moment that is truly illustrative of a doubled consciousness, of *being both self and other.*

The scene begins with two people at the kissing/touching stage of amorousness. Then, just as sexual arousal reaches that peak of excitement where penetration occurs, Evan's perceptions radically alter; the two lovers seemingly merge identities and then *exchange* selves.

> "As I mount her and we begin to move, I press my lips to hers but do not feel flesh, neither hers nor my own. It feels as though my mouth has fallen asleep. My lips, then the back of my neck, then my fingertips buzz with a deep electrical pulse. I try to lift my mouth from hers in

order to whisper something obscene or sweet into her ear, but I cannot raise my head. It is as if another body lies upon mine. I am pressed between succubus and flesh, can move nothing but my hips though it becomes more difficult with each motion. My penis is impossibly large. I feel it in her stomach, into her rib cage. It widens and spreads, filling her body cavity, till I can no longer move [. . .] I feel my heartbeat through my penis, it grows stronger until I can almost hear it. It beats heavily, as though pushing oceans of blood. The electrical pulse grows stronger. My body fizzes like acid on unfeeling skin. *I feel the penis moving again, moving in me. It feels unconnected.*[. . .] *I buck my hips twice. I feel the penis slide from my chest to my stomach. I try to lift myself again, but cannot move backward at all. I feel the earth pressing my back and the penis slide from my stomach to the outside of my vagina. This hurts a little, something I had not expected. It plunges back into me and Evan moves slowly.*[. . .] *I look at Evan, and he looks afraid, wild and afraid. This is also something I had not expected.*" (132–33; emphasis added)

This arresting scene deftly captures the reader's attention for it not only represents the throes of sexual climax, it also gives readers a rather unique voyeuristic perspective, permitting us to feel and to witness, simultaneously, both the male and the female position, if you will, of this sexual encounter. But while Evan is apparently conscious of and frightened by their apparently corporal as well as metaphysical exchange, Aminata is not. She shares neither his confusion nor his apprehension. To his rapid-fire questions, "'What are you, woman? What is this? Did you feel, did you see, do you know?'" she can only respond that with respect to sexual intimacy, he is her teacher in this aspect of her life just as he is when teaching her English (134–35).

Aminata's grasp of English is superior to Evan's grasp of the intricacies of village life in N'Gor. All manner of things have happened to him while he has lived in the village, many of them of supernatural origin and thus inexplicable by Western logic. Evan has found dead lizards scattered about his room or tucked into his belongings; bound chickens have appeared in his room; his excruciating headaches narrow to the point where he feels as if an ice-pick is drilling into his skull causing him to leak air, sounding to himself as if he is emitting a high-pitched squeal as he moves (68). Even his nightly dreams are more like nightmares involving swirling images—vortices and hurricanes. Caught up in and spun around by the array of mysterious forces he finds himself facing, Evan turns to Aminata for answers. She explains: "'Someone, I don't know who or why, has sent a jinn on you. Jenni are dangerous.

They are called up from hell with the parts of dead people, blood, herbs. There are many kinds, but the kind that follows you means to kill you or drive you crazy'" (121–22). This revelation, coupled to the story Aminata tells about a Frenchman afflicted with a jinn whom her father tried to cure and was later forced to kill, unsettles Evan even further. Having gone to Africa in search of himself, he confronts a world that destabilizes him further, a world where a woman tells him quite earnestly that in order for him to fight the jinn affecting him, he must do most of the work in tracking it down to its source (the person who set it on him) and make that individual stop. If he cannot, he must kill. This is the truth he must assimilate and the expectation he must meet if he is to survive Senegal.

Camus's *The Stranger* and McKnight's *I Get on the Bus* are like two bowls of steaming hot cereal. The key difference is that one is basic grits while the other is a thick, rich oatmeal with raisins and bananas cooked into it—both are good but one has much more fiber. Camus's Meursault never tries to understand the native Algerians. Though he lives in Algiers and is definitely affected by the Algerian climate, the physical environment, he remains a displaced Frenchman who barely even notices the Arab inhabitants—until he kills one. By contrast, Evan tries as hard as he is able to comprehend the different aspects of Senegalese life that he sees; but, just as Meursault remains aloof and unfathomable to those around him, so Evan remains the alienated outsider, unable to penetrate the mysteries of the country. What the two protagonists also share are similar responses to certain physical stimuli and a roughly similar fate. Additionally, their lives in Africa are framed by familiar symbols used in roughly equivalent ways.

In both novels, the protagonists suffer from intense, blinding headaches and the intense effects of heat and the sun. In the space of three pages *The Stranger* presents a series of images showing the stifling atmosphere that dooms Meursault. While standing at the foot of a staircase leading to the beach house of an acquaintance, his head is "ringing from the sun," making him unable to climb the stairs. Because "the heat [is] so intense . . . [a] blinding stream falling from the sky," he decides to walk the beach rather than climb the stairs. As he walks, he feels his "forehead swelling under the sun . . . [and] the heat pressing down." All he wants to do is escape the sun, find a cool place and rest by the water. Unfortunately, the cool spring he walks toward is already occupied by the Arab man with whom he has been involved in a previous altercation. Meursault recognizes that he could avoid any further dispute by simply turning around and returning to the beach house, but the effects of the sun aggravate his physical and emotional state. He does not alter his course. Now he feels "the whole beach, throbbing in the sun" pressing down on him. To aggravate him further, the Arab apparently sits in the shadows with his hand on the knife in his pocket.[10] To Meursault, peering from sunlight into shadow, the Arab is laughing at him. Moreover, the sun is now burning his face and his cheeks, and making sweat accumulate over his eyes. Finally, to bring matters to a head, it is the sun that forces Meursault to leap to a seemingly implausible connection: "'The sun was the same as it had been the day I'd buried Maman, and like then, my forehead was especially hurting me, all the veins throbbing under the skin. It was this burning, which I couldn't stand anymore, that made me move forward'" (57–59). When he continues toward the Arab, the sweat drops into his eyes and blinds him; through the dazzling light of sun on sweat, salt, and tears, he thinks he sees the Arab flash his knife and, in what seems initially self-defense, he shoots him. The first shot probably kills; he then shakes off the effects of "sweat and sun" and fires four more times "into the motionless body" (59).

The murder of the Arab generates heated critical debate. Some critics see Meursault's actions as those of "an irrational, unintelligent child,[. . .] who kills a man because he wants attention from society" (Scherr 150). Others have seen his action as moronic or psychologically warped. But regardless of his logic, or lack thereof, at the time of the crime, Meursault does actually kill a man. He is then arrested, tried, convicted (and subsequently executed) for two reasons that have little to do with the murder. First, he seems largely to have been convicted for evincing an inappropriate emotional response to the death of his mother. His court-appointed lawyer tells him that his case "is a tricky one" because investigators had learned of his mother's death and that he "had 'shown insensitivity' the day of Maman's funeral." The lawyer believes this "embarrassing" lack of feeling provides "a strong argument for the prosecution." He then explicitly asks whether Meursault "felt any sadness that day" but the question appears both tactless and invasive. "'I would have been very embarrassed if I'd had to ask it,'" Meursault tells us. Finally he proffers an answer, but it is clearly not what the attorney wants to hear. Using the almost same wording he used when speaking to Marie, he says, "'I probably did love Maman, but that didn't mean anything . . . . [A]ll normal people have wished their loved ones were dead.'" His lawyer becomes disturbed and makes him promise not to reveal such sentiments in court. Meursault then tries to explain himself more clearly. Listless and tired the day his mother was buried; he was not particularly aware of his surroundings. "What I can say for certain," he tells the lawyer, "is that I would rather Maman hadn't died." This unvarnished declaration, lacking in what is supposed to be "natural feelings," does not pacify his lawyer who abruptly announces, "That's enough." And even though it is Meursault who points out that this line of questioning had nothing to do with his case, the lawyer still appears angry and seems to find him distasteful or "slightly disgusting" (64–65).

The second reason Meursault commits his crime is pure existentialism. At the moment he kills, his universe is a purposeless, hostile environment. In those circumstances, he does what McKnight's Evan Norris announces he will do; that is, he has "let [that] hot sun and [those] strange people (the Arabs) have their ineffable effect" on him. (McKnight, *Bus* 3). In other words, the stifling heat and the piercing, blinding sun have affected his capacity to think or act rationally. A year after his arrest, a year spent in jail, he is tried and forced to come to grips with the absurdity of being judged guilty, not for killing a man but essentially for failure to cry at his mother's funeral; for his failure to accept a state sanctioned God; for his solipsism, his lonely but keen awareness of life's futility, his conviction that nothing in life matters (Camus 121). Following a confrontation with the priest who comes to offer him some Christian comfort before his execution, Meursault finds that his rage has cleansed him and "rid [him] of hope. . . . " Ironically, it is the absence of hope that allows him to feel "happy again." In one of his final observations, Meursault tells us, "I opened myself to the gentle indifference of the world" (122).

While Meursault's execution is sanctioned by state and law (though he is convicted for the wrong reasons, he does kill a man), Evan Norris's death is a more complicated, more private execution, if indeed it is an execution and not a suicide—there is sufficient ambiguity to call the question. Evan not only faces an indifferent world, one which is more overtly hostile toward him, he yields up his life for a crime he never committed; he gives it up because of his continuing passivity, his continued inability to learn or to struggle, his gullibility. He never comprehends the veiled mysterious and dangerous cultural forces playing upon his gullibility in Senegal, and he dies because of a divided self-consciousness that has kept him forever on the fringes, living the life of the outsider with no true understanding of the complexities and depths around him.

McKnight makes a brief but telling allusion to French philosopher Michel Foucault that may shed some light on Evan's indirection.[11] In a land where belief in jinni and demm and tere[12] (another element of the occult in Senegal) are real, where one person is able to consume the soul and merge with the essence of another before devouring him, Evan is unable to navigate between realities, unable to discern what is truth, and unable to uncover where the power lies or who wields it. Because he has no will to power for himself, and he does not recognize the relationship between power and knowledge, he is continually manipulated by those around him, from the black American expatriate Africa Mamadou Ford (formerly *Alvin* Ford, who tries to mentor him), to Aminata, to virtually everyone connected to her or to her family.

Lamont, the man Aminata's father has arranged for her to marry, tries to convince Evan that Ford is evil, that he has been possessed by a jinn, and that Evan should kill him. When Evan protests that he is "not going to kill Ford," despite Lamont's attempted blackmail and his implication that he will go to the Senegalese police and swear that he witnessed Evan killing the beggar, Lamont makes it clear that Evan has no options (216). He insists that Evan not only has a jinn but that he has become a demm, a soul eater, and therefore he will do as Lamont directs him.

> "Evan, listen to me, boy. Ford is breakfast. Ford is lunch. Ford is dinner. Eat and he dies, boy. Eat and you live. It's simple. You've got to learn how or it'll kill you. If you don't eat the soul, well, you'll starve to death." (218)

Because throughout the novel Evan has remained rootless, without grounding, beset by doubt, angered by questions without answers, suffering from his fears and insecurities, disturbed by his own flickering sense of "blackness" (165)—because he is a man who believes in everything from his parents' teachings to the Protestant work ethic to the Wizard of Oz, Evan believes that he has eaten Ford. "'For there is no doubt—I am digesting Ford. I do not feel bones shift or hair curl out or pull in as happens in [. . .] horror films, but it is between seeing and not seeing, between remembering and not remembering, between hunger and no hunger that he unfolds, unravels before me. It is exquisite'" (282–83). His problem becomes that he has taken in so much that he is full. He cannot digest another word, another lesson, another story, another lie. By the time Lamont suggests that Evan is not really poisoned, that he has merely been taught "another lesson" and thus is not actually about to die for having consumed and merged with Ford, Evan no longer believes in anything anyone says. His absence of faith or hope in some respects mirrors Meursault's; in other ways it differs, for he affirms nothing.

I Get on the Bus concludes with a troubling ending for some. Senegal, ultimately, has not been kind to Evan—he has fooled himself and has been duped and betrayed by virtually everyone he has met. No one comes to rescue him, nor can he save himself. Just as he predicted, his one act of agency has been to permit the hot Senegalese sun and the Senegalese "people to have their ineffable effect" on him. Unfamiliar with and unable to fathom the customs of the place, he has remained a stranger, a man who, whenever assailed by fears and doubts, gets back on the bus. Urged by Lamont, who is standing above an immobilized Evan holding a machete, to get up, to fight a little, to struggle for his life, an Evan now *merged with* Ford makes no effort. He simply lies there. Apparently he sees the lights of an oncoming bus reflecting off of Lamont's features. A voice (Evan's? or Ford's?) then emerges from the supine body to make this penultimate comment, "'Sometimes, you know, sometimes I really hate being black'" (296). At that point Lamont, we are told, "grunts once"—whether in agreement with the statement or because he has brought his blade down, we don't know. But the last sound Evan hears evidently becomes his ticket to ride for following that solitary grunt, he makes the closing statement of this richly layered and elegant text: "'[A]nd I am on the bus, and I am on the bus for good'" (296).

From the rhythms used to capture readers; to the skillful prose that takes us into the heart of Senegalese village life (with its adherence to mysterious animistic belief systems) and Francophone Africa; to its energy in recasting a lost African American as a convincing existential character, adapting the model of Albert Camus's Meursault (rather than that of Richard Wright's murderous Cross Damon of *The Outsider* [1953]), Reginald McKnight's *I Get on the Bus* makes for a spellbinding, emotionally engaging, and intellectually stimulating literary project. With this first novel, McKnight has both changed and charged the canon while simultaneously enriching it. As readers follow a hapless Evan Norris, a man condemned because he will not play the expected game, from America to West Africa in his fruitless search for meaning, we can indeed see that he is a stranger on the bus.

Notes

1. For a better understanding of how a linguist would treat the elements presented in the passage I am indebted to my colleague, Dr. Ronald Lunsford of the UNC–Charlotte English Department, who graciously gave his time to be sure I had my facts, and my linguistic vocabulary, right. I also thank Dr. Jeffrey Leak at UNC–Charlotte and Dr. Helen R. Houston at Tennessee State University for reading earlier drafts.

2. E-mail exchange from McKnight to Sandra Y. Govan, May 22, 2005.

3. According to Aminata, a *marabou* is similar to a doctor or a healer. Supposedly, he heals people, gives advice or helps people understand the Quoran. But Evan is also told that marabous "can fly, stop time, make love potions, invoke good or evil spirits and make the do all kinds of weird things" (48–49). *Jinni* are the African equivalent of the Western "genies" (43) and *demm* are "soul-eaters"; they are the "crazy people who eat other people's souls," Aminata tells Evan (48).

4. Regarding the origins of the term *cultural mulatto*, McKnight believes that he and Trey Ellis "coined the term independently since we are generationally and culturally coterminous" and that because he was "an Air Force brat," with wide experience living in the integrated settings, he would perforce be "strongly influenced by a variety of sub-cultural streams." E-mail, May 22, 2005. Trudier Harris defines the term, as it applies to literary characters, more explicitly. Such characters "generally adhere to the values of the American dream." Typically, they "reflect the era of their creation by being college age or slightly older," and they are college educated, well traveled, and usually "consider their blackness coincidental rather than essential" (536). See the "New Cultural Mulatto" in *The Oxford Companion to African American Literature*.

5. Having been raised without knowing his racial identity, Johnson's mulatto narrator has to experience the racial and cultural barriers caused by segregation when he goes first to Atlanta, then Jacksonville, then Harlem; if we discount the prologue, Ellison's narrator first discovers for himself the dangers of the racial and cultural divides when he addresses the local civics club, his town's "leading white citizens" group and is forced to participate in a battle royal (*Invisible Man* 17).

6. E-mail to Sandra Y. Govan, May 31, 2005.

7. McKnight's depiction of Evan's fellow Peace Corps volunteer Ruth Barron is one of the most damning indictments of a black woman teacher in African American literature. From Evan's perspective, Ruth is not only a miserable excuse for a human being, she is also a perfect example of the Peter Principle:

> She taught for twenty-five years in the Detroit public school system before they discovered how monumentally incompetent she was. They retired her, but, perhaps figuring her level of incompetence for government work, wrote loquaciously gooey letters of recommendation to the Corps for her. Ruth is cruel, megalomaniacal, insane, and despises children—particularly African children. She mocks them when they mispronounce words in either French or English. She forbids them to speak in any language indigenous to Africa on the school grounds. She teases children who suffer speech impediments, limps, missing limbs, skin rashes, threadbare clothes. (29–30)

8. A father's inability to articulate his love, particularly for male offspring, is perfectly consistent within the African American literary canon. Neither the father

nor the dying grandfather in *Invisible Man* tells the protagonist that they love him; the white father in Johnson's *Autobiography of an Ex-Colored Man*, rather than profess any love, hangs a coin attached to a gold chain around his son's neck. This token of his "love" is an ambiguous symbol at best. The father seems to be either dead or absent in most canonical African American novels. The exception to this rule of thumb that I can think of occurs with Anthony Grooms's 2001 novel, *Bombingham.*

9. While Evan regrets suggesting to his mother that Wanda has some "unspeakable problem" and that this is why he cannot marry her, he admits to himself that she has no problems he knows about. But still he announces, "'I will not marry her.'" However, with his next breath the declarative "will not" shifts to the more equivocal, "'At least let me say that I should not'" (28).

10. We know this man carries a knife and has wounded Raymond with it, after a fight Raymond had provoked.

11. In a hallucinatory conversation with his mother, Evan refers to Wanda as being as "tough as Foucault." Asked "Who?" by his mom, he replies that Foucault is "just some guy," but his real point is Wanda's ability to be honest, to cut "beneath [his] bullshit" (288).

12. Aminata uses the Wolof term, *tere,* also called *gris-gris,* to describe a protective goatskin belt she asks Evan to wear. The *tere,* which also signifies a book, is filled with powerful herbs and verses from the Quoran (201).

Works Cited

Camus, Albert. *The Stranger.* 1942. Trans. Matthew Ward. New York: Vintage International, 1989.
Champion, Laurie. "Reginald McKnight." In *Contemporary African American Novelists—a Bio-bibliographic Critical Source Book.* Ed. Emmanuel S. Nelson, 314–18. Westport, CT: Greenwood Press, 1999.
Cullen, Countee. "Heritage." In *American Negro Poetry.* Ed. Arna Bontemps, 83–86. New York: Hill and Wang, 1963.
Brombert, Victor. "Camus and the Novel of the 'Absurd.'" *Yale French Studies* 1 (1948): 119–23.
Du Bois, W. E. B. *The Souls of Black Folk.* 1903. New York: Vintage, 1990.
Ellis, Trey. "The New Black Aesthetic." *Callaloo* 38 (Winter 1989): 233–43.
Ellison, Ralph. *The Invisible Man.* 1952. New York: Vintage Books, 1989.
Fabre, Michel. *The Unfinished Quest of Richard Wright.* New York: William Morrow, 1973.
"Foucault, Michel." *Wikipedia.* January 28, 2006. http://en.wikipedia.org/wiki/Michel_Foucault.
Giddings, Paula. "Reginald McKnight." *Essence* 21 (March 1991): 40.
Johnson, James Weldon. *The Autobiography of an Ex-Colored Man.* 1912. New York: Hill and Wang, 1960.
Megan, Carolyn E. "New Perceptions on Rhythm in Reginald McKnight's Fiction." *Kenyon Review* 16 (1994): 56–12.
McKnight, Reginald. "Confessions of a Wannabe Negro." *Lure and Loathing: Essays on Race, Identity, and the Ambivalence of Assimilation.* Ed. Gerald Early, 95–112. New York: Penguin, 1993.
———. *I Get on the Bus.* Boston: Little Brown, 1990.
———. E-mail to Sandra Y. Govan, May 22, 2005.

———. E-mail to Sandra Y. Govan, October 26, 2005.
O'Brien, Conner Cruise. *Albert Camus of Europe and Africa*. New York: Viking Press, 1970.
O'Brien, George. "I Get on the Bus." *Masterplots II*. African American Writers Series, vol. 2. Ed. Frank N. Magill, 563–68. Pasadena, CA: Salem Press, 1994.
"Reginald McKnight." *Contemporary Authors*. Vol. 129. Ed. Susan M. Trosley, 297. Detroit: Gale, 1990.
Rhein, Phillip H. *Albert Camus*. Boston: Twayne, 1969.
Scherr, Arthur. "Camus's *The Stranger*." *Explicator* 59, no. 3 (Spring 2001): 149–53.
Thrody, Phillip. *MacMillan Modern Novelist: Albert Camus*. London: MacMillan, 1989.
———. "A Note on Camus and the American Novel." *Comparative Literature* 9, no. 3 (Summer 1957): 243–49.
Walsh, William. "We Are, in Fact, a Civilization: An Interview with Reginald McKnight." *Kenyon Review* 16 (1994): 27–42.
Wright, Richard. *The Outsider*. New York: Harper, 1953.

8 Re-Imagining the Academy

Story and Pedagogy in Contemporary African American Fiction

ELEANOR W. TRAYLOR

When literary historians of the third millennium look back to discover "the creative, generative power of language in a particular historical period,—say between 1970 and the turn of the century—the power that manifested itself in the schools, successions, academies, societies, colleges, orders" (Greenblatt 477), the specific concentration of the literary genius on a mode of communication, they will find *story*. Not myth, story. They will see an empathetic disengagement from "the diagrams of ritual, which presuppose total and adequate explanation of things as they are and were," a disruption of a "sequence of radically unchangeable gestures," a disenchantment with "agents of [assumed] stability [that] call for the absolute" (Kermode 39). Rather, they will find a tendency toward fictions (stories), fictions "consciously held to be fictional" in the enterprise "of finding things out," a preoccupation with "fictions as the agents of change," fictions in the project of making "sense of the here and now, changing as the needs of sense making change" (39). They would also discover in these fictions, consciously held to be fiction, a total erasure of mythic binaries, as between the oral and the inscripted; the philosophical and the actual; the creative imagination and scholarly research; the political and the aesthetic; teaching and institution building; reading and writing; poetry and theory; the local (village) and the global (cosmopolitan). They would certainly encounter a distinct and prevalent attitude toward story as a vehicle of communication that might be phrased this way:

Stories are important. They keep us alive. In the ships, in the camps, in the quarters, fields, prisons, on the run, underground, under siege, in the throes, on the verge—the storyteller snatches us back from the edge to hear the next chapter. In which we are subjects. We, the hero of the tales. Our lives preserved. How it was; how it be. Passing it along in the relay. That is what we do: to produce stories that save our lives. [. . .] I argue then and in "Faith" as well that immunity to the serpent's sting can be found in our tradition of struggle and our faculty for synthesis. The issue is salvation. I work to produce stories that save our lives. (Bambara, "Salvation" 41–47)

Or this way:

[G]ood literature is disturbing in a way that history and social science writing frequently are not. It inspires distrust of conventional pieties and exacts a frequently painful confrontation with one's own thoughts and intentions. [. . .] Literary works that promote identification and emotional reaction cut through those self-protective stratagems, requiring us to see and to respond to many things that may be difficult to confront—and they make this process palatable by giving us pleasure in the very act of confrontation. (Nussbaum 356)

Nor would future historians fail to notice a *hypogram* (according to Michael Riffaterra, a deep-level meaning or unifying structure) that characterizes the universe of these fictions—a universe whose metalanguage serves possibilities and is, therefore, as poetical as theoretical. They would see this hypogram manifest in various images. They would see it in an image Miz Eva, in Earl Lovelace's *The Wine of Astonishment* (1982), calls "we church." In this novel that recreates "the history of a spiritualist's community [in Trinidad] from the passing of the [British] Prohibition Ordinance of 1917 [banning Miz Eva's Church] until the lifting of the ban in 1951" (Thorpe viii) through the eyes of Miz Eva, the central vision and narrator of the novel, we see the little church and its surrounding situation. Indeed, through her sensibility do we apprehend the meaning of "we church" for its members. Miz Eva says:

"We have this church. The walls make out of mud. The roof covered with carrat leaves; a simple hut with no steeple or cross of acolytes or priests or latin [sic] ceremonies. But is our own. Black people own it. Government ain't spent one cent helping us build it or put bench in it or anything; the bell that we ring when we call to the spirit is our money that pay for it. So we have this church. We have this church where we gather to sing hymns and ring the bell and shout hallelujah and speak in tongues when the Spirit come; and we carry the Word to the downtrodden and the forgotten and the lame and the beaten, and we touch black people soul. We have this church where in this tribulation country far away from Africa, the home that we don't know, we can come together and be ourselves." (Lovelace 32–33)

In "we church," you can "'hear your own voice [. . .] feel your own spirit, and catch your own power [. . . .] shout hallelujah and speak in tongues when the Spirit comes; and [. . .] carry the Word to the downtrodden and the forgotten and the lame and the beaten, and touch black people soul'" (32–33).

Indeed, future historians would comprehend the hypogram of the church not as a dogma or land; not as an army, not as a flag, but as a transgressive space defying arbitrary, hegemonic destruction. They would understand it as a place of authentic human feeling—the residence of language that admits the existence of the human heart, that sentient drum beating one insistent message: "[T]his is your urgency: Live! / and have your blooming" (Brooks 453).

Here in the gathering of "we church," the historian would witness the daily round of life whose expression we may call the Humanities. No walls or boundary lines restrict "we church." It is a community of memory and shared experience where all the old stories begin, are recalled, are transformed anew. It is here where "the old decapitations and dispossessions" 445) are remembered, where the small and large victories of being are rehearsed; "something profound and unanswerable [stirs] in the consciousness of all" (Baldwin 122). Here, the litany admits no categorical distinction between the aesthetic and the ethical: "[T]he apostle of Beauty thus becomes the apostle of Truth and Right . . . by inner and outer compulsion. Free he is but his freedom is ever bounded by Truth and Justice" (Du Bois, "Criteria" 296). And here, a common faith abounds: "[T]he world is full of [beauty] . . . its variety is infinite, its possibility endless. In normal life all may have it" (292). "Yet," the congregation shares a tacit understanding: "the mass of human beings are choked away from [beauty] and their lives distorted and made ugly" (292). Thus, "we church," the historians would hear, intones the common query: "[W]ho shall right this well-nigh universal failing? Who shall let this world be beautiful?" (292). It is here, the witness would conclude, where "our endless connections with and responsibilities for each other"

(Baldwin 122) are somehow clarified by the memory of our particular passage through the world.

Being interested in the traces of texts arising from "we church," the witness would uncover a vocabulary of images naming major and broad-reaching conditions of modern humanity: *the veil* (Du Bois), the distorting, warping, dwarfing myopia preventing a clear vision of reality; *the river* (Hughes), the stream of consciousness mapping the journey back, the journey forward; *the native son* (Wright), the dispossessed and dispossessing pariah denied the rites of passage essential to self-knowledge and, therefore, self-fulfillment; *the conjurer* (Chesnutt and Bambara), the healing power of insight and imagination; *invisibility* (Ellison), the denial of authentic being; *the slave* (Baraka), a delusion; *the bluest eye* (Morrison), the dementia of delusion; *Sula* (Morrison), the conundrum of modern woman; *the ark of bones* (Dumas), the ship of memory, resisting deluge, conveying "the whole house of thy brothers" (Dumas *Ark* 6).

The scholar-witness would hear in the texts that speak from the present of "we church" the resonance of a remote humanistic past: the rage of Achilleus, the plight of Andromache, the bold assertion of Antigone, the vengeance of Medea, the mission of Moses, the dreams of Joseph, the insistence of Job, the courage of Judith, the quest of Dante, the outrage of Caliban, the arrogance of Prospero, the triumph of Sundiata, the quaking soul of the Gita. All these memories are alive in "we church." But, as the witness would know, memory "involves not just an act of retrieval by the mind of the poet, but simultaneously the perception of what lies before him and her in the present as deficient, as a vice, a lack that memory will fill" (Vance 382).

The hypogram that the scholar-witness might surely deduce from the imagistic-lode of "we church" would unveil as an imagined or reimagined curriculum. Such a portrait would be corroborated by a startling representation of an Academy presenting itself in a touchstone fiction, published near the millennium, entitled *The Salt Eaters* (1980), by Toni Cade Bambara. This elaborate story actually constructs a cross-disciplinary, cross-cultural institution called "The Academy of the Seven Arts," which, in design and spirit, is

> a place where imaginings may be made real and realities disclosed as the products of imagination [. . .] a place where "the made-up and the made-real touch," where skepticism and faith struggle bitterly over the substance of things hoped for and the evidence of things not seen. (Greenblatt 478; the enclosed quote is from Elaine Scarry's *The Body in Pain*)

If the Academy of this fiction falters in the novel, as it does, the fault is not the design, but the faint heart of the builders. "The Academy of the Seven Arts" in *The Salt Eaters*, a witness may note, is a complementary re-vision of another fiction, a story called *Ark of Bones* (1974), by Henry Dumas, where the hypogram images as a huge white ark sailing the waters of American literature as if interfacing or complementing a huge white whale. This ark, gathering up in its metonym a well-established creation story, is itself a story boat rescuing stories that should not be forgotten; it is foremost a "Glory Boat [. . .] the house of generations. Every African who lives in America has a part of his soul in this ark" (10, 15).

Yet perhaps the most extraordinary manifestation of this hypogram, the scholar-witness would find, is a fiction published in 1998 by Toni Morrison entitled *Paradise*. Here, there appears a *convent* living in its ruins. This convent has endured three transformations, each change caused by a need to make sense of its present being. Its ruins, actually, become the space for the advent of wonderful emergent identities, for the inhabitants of the convent discover an obligation to find things out. Doubtless, the witness would be drawn to an emblematic scene in this novel where old stories are reenacted. The scholar-witness would likely experience here a site of pedagogy where something very like "a change in the economy of desire" takes place, creating "a different relationship between man and gods, man and man, man and the world, man and woman" (Irigaray 120). The witness might learn from this pedagogical scene that

> [o]ur own age, which is often felt to be the one in which the problem of desire has been brought to the fore, frequently theorizes about this desire on the basis of certain observations about a moment of tension, situated in historical time, whereas a desire ought to be thought of as a dynamic force whose changing form can be traced in the past and occasionally in the present, but never predicted. Our age [could] only realize the dynamic potential in desire if the latter is referred back to the economy of the interval, that is if it is located in the attractions, tensions, and acts between form and matter, or characterized as the residue of any creation or work, which lies between what is already identified and what has still to be identified. (120)

From this fiction, these stories that seek to find things out, our witness would surely contextualize the dynamics of the decades in which they appeared. The visiting scholar would, of course, seek sources that elaborate such events in the social, political, and economic surrounds but especially within the American Academy in which the authors here mentioned, all university professors, wield influence. These decades would reveal the rise of interdisciplinary Black Studies, African American Studies, the introduction of the heretical text, as James Baldwin has put it, into the congregation (canon) of the always-already chosen righteous, and the "ferment that might be called the Era of Grand Theory." It would be clear then that "[b]y the end of the 1960s, [. . .] the road to the culture wars of the late 1980s and early 1990s" (Richter 20) had been paved.

Yet another narrative, this one *diegetic*, would come to the attention of the witness concerned to contextualize widely the powerful activity of the creative imagination, the literary genius of this time. This narrative, an analysis of the real-world Academy, by the late professor Bill Readings, offers a "structural diagnosis of contemporary shifts in the University's function as an institution" entitled *The University in Ruins*. It argues that "it is no longer clear what the place of the University is within society nor what the exact nature of that society is, and the changing institutional form of the University is something that intellectuals cannot afford to ignore" (2). Briefly stated, the argument holds that "the process of economic globalization brings with it the relative decline of the nation state as the prime instance of the reproduction of capital around the world" and that "the University is becoming transnational" (3). Thus, by the light of globalization, the university has lost its historical reason for being, for its two defining projects, which Du Bois articulated at the turn of the twentieth century in "The Field and Function of the Negro College"—the Enlightenment and the training of citizens in the culture of the nation-state—are now unreliable narrators of its identity.

What is undeniable is that in matters of identity, the twenty-first century is *a*- or *in*-temporal. I avoid Readings's term *post-historical* because it resonates, as a colleague notes, the multitude of codicil sensibilities and philosophic stances important to historical developments in the academy that we know as post-Freudian, post-Marxist, poststructuralist, postdeconstructionist, postcolonial, and so on. But these stances may do little to explain the emergent identities already imminent in the gulf of transition—our world space. And yet, in addition to the work of imminent scholars with whom these approaches to reading and writing and seeing the world are most often associated, if the witness were to comprehend these pedagogical approaches as the outcome of their unacknowledged but antecedent practices in the migrant and existential *blues*, the solo and intertextual design of *jazz*, the congregational call and response of *gospel*, the I/we voice and address of nineteenth-century and continuing emancipatory African American narratives, the witness would come near to envisioning an Academy, especially in the light of its hypogram in literary imagination, as frame for a humanities-driven interdisciplinary *situs* of being.

If Du Bois, philosopher of identity, defined the problem of the twentieth century as "the colorline" and its characteristic identity "double consciousness" (*Souls* 2), the problem of the twenty-first century, before and certainly after the horror of September 11, 2001, may be the global recognition of uncertainty. This emergent identity—uncertainty—may announce a new character in this era of human concerns and resourcefulness. By this light, the fictions mentioned here and that my students read become challenges testing the pedagogical mission, objectives, and outcomes assessment of our seminar in Contemporary African American Narrative. The mission that drives the seminar is one purporting simply "to find things out," and the objective, based on a broad endeavor as phrased by one of our novelists, is an exploration of "how to carve away the accretions of deceit, blindness, ignorance, paralysis, and sheer malevolence embedded in raced language so that other kinds of perception [are] not only available but [. . .] inevitable" (Morrison, "Home" 7). In this way, contemporary African American fictions may be understood as discourse-altering events. In fact, this enterprise is not only discourse altering; it is profoundly discourse making.

Paradise, as a dialectical conversation between two worlds of being, is a case in point. A discourse-making event is, in fact, a resolution of the conversation. Moreover, the portraits or scapes inside the novel's frame may include various sights (sites). I read one of these as a site of teaching and learning that approximates an Academy—one that addresses the issue of identity and its implications that critics have posed. The novel describes two locales. The town of its setting, called alternately Haven and Ruby, whose description some of its readers see as a rescription of the national epic, is one domain. The other is a ruined institution called the Convent, which, having lost its reason for being—its proprietor, the church, and its missionary charge—is living among its ruins. Its ruins then become the space for the advent of wonderful emergent identities. It is here that I come to my reading of what I determine to be the emblematic scene of *Paradise*—the scene in which it acts as a fiction that reconfigures the millennial Academy. I might add that nothing could have driven me more quickly to the cellar floor of this scene than the struggle with the politics of difference or identity (the Canon debates/

the Culture Wars) waged in academic departments all over the world. The number of times I have shuttled between Haven and the Convent (defining them differently) are innumerable. I have read this scene each time by the light of my own psychic state.

I have also alternately read this scene by the light of Gloria Anzaldua's observations in *Making Face, Making Soul,* as she reminds us:

> "Face" is the surface of the body that is most noticeably inscribed by social structures, marked with instructions of how to be [. . .]—We are "written" all over, carved and tattooed with the sharp needles of experience [. . .]—In sewing terms "interfacing" means sewing a piece of material between two pieces of fabric to provide support and stability [. . .]—Between the masks we've internalized, one on top of another, are our interfaces. The masks are already steeped with self-hatred and other internalized oppressions [. . .]—We rip out the stitches, expose the multi-layered "inner face." [. . .] We begin to acquire the agency of making our [face]. You are the shaper of your flesh as well as of your soul. (xv–xvi)

I have read it in terms of the question raised in *Schindler's List:*

> Question: Do I have to invent a brand new language?
> Answer: Yes, I think so.

And I have read it by the desire expressed in Morrison's *Jazz:*

> I want to be the language that wishes him well, speaks his name, wakes him when his eyes need to be open. (161)

I have read it also as it addresses T. M. Luhrmann's phrase "creativity forced by its tensions" (193); as it addresses "a new freedom of identity" in the construction of "a life aimed towards the good, in which one is able to love and to work, to find joy" (205); as it addresses Leela Gandhi's query

> whether it is possible to recuperate the (theoretically founded) ethical claims of cosmopolitanism without abandoning altogether the affective urgency and immediacy of cultural nationalism and in so doing reclaim the latter housing it anew within a politics of transcultural friendship. (31)

And I read it again in *Paradise,* as another phase of a spiritual biography that encourages my own passages toward enriched identity.

The scene begins:

> The table is set; the food placed. Consolata takes off her apron. With the aristocratic gaze of the blind she sweeps the women's faces and says, I call myself Consolata Sosa. If you want to be here you do what I say. Eat how I say. Sleep when I say. And I will teach you what you are hungry for. (262)

Consolata Sosa, called Connie, has achieved the confidence of her voice—an authority the four women, to whom Connie is refuge and safe harbor, the initiates of the novel, have heretofore never heard. They are startled by both the timbre of her voice and the changed features of her face:

> higher cheekbones, stronger chin. [. . .] Had her eyelashes always been that thick, her teeth that pearly white? Her hair showed no gray. Her skin is smooth as a peach. (262)

The women have come to know and love Connie as "a sweet unthreatening old lady who seemed to love each one of them best; who never criticized, who shared everything but needed little or no care; required no emotional investment; who listened, who locked no doors and accepted each as she was" (262). She is to them an "ideal parent, friend, companion in whose company they were safe from harm . . . [a] perfect landlord who charged nothing and welcomed anybody"; she is also "Granny Goose who could be confided in or ignored, lied to or suborned . . . [a] playmother who could be hugged or walked out on, depending on the whim of the child" (262). Is this a portrait of the fully evolved teacher or of a book, or is it a reinscription of the central image in the fiction of contemporary Black women writers: a praise song and especially a commemoration of Minnie Ransom invigorated by her familiar, Old Wife, in Toni Cade Bambara's *The Salt Eaters*? Like Minnie and like contemporary African American fiction, Connie's portrait in *Paradise* is all three—imbued with that knowledge customarily consigned to science (Bambara, *Salt Eaters* 145). A signal achievement, then, of contemporary African American fiction is that it is a teacher, a "clairvoyant, clairaudient, clairfeelant, clairdoent" (146) who knows "each way of being in the world and could welcome [us] home again to wholeness" (48). This fiction discovers itself, even as it draws unto itself from within itself its fullest cultural inheritance.

Like the academy under construction in *The Salt Eaters*, "where the performing arts, the martial arts, the medical arts, the scientific arts, and the arts and humanities" (120) form a coherent curriculum, the metanarrative that is contemporary African American fiction signals for commemoration and readerly insight texts, ancient and contemporary, that resonate its contradictory or affirmative discourses: from the cave where Plato situates the problem of knowledge; the Zoroastrian vision of redemption; the *Book of the Dead;* the descent of the Homeric and Virgilian travelers; the Cartesian, Aristotelian, and Acquinian oppositional binaries; the Old and New Testaments; the infernal and paradisiacal visions of Dante, Milton, and Goethe; (the post-Hiroshima discoveries of) *The Dead Sea Scrolls* and *The Nag Hamadi* Gospels, to the restatement of the modern angst disclosed in Chinua Achebe's *Things Fall Apart*. In fact, if, as some of my students read it, contemporary African American fiction is "the place where the building never ceases" and "literary genres are tested for their limits," then in its intertextual design (texts of which are only hinted at here), this fiction presents a model for the millennial university. In the emblematic scene we glimpse in *Paradise, the teacher* who shows us "how to learn to see yourself for yourself" (273) and to hear the singing of a *paidia* where rhetoric and poetic combine to inform "what neither history or memory can say or record" (272); *the initiates* or *the students,* "written all over [. . .] carved and tattooed with the sharp needles of experience [. . .] steeped with self-hatred and other internalized oppressions" (Anzaldua xv–xvi); the *debatment* or the ceremony of displacement, cleansing, and advent; *the dance of joyful awareness* in which the individuated and informed consciousness is able to re-form community. We witness a *site of the possibilities* of our being together—a fulfilled desire of the world soul. *Paradise* traces this ceremony of transformation from antecedent fiction as various as Ellison's *Invisible Man,* Baldwin's "Sonny's Blues," Dumas's *Ark of Bones,* Gayl Jones's *Corregidora,* Leon Forrest's *There Is a Tree More Ancient than Eden,* and Alice Walker's *The Color Purple*. All these and more may be read as fruitfully presenting stages in the ritual of transformative decolonization.

When literary historians of the next millennium look back to discover "the creative, generative power of language" in world literatures, they will likely find contemporary African American fiction as the world's beacon. A brief narrative might furnish a scholar-witness from a distant age an example of some real-world outcomes proceeding from the generative power of language typical of the literary genius of our own era.

Majda, my student from Syria, had barely sat down before she began to weep. She had come to my office to present to me her proposal for a master's thesis. As I quickly rose to embrace her, hoping to ease whatever anguish she was suffering, she sobbed out words, each of which shook her body. She moaned, "Professor, it is not easy being Muslim in America today." Majda had endured a slight on her way to my office. She had come to the graduate program in English at Howard University to earn a Ph.D., specializing in African American literature. She decided to earn a master's degree first. She wanted to be sure that certification took place along the way she had mapped [. . .] "just in case." I spoke to her softly, saying: "Majda, it has never been easy to be Black in America." After a long tremor, she replied: "This is the reason I am here—to study a literature that has saved my life." In fact, Majda's proposal, a chapter of which is included in this collection, argues for *Paradise* as a new version of the ancient frame narrative *Alf Laylah wa Laylah* (The Arabian Nights) "to demonstrate how the frame narrative is a contingent form" and to show how, like *The Arabian Nights, Paradise* is "a new frame narrative that defers death and longs for rebirth and self-reconstruction." Majda's argument reminds us that "[s]cholars have missed a comprehensive comparative study between two frame narrative cycles: Arabic frame narratives and African American frame narratives." She claims, "This study will highlight the affinity between the Arabian and African American outlook and mode of narration and organization that reflect shared traditions, especially that African tales are plentiful in *Alf Laylah Wa Laylah*."

I love the way Professor Stephen Greenblatt concludes his stunning essay "What Is the History of Literature?" from which I have quoted. He turns us toward the scene from *Hamlet* where Horatio admonishes the ghost to speak. Greenblatt then reminds us wonderfully, "It is the duty of the scholar to speak to the dead and make the dead speak." I turn now to another scene, the one where the women visit the tomb on resurrection morning. There they hear the voice of an angel asking the question: "Why seek ye the living among the dead?" Majda, and her colleagues in the Academy at millennium, has heard the voice of an angel and brought home the good news. Her voice, like their voices, disengages from presumptions of an "adequate exploration," from assumptions of "the absolute"; she and they and we rise and join the "we church" and continue the activity of mapping the salvaging language of story traced throughout millennial African American fiction now reshaping the Academy.

Works Cited

Anzaldua, Gloria, ed. "Haciendo Caras, Una Entrada: An Introduction." In *Making Face, Making Soul: Haciendo Caras*, xv–xviii. San Francisco: Aunt Lute Foundation, 1990.
Baldwin, James. *The Evidence of Things Not Seen*. New York: Holt, 1985.
Bambara, Toni Cade. *The Salt Eaters*. New York: Random House, 1980.
———. "Salvation Is the Issue." In *Black Women Writers (1950–1980): A Critical Evaluation*. Ed. Mari Evans, 41–47. Garden City, NY: Anchor Press, 1984.
Brooks, Gwendolyn. *Blacks*. Chicago: Third World Press, 1987.
Du Bois, W. E. B. "Criteria of Negro Art." *Crisis* 32 (October 1926): 290–97.
———. "The Field and Function of the Negro College." In *The Education of Black People: Ten Critiques , 1906–1960*. Ed. H. Aptheker, 83–102. Amherst: University of Massachusetts Press, 1973.
———. *The Souls of Black Folk*. New York: Bantam Books, 1989.
Dumas, Henry. *Ark of Bones*. New York: Random House, 1974.
Gandhi, Leela. *Affective Communities: Anticolonial Thought, Fin-De-Siècle Radicalism, and the Politics of Friendship*. Durham: Duke University Press, 2006.
Greenblatt, Stephen. "What Is the History of Literature?" *Critical Inquiry* 23.3 (Spring 1997): 460–81.
Irigaray, Luce. "Sexual Difference." In *French Feminist Thought: A Reader*. Ed. Toril Moi, 118–30. New York: Blackwell, 1987.
Kermode, Frank. *The Sense of an Ending: Studies in the Theory of Fiction*. New York: Oxford University Press, 1967.
Lovelace, Earl. *The Wine of Astonishment*. London: Heinemann, 1985.
Luhrmann, T. M. *The Good Parsi: the Fate of a Colonial Elite in a Postcolonial Society*. Cambridge, MA: Harvard University Press, 1996.
Morrison, Toni. "Home." In *The House That Race Built*. Ed. Wahneema Lubiano, 3–12. New York: Pantheon Books, 1997.
———. *Jazz*. New York: Knopf, 1992.
———. *Paradise*. New York: Knopf, 1998.
Nussbaum, Martha C. "The Literary Imagination and Public Life." In Richter 356–65.
Readings, Bill. *The University in Ruins*. Cambridge MA: Harvard University Press, 1996.
Richter, David H. *Falling Into Theory: Conflicting Views on Reading Literature*. New York: Bedford/St. Martin's Press, 2000.
Scarry, Elaine. *The Body in Pain: The Making and Unmaking of the World*. New York: Oxford University Press, 1985.
Thorpe, Marjorie. Introduction. In Lovelace ix–xii.
Vance, Eugene. "Roland and the Poetics of Memory." In *Textual Strategies: Perspectives in Post-Structuralist Criticism*. Ed. Josué V. Harari, 374–403. Ithaca, NY: Cornell University Press, 1979.

The Contributors

Originally from Syria, **Majda Ramadan Atieh** earned her MA and Phd degrees with honors in African American Literature from Howard University. She is currently a lecturer at Tishreen University, Lattokia, Syria.

Sandra Govan is professor of English at the University of North Carolina, Charlotte. She received her PhD from Emory University. Her latest article on Octavia Butler appeared in the *African-American Encyclopedia*.

Tara T. Green is an associate professor of the Department of African American Studies at UNC-Greensboro. Her research specialty is African American Literature with a developing interest in Caribbean and West African women's literature.

Jennifer A. Jordan is associate professor of English at Howard University. She holds a PhD in American Literature from Emory University. She has taught in the English and Afro-American studies departments at Howard. Her various articles, lectures, reviews, and bibliographies have made important contribution in the area of African American literary criticism, with special emphasis on the novel, contemporary black women writers, and the interrelationship of politics and literature.

Mildred R. Mickle is assistant professor of English at Pennsylvania State University, Greater Allegheny. She received her PhD from the University of North Carolina. Her research interests include African American poetry and speculative fiction.

Eleanor W. Traylor is professor and chair of the department of English at Howard University. She is the co-editor of *The Black Woman: An Anthology*, with Tonie Cade Bambara (Washington Square) and author of *Broad Sympathy: The Howard University Oral Traditions Reader* (Ginn).

Reggie Scott Young is associate professor of English at the University of Louisiana, Lafayette. He received his PhD from the University of Illinois at Chicago in 1990. He compiled and edited *Mozart and Leadbelly: Stories and Essays by Ernest J. Gaines* (Knopf 2005) and *This Louisiana Thing That Drives Me: The Legacy of Ernest J. Gaines* (University of Louisiana Press, 2009).

Dana A. Williams is associate professor of African American literature at Howard University. She is the author of *In the Light of Likeness—Transformed: The Literary Art of Leon Forest* (The Ohio State University Press, 2005) and co-editor of *August Wilson and Black Aesthetics* (Palgrave) with Sandra G. Shannon.

Index

A

Achebe, Chinua, 7, 169. See also *Things Fall Apart*
acknowledgment, 1, 25, 28, 95
African American, 1, 2, 4–9, 11–30, 38, 40–41, 44, 49–50, 52–53, 56–57, 61–62, 65, 79, 81–84, 96, 99–102, 110, 115, 123, 136–39, 142–45, 148–49, 156, 165–66, 168–70, 173–74, 31n1, 31n6, 32n7, 32n8, 32n9, 32–33n10, 33nn12–15, 58n1, 58n13, 116n3, 116n5, 157n7, 157–58n8
African American Literary Criticism, 1773 to 2000 (Ervin), 31n1
African diaspora, 83
Africanisms, 8
Africanist, 38, 40, 44, 116
African Renaissance, 55
Afro-American Literature: The Reconstruction of Instruction (MLA), 31
Afrocentricity, 38, 53, 55–56. See also Afrocentrism
Afrocentrism, 38, 53. See also Afrocentricity
ahistorical, 107
Alf Laylah Wa Laylah [Arabian Nights] (Morrison), 119, 123–24, 126–34, 170
Allen, Jeffery Renard, 32
American Adam myth, 101, 104, 112
American Book Awards, 40
American Dream, 51, 157
Americanisms, 8
antifeminist, 44
anti-White, 43–44, 58
Anzaldua, Gloria, 167
archvillain, 51
Atieh, Madja R., 5, 173
Atonism, 44
Audubon, John James, 55
The Autobiography of Miss Jane Pittman (Gaines), 28, 33n14, 32n8

B

Babb, Valerie, 31n4, 33n14
Baker, Houston, 2, 36–37, 41–42, 44
Baldwin, James, 12, 35, 110, 162–63, 165, 32n7, 117n14
Bal, Mieke, 132
Bambara, Toni Cade, 7, 9, 15, 84, 161, 163, 168, 174, 116n10. See also *The Salt Eaters*
Baraka, Amiri, 7, 38, 40–42, 45–47, 49, 52–53, 56–57, 58n8, 58n9, 58n11, 58–59n15. See also Jones, Leroi; *Un Poco Low Coup*
Beavers, Herman, 19–21, 34
Before Columbus Foundation, 39, 40, 50, 54, 60
Bell, Bernard, 8, 79
Beloved (Morrison), 103, 119
Berger, Art, 41
biblical, 33, 54, 65–66, 112
biracial, 142
black, 11–12, 14, 38, 42–43, 49, 51–52, 57, 161, 165, 168, 170, 117n11
Black aesthetic, 11, 14, 17, 41–42, 44,

49, 52, 60
Black American Literature Forum, 31, 36, 81
Black Arts aesthetics, 25
Black Arts era, 14–16, 35
Black Arts Movement, 3, 9, 14–16, 22, 25–27, 31, 33, 37, 41–46, 48–48, 52–54, 56–57, 60, 98
Black Arts Repertory Theater/School, 41, 58
black community, 11, 22, 115
black consciousness movement, 42
black experience, 22, 28
Black Metafiction: Self-Consciousness in African American Literature (Jablon), 24
Black Nationalist Movement, 31, 43, 58
blackness, 6, 12, 28, 46, 73, 102, 142, 144, 155, 157
Black Power Movement, 57
Blacks in Eden (Greene), 65
Black Studies, 11–12, 14, 22, 52, 165
Black World, 34, 37, 42–44, 56, 58nn5–6
Boogeyman, 87
Book of Thoth, 43
Bordo, Susan, 93
boutique multiculturalism, 39, 50, 58n2
Boyce Davies, Carole, 38, 39, 53, 55, 84
Bradley, David, 137
Breath, Eyes, Memory (Danticat), 82–85, 97
Brombert, Victor, 144–45
Brooks, Gwendolyn, 56, 162
Brown, William Wells, 100
Butler, Octavia E., 3–4, 32, 63–80. See also *Fledgling*; *Survivor*
Byerman, Keith, 31n1

C

Callahan, Bob, 39, 50, 60
Camus, Albert, 6, 136, 143–47, 149, 152, 154, 156. See also *The Stranger*
Chairman Mao, 58n14
Chestnutt, Charles, 17, 163
Church Committee, 58n12
Church, Frank, 58n12
Clark, Keith, 26

Clayark, 64–65, 69–70, 76
Clifton, Lucille, 15
coexistence, 3, 37, 38, 66
COINTELPRO, 49, 61, 58n12
Coleman, James W., 22, 32n9, 34n15
The Color Purple (Walker), 4, 84, 97, 169, 117n11
coming-of-age, 4, 85, 99–105, 108, 110–11, 115, 116n1, 116n4, 116n6, 116n7
Communist Party, 57
Connor, Kimberly Rae, 17
Conrad, Joseph, 140
co-opt, 69
Cullen, Countee, 6, 136–37, 140

D

Danticat, Edwidge, 4, 82–84, 90, 92–93, 95–97, 98n1. See also *Breath, Eyes, Memory*
Delany, Martin R., 32n8
Delany, Samuel, 8, 32n8
demm, 140, 155, 157
Dessa Rose (Williams), 24
dialogue, 1–2, 26
diaspora, 8, 82, 95
dis/ease, 3–4, 62–71, 74–76, 79
double-consciousness, 6, 56, 138–40
Douglass, Frederick, 18–19, 100
DuBois, W. E. B., 6–7, 18, 56, 102. See also *The Souls of Black Folk*
Due, Tananarive, 8
Dumas, Henry, 2, 7, 14–19, 21–25, 28, 30, 116, 163–64, 169, 31nn3–4, 33n12, 34n15
Duvalier, François, 82
Duvalier, Jean-Claude, 82

E

Eden (Vernon), 4, 99–100, 102–4, 110, 115
Edenic, 65–67. See also Garden of Eden
Ellis, Trey, 142, 157n4
Ellison, Ralph, 2, 6–7, 17, 19–21, 27, 32–34, 39, 143, 157, 163, 169. See also *Shadow and Act*
emancipatory, 1, 166. See also liberatory

ennui, 137, 146
Erdrich, Louise, 40
Ervin, Hazel Arnett, 31n1. See also *African American Literary Criticism, 1773 to 2000*
Eurocentrism, 13, 38, 59
Evans, Mari, 56
Everett, Percival, 8
Exorcising Blackness: Historical and Literary Lynching and Burning Rituals (Harris), 113
extraconstitutional, 58n12
extraliterary, 13, 15, 17, 27, 31, 119–20

F

Faris, Wendy B., 129, 133
Fisher, Dexter, 31n1
Fish, Stanley, 39
Fledgling (Butler), 3–4, 62–64, 70–71, 74–75, 77, 80
Forrest, Leon, 8, 169
Fortune, T. Thomas, 46
Foucault, Michel, 155, 158n11
Francis, Donette A., 87, 95
Francophone, 28, 156
Free-Lance Pallbearers (Reed), 3, 37, 43–44, 47–49, 51

G

Gaines, Ernest J., 2, 11, 15, 17, 19, 24, 32, 174. See also *The Autobiography of Miss Jane Pittman; A Lesson before Dying; Mozart and Leadbelly: Stories and Essays*
Garden of Eden, 65–66, 69. See also Edenic
Garvey, Marcus, 46, 48, 136
Gates, Henry Louis, Jr., 2, 11–14, 23, 30–33, 43, 61, 100–101
Gaudet, Marcia, 31n4
Gayle, Addison, 37, 41–42
Gibson, Donald, 14, 16, 26
Girard, René, 144
Gould, Stephen Jay, 76–77
Govan, Sandra Y., 5–6, 70–71, 173, 32n8, 157n6
Greene, J. Lee, 65–67
Grossman, Judith, 124, 128

Guterl, Matthew, 48

H

Harjo, Joy, 40
Harlem Renaissance, 9, 59, 137
Harris, Trudier, 15, 23, 30, 113–14, 157n4. See also *Exorcising Blackness: Historical and Literary Lynching and Burning Rituals*
Harrison, Elizabeth Jane, 104, 117n11
Har-You, 58n8
Hernton, Calvin, 41, 45
Himes, Chester, 25
Holloway, Karla F. C., 12, 83–84, 97, 32–33n10
Holocaust, 51
Hooker, John Lee, 27, 29
hooks, bell, 63
Hopkinson, Nalo, 32
Howe, Irving, 19–20
Hughes, Langston, 7, 19, 163
Hurston, Zora Neale, 17, 23, 102
hypogram, 161–64, 166

I

I Get on the Bus (McKnight), 6, 136, 140, 142, 144, 152, 156
integrationalist, 12
intertextual, 1–2, 13, 24, 26, 144, 166, 169, 31n1
intracultural, 74
Ippolito, Emilia, 83–84

J

Jablon, Madelyn, 24–26, 29. See also *Black Metafiction: Self-Consciousness in African American Literature*
Jacobs, Harriet, 100
Japanese by Spring (Reed), 3, 37, 46–48, 50–53, 55
Jazz (Morrison), 119, 167
Jes Grew, 44
Jimoh, A. Yemisi, 34
jinni, 140, 155, 157n2
Joe Turner's Come and Gone (Wilson), 15
Johnson, Charles, 8
Johnson, James Weldon, 6, 142–43,

157n5, 157–58n8
Johnson, Lyndon, 43
Jones, Edward P., 8
Jones, Gayl, 8, 169
Jones, LeRoi, 17, 38, 49, 33–34n14, 58n11. *See also* Baraka, Amiri
Jordan, Jennifer A., 3, 46, 54, 173, 58n1, 58n7
Joyce, Joyce Ann, 2, 11–12, 20, 30, 56

K

Karenga, Maulana "Ron," 46, 49, 52, 56, 58n14, 58–59n15. *See also* Kwanzaa
Kelley, William Melvin, 8
Kenan, Randall, 75
A Killing in This Town (Vernon), 4, 99–100, 102, 110, 113–15
Konch (journal), 40
Kwanzaa, 47. *See also* Karenga, Maulana "Ron"

L

Laguerre, Michel S., 92
Lang, John, 33n14
Leadbelly tradition, 17, 21, 29, 31n5
A Lesson before Dying (Gaines), 2, 17, 24–26, 28
Lewis, R. W. B., 101
Lewis, Wyndham, 145
liberatory, 1. *See also* emancipatory
lifeblood, 34n15
Little Red Book, 58
Logic (Vernon), 4, 99–100, 102, 107, 115
Loichot, Valerie, 93
Lorde, Audre, 100, 116n4
Lovelace, Earl, 161–62
Lowe, John, 32–33
Lubiano, Waheeman, 33
Luhrmann, T. M., 167
The Lynchers (Wideman), 114

M

Mackey, Nathaniel, 8
Madhubuti, Haki (Don L. Lee), 43–46, 56, 59, 58n7
Major, Clarence, 8

makeshift, 99
Mama Day (Naylor), 24
marabous, 140, 157
Marshall, Paule, 4, 83. *See also Praisesong for the Widow*
masterworks, 27
McCullers, Carson, 116n10
McKay, Nellie, 14, 23, 29, 32, 35–36
McKnight, Reginald, 6, 136–47, 149, 152, 154–56, 157n2, 157n4, 157n7, 158. *See also I Get on the Bus*
Megan, Carolyn E., 138
meklah, 64–70, 76, 78, 79
Melville, Herman, 51, 101
metacommunication, 120–23
metafiction, 24–25
metalanguage, 161
metastatements, 123
Mickle, Mildred R., 3–4, 63, 173
Mikics, David, 60, 58n13
misreading, 2
Missionaries (*Survivor*), 64–69
Mitchell, Carolyn A., 22
Modern Language Association, 31
Morrison, Toni, 5, 7, 9, 15–16, 22–23, 29, 32–33, 40, 45, 83, 99, 101–3, 119, 121–24, 127, 131–32, 134, 163–64, 167, 116 nn2–3, 116nn9–10, 117n11, 117n15. *See also Beloved; Jazz; Paradise*
Mosley, Walter, 25
Mozart and Leadbelly: Stories and Essays (Gaines), 18, 20, 24, 31, 33, 174
Muhammad, Elijah, 57
multiculturalism, 3, 37–40, 48–53, 55–56, 58nn2–4, 58–59n15
multifocal, 39
multilayered, 127, 137
multitiered, 142
Mumbo Jumbo (Reed), 37–38, 43–46, 48–52, 54–55
Mu'tafikah, 49–51, 58n13

N

Nation of Islam, 43, 46, 53, 57, 58
Native Son (Wright), 9, 24–26, 163
Naylor, Gloria, 4, 8, 23–24, 32, 36, 84. See also *Mama Day; The Women of Brewster Place*

Neal, Larry, 13, 42, 48–49, 53–54, 58n14
neocolonialism, 39, 49
neoconservative, 44
neo-Nazi, 51
New Literary History, 11
New World, 12, 21, 66, 69, 75
neosocialism, 43
non-black, 28
nonfiction, 27
noninterference, 66
nonlinear, 126, 127–28
nonnative, 65
nonpurist, 110
nonsecular, 34n15
nonwritten, 18, 21
the North, 18, 125
The Norton Anthology of African American Literature (Norton Anthology), 2, 14, 16, 82

O

O'Connor, Flannery, 116n9
Onodera, Bob, 39
Oprah's Book Club, 28, 82
Oren, Michael, 41, 46–47
Organization of Black American Culture (OBAC), 56
Ortiz, Simon, 39
overarching, 9

P

Pan-African, 58n7
Paradise (Morrison), 5, 7, 119–28, 131–34, 164, 166, 168–69
paraliterature, 8
pastoral Gothic, 107
Peace Corps, 6, 136, 140, 147–48, 157
Poindexter, Jane, 41
postcolonial, 165
postdeconstructionist, 165
post-Freudian, 165
post-Marxist, 165
poststructuralist, 165
Powell, Timothy, 39, 58n3
Praisesong for the Widow (Marshall), 4, 84
precivilization, 104

preempt, 64
Prejean, Helen, 27
pro-black, 50
Protest Movement, 9
pseudoscience, 24

Q

qasida, 127
Quilt (journal), 40

R

Ralph Ellison: A Biography (Rampersad), 20
Rampersad, Arnold, 20. See also *Ralph Ellison: A Biography*
Raynaud, Claudine, 102
Readings, Bill, 165
Reconstruction era, 21
Reconstruction Movement, 28
Reconstructionist, 13, 23, 31n1, 31nn3–4
re-create, 107, 112
Reed, Ishmael, 3, 15, 37–57, 58nn4–6, 58n13. See also *Free-Lance Pallbearers; Japanese by Spring; Mumbo Jumbo; Yellow Back Radio Broke-Down*
Reed, Cannon and Johnson (publishing house), 40
reenact, 164
reenvision, 4
reestablish, 71
reimagined, 107, 163
religiocosmic, 32
religious right, 47, 51
rememory, 7, 103, 116n3
Riffaterra, Michael, 161
right-wing (adj.), 44, 47
rhythm-and-blues (adj.), 46
Robinson, Tracy L., 91–92, 97
Rodgers, Carolyn, 56

S

The Salt Eaters (Bambara), 7, 163–64, 168–69
Sanchez, Sonia, 1, 9. See also *Uh Huh, But How Do It Free Us?*

Santeria, 95
Sartre, Jean-Paul, 145
Scherr, Arthur, 144–46, 153
Seale, Bobby, 49
Shadow and Act (Ellison), 19–20
Shange, Ntozake, 100, 116n4
Shriver, Sargent, 43
signifyin(g), 27, 100–101
Simpson, Lewis P., 107. See also *3 by 3: Masterworks of the Southern Gothic*
Soitos, Stephen F., 25
The Souls of Black Folk (DuBois), 18, 102, 138, 158
the South, 16–18, 20, 26, 28, 104, 107, 109, 125
Southern environs, 22
Southern experience, 18, 28
Southern folk culture, 18, 32
Southern folk perspective, 17
Southern heritage, 21
Southern literary, 16
Southern literature, 16, 22
Southern narrative, 26
Southern origins, 27
southern region, 19
Southern settings, 22
Southern states, 18
Southern writing, 22. *See also* Southern writer
Southern writer, 22, 103, 107, 116n2
southerner, 28
speciesism, 62–63, 65, 67–68
Spirit House, 47
Stepto, Robert B., 31n1
straightforward, 102
The Stranger (Camus), 6, 143–46, 149–50, 152, 158
Survivor (Butler), 3–4, 62–67, 70–71, 75–80, 95
symbiology, 53
symbionts, 64, 70–74, 77

T

tere, 155, 158n12
Things Fall Apart (Achebe), 7, 169
Third World Press, 56
Thomas, Lorenzo, 46
3 by 3: Masterworks of the Southern Gothic (Simpson), 107
Thrody, Philip, 146
Todorov Tzvetan, 124
Toomer, Jean, 17–18, 22, 100, 116n4, 31–32n6
Toure, Askia Muhammad, 53
toward, 4, 7, 12, 40–41, 49, 54, 62–63, 77, 85–87, 93, 95–97, 99–100, 138, 146, 149, 152–54, 160, 167–68, 170, 34n15
traditionless, 114
Traylor, Eleanor W., 5–7, 116n3, 173
Twain, Mark, 22, 101, 116n7

U

Uh Huh, But How Do It Free Us? (Sanchez), 1, 19
Ullrich, David, 119, 121, 123–24
Umbra, 41, 46, 60
undergird, 107
University of Louisiana at Lafayette, 24, 174
Un Poco Low Coup (Baraka), 40

W

Walker, Alice, 4, 8, 15, 45, 83–84, 97, 169, 116n9, 117n11. See also *The Color Purple*
War on Poverty, 43, 58n8
Washington, Booker T., 43, 45–46
Welburn, Ron, 12–13
Welty, Eudora, 116n9
What Moon Drove Me to This (Harjo), 40
white, 51, 103–6, 110–111, 113–15, 116n6, 117n13, 117n15
Whiteness, 102, 145
Wideman, John Edgar, 8, 15, 29–30, 114, 32n8
Wiederman, Michael W., 93
Will, George, 50
Williams, Dana A., 15, 174
Williams, Sherley Anne, 24. See also *Dessa Rose*
Wilson, August, 15, 174. See also *Joe Turner's Come and Gone*
Wilson, Colin, 146
Winfrey, Oprah. *See* Oprah's Book Club

Wolf, Paul, 58n12
The Women of Brewster Place (Naylor), 4, 84
Wong, Shawn, 39
Wooden, Carl, 31n4
Wrestling Angels into Song: The Fictions of Ernest J. Gaines and James Alan McPherson (Beavers), 19
Wright, John S., 33n12
Wright, Richard, 2, 6–7, 9, 19–21, 24–27, 42, 57, 102, 110, 113, 156, 163, 33nn13–15, 117n14. See also *Native Son*

Y

Yardbird Reader (journal), 40
Y'Bird (journal), 40
Yellow Back Radio Broke-Down (Reed), 43–44, 47, 49, 52, 54–55, 61
Young, Reggie Scott, 2–3, 7, 174, 31n5

www.ingramcontent.com/pod-product-compliance
Lightning Source LLC
Chambersburg PA
CBHW031629160426
43196CB00006B/338